Joseph Parrish Thompson

The Theology of Christ

From His Own Words

Joseph Parrish Thompson

The Theology of Christ
From His Own Words

ISBN/EAN: 9783337166984

Printed in Europe, USA, Canada, Australia, Japan

Cover: Foto ©Lupo / pixelio.de

More available books at **www.hansebooks.com**

THE

THEOLOGY OF CHRIST,

FROM HIS OWN WORDS.

A Deo docetur, Deum docet, et ad Deum ducit.—THOMAS AQUINAS.

By JOSEPH P. THOMPSON.

NEW YORK:

CHARLES SCRIBNER & CO.,

1871.

TO

REV. LEONARD BACON, D.D., LL.D.,

THE COUNSELLOR OF MY YOUTHFUL MINISTRY, THE CO-LABORER OF MY
RIPER YEARS,

THE CONSTANT AND FAITHFUL FRIEND,

THIS VOLUME IS GRATEFULLY INSCRIBED,

IN RECOGNITION OF A LIFE ILLUSTRATING, BY PRECEPT AND EXAMPLE,

THE DOCTRINE OF CHRIST.

PREFACE.

RECENT discussions of Christianity as a Faith
have revolved about Christ as a Person; and the
Life of Christ, that formerly was shaped into biog-
raphy for the instruction of the young and the
edification of the devout, has become an effective
weapon of theological polemics. But while within
the sphere of theology this new significance has
been given to the Life of Christ, the *Theology of
Christ* Himself has hardly received the distinction
due to it as the formative power in the Christian
system both as to faith and to practice. The doctrine of Christ was of the very essence of His life,
and constitutes the true and vital Christianity.
" I am the *light* of the world; he that followeth Me
shall not walk in darkness, but shall have the light
of *life.*"

This book does not attempt to delineate the life
of Christ, but *to evolve, directly and exclusively from
His own words, the Doctrine that He taught.* Theology has been too much the name of speculative
systems, the product of philosophy applied to the
Scriptures, or of some spiritual experience evolved
from an individual soul and then supplemented
from the Scriptures. But in the teaching of Christ,

theology is declarative in its form, and directly
practical in its intent. He sets forth the truth of
God, and all things spiritual and divine, with a specific cast of doctrine, and a subjective relation of
system, yet without the formulas of logic or the
definitions of philosophy. Hence a truly Christian
theology must be derived from the interpretation
of His words by the laws of exegesis, and the collation of detached sayings in their relations to the
whole course of His teaching. This has been
attempted in the volume which is here given to
the public.

It is no easy task to withdraw one's mind from
the phrases and methods of theology with which
it has long been familiar, and to concentrate it upon
the interpretation of words spoken eighteen centuries ago; it is as difficult at least as to extract from
Plato and Xenophon the pure words of Socrates,
and to hold these apart from all later speculations,
for independent investigation. This, however, the
author has sought to do; and he hopes that his
book will be found as free from any unconscious
bias of preconceived opinions or beliefs, as it is
from the terminology of any theological system or
school.

It is believed that such a development of the
Theology of Christ as is here attempted is new in
English literature : and only within a recent period
has Germany, so prolific in every form of Biblical
and Theological criticism, produced anything in
this distinct department of Christian science.

Among the most important of these recent works
are Dr. F. C. Baur, *Vorlesungen über N. T. Theo-*
logie—a work conceived in the spirit of the Tübingen school of criticism; Drs. Schmid and Weizacker,
Bib. Theologie des Neuen Testaments; Dr. B. Weiss,
Lehrbuch der biblischen Theologie des Neuen Testa-
ments: and Dr. J. J. Van Oosterzee, *Die Theologie*
des Neuen Testaments, translated from the Dutch.
A particular account of the last two works will be
found in the Appendix. There are also isolated
comments and discussions upon the doctrines of
Christ in several of the recent works upon His life.

The author has assumed the genuineness of the
Gospel of St. John. This has not been done, however, without a careful study of the controversy
touching the fourth Gospel; and the reader who
cares to investigate that question will find materials in the Appendix.

It is hoped that this treatise will commend itself
to the Faith and Charity of the universal Church;
and also that it will find a specific use as a text-
book for Bible Classes, and for classes in the English
course in Theological Seminaries.

With the prayer that it may guide and help
some in the knowledge of the Truth as declared by
" the Teacher come from God," it is humbly offered
unto the Head of the Church, as the fruit of years
of study in His Word.

NEW YORK, *Sept.* 10, 1870.

CONTENTS.

CHAPTER XIV.

CHAPTER XV.

CHAPTER XVI.

CHAPTER XVII.

THE THEOLOGY OF CHRIST.

CHAPTER I.

CHRIST A PREACHER.

CHRIST was a Preacher. He began His public life by preaching in the synagogues of Galilee; He closed it by preaching in the porch of the Temple at Jerusalem. He who was Himself the matter of the Gospel in the preaching of the apostles, and is now the constant theme of evangelic preaching, was the first preacher of His own Gospel, and made preaching the chief function of His life. That He manifested God by works of power, that He exhibited a perfect Humanity through a sinless life of love, that He constituted a new community to be known as His Church, that He suffered and died for a testimony unto the truth and for the redemption of mankind—all this does not exhaust nor embody the story of the mission of Christ as given in the Gospels. From first to last He is there the Preacher.

Baptism was appointed by Him as the rite of initiation into His kingdom; but "Jesus himself baptized not."[1] John had insisted hardly less upon baptism than upon repentance; but after that John was put in prison, Jesus, taking up the work of reformation, came into Galilee, not baptizing with water, but "preaching the Gospel of the kingdom of God, and saying, the time is fulfilled, and the kingdom of God is at hand; repent ye, and believe the

[1] John iv. 2.

1

Gospel."[1]   The priestly office was exalted by Him into a spiritual mediatorship, when He made direct personal intercession with the Father for His disciples,[2] yet He neither offered sacrifices nor founded a priesthood, but Himself preached and commissioned others to preach, "the Gospel of the kingdom."[3]   A king He was, with authority to give laws and to change customs and institutions in religion, in society, in the state—in all this demanding the homage of the souls of men,—yet He wore no semblance of royalty, but rested the evidence of His kingship in that He "came into the world that He should bear witness unto the truth,"[4] and the evidence of His Messiahship upon the fact that "the poor have the Gospel preached unto them."[5]   While He founded a Church, and made provision for its officers, its sacraments and its discipline,[6] He enjoined it upon His apostles to teach His commandments, and "that repentance and remission of sins should be preached in His name among all nations."[7]

Preaching being the characteristic feature of the life of Christ, no true understanding of His mission can be had without a knowledge of what He preached as the truth of God.   The Gospels which give us the record of His life contain also a Gospel which He preached; and this Gospel comprises not only the rules of practical morality, the lessons and precepts of humanity and religion, but the Doctrines of a Positive Theology.   It is sometimes alleged that Christ taught personally none of those doctrines which are commonly set forth by the Church in her creeds as distinctive of the Christian faith, but directed His teachings to practical life, inculcating the virtues, graces and charities that would reform, adorn and bless society, and elevate mankind :—that the doctrines of regeneration and atone-

---

[1] Mark i. 14, 15.   [2] John xiv. 16, and c. xvii.   [3] Mat. ix. 35, x. 7, xi. 1.
[4] John xvii. 37.   [5] Mat. xi. 5.   [6] Mat. xvi. 18, 19.
[7] Mat. xxviii. 20 ; Luke xxiv. 47.

ment, of the divinity of Christ and the personality of the
Holy Spirit, were woven out of His sayings by speculative
minds among His followers, after Jesus had finished His
personal testimony of truth and goodness,—that such doctrines owe more to St. Paul and St. Augustine than to
Christ, and belong not to the original substance of the
Gospel, but to a philosophical theology that has grown up
around it. This notion is somewhat favored by a common
method of teaching theology—stating doctrines in technical
terms and with scientific nicety, tracing their development
in the history of the Church and of schools of philosophy,
and finally authenticating them by citations from the
Scriptures used mainly as proof-texts. For this purpose
the writings of Paul, as the logical expounder of the
Christian faith, are drawn upon more largely than other
portions of the New Testament;—the Pauline conception
being taken as the basis of the Christian dogmatics, and
the words of Jesus being used to verify the statement
of His doctrines in the form of theological propositions.
To reverse this method is to derive the Christian Theology
primarily and directly from the words of Christ—a process
in which we have to do not with the creeds of the Church
nor the formulas of the theologians, but simply with the
principles of interpretation. So far as the very words of
Christ have been preserved, these form the essence of Christianity, just as the original sayings of Socrates as preserved
by his disciples are the substance of the Socratic wisdom.
To the first preacher of Christianity must we look for the
freshest, truest, best conception of the system. In His
words we find a proper theology—not formulated, indeed,
nor systematized, yet expressed in doctrines to be severally
believed,—doctrines set forth with a certain gradation of
time and thought, or in a certain order of development
—and these doctrines interwoven with the whole texture
of the precepts and promises of the Gospel.

The study of the doctrines preached by Christ may exhibit the Christian faith in a phase differing somewhat from that presented through any sect or school; especially will it give to that faith a life and warmth, a power of renewing and edifying, that is too much suppressed under the technicalities of creeds. To many the very word "doctrine" brings up reminiscences of the Catechism as a school-boy task, or of a formal text-book in theology, of dry, stiff propositions, having neither spiritual warmth nor practical utility. But the doctrines that Christ preached have as direct a bearing upon our lives as His precepts; and, if we will but suffer it, will come home to our hearts with the emphasis of positive practical duties. Indeed the duties of the Christian life derive their obligation from the doctrines that make up the Christian faith. There is a good deal of cant now-a-days about "preaching Christ." In a great Christian Convention it was said lately, "the churches are dying of Theology; ministers must preach Christ," and the sentiment was received with applause. But Christ Himself preached theology, and it is not possible to preach Christ except one shall preach the doctrines that He taught and that are the substance of His gospel. Shall one preach that Jesus is the Saviour of mankind? But this is a doctrine, to be illustrated from His life and death, and confirmed by His own words. Shall one preach that men must repent and believe, that they may be saved? But this again is a doctrine, to be expounded, proved, enforced. Shall the preacher, with Paul "determine not to know anything, save Jesus Christ and Him crucified?"[1] But the relation of Christ's death to our salvation, of all doctrines most requires clearness of statement and cogency of proof. If the Church is languid and feeble in face of Rationalism, Ritualism, and Materialism, it is for lack of a vigorous grasp of the doctrines of the gospel. Preaching has run

[1] 1 Cor. ii: 2.

too much to the superficial, the fanciful, the sensational; men go to Church that they may be pleased and excited rather than instructed, for some transitory play upon the imagination and emotions rather than the lasting conviction of the understanding; whereas what most they need is that the intellectual and moral nature be lifted up to the great thoughts of Christ, and so filled with His Spirit. Christ is best preached in the grand doctrines whereby He Himself preached the Gospel of the Kingdom of God.[1]

[1] On Christ as a teacher of Theology, see Dr. B. Weiss, *Lehrbuch der Biblischen Theologie des Neuen Testaments;* and Dr. J. J. Van Oosterzee, *Die Theologie des Neuen Testaments*. A good abstract of this latter work, with translations, is given in the *American Presbyterian Review* for July, 1870. This author says, " To the teaching of the Lord we must ascribe a definite *soteriological* character. In other words, all that the Lord announces respecting God and man, sin and grace, the present and the future life, all, especially that He testifies respecting Himself, stands in direct relation to the *salvation* that He came to reveal and bestow. It is not so much religious truth in general as specifically saving truth that is brought to light by Him. The possibility of exhibiting the instruction of our Lord, with all its riches, as one whole lies just here, that it manifests from beginning to end the character of Gospel. Luke iv. 16, 22; John vi. 68."

CHAPTER II.

"NEVER man spake like this man,"[1] said the officers who being sent to arrest Jesus were themselves arrested by the spell of His words. This spontaneous testimony of His contemporaries is also the deliberate verdict of history. All the ages since have not produced a competitor nor even a successor of Jesus as a teacher of wisdom and truth. His preaching always made upon His hearers the impression of something extraordinary in its character and peculiar to Himself. At His first discourse at Nazareth, the home of His youth, "all bare Him witness, and wondered at the gracious words which proceeded out of His mouth."[2] Nor was this the novelty of a first appearance, for the surprise was none the less when, a year later, after His preaching was widely known, He again taught at Nazareth "insomuch that they were astonished and said, Whence hath this man this wisdom and these mighty works? Is not this the carpenter's son? Whence hath this man all these things?"[3] At Capernaum, where He preached so constantly, "they were astonished at His doctrine, for His word was with power."[4] The same effect was produced by the sermon on the mount, at the close of which it is said "the people were astonished at His doctrine; for He taught them as one having authority, and not as the scribes."[5]

Once, for the purpose of entrapping Jesus, the most adroit and learned among the Jews concocted questions of casuistry, touching politics, theology, and morality, to be

[1] John vii. 46. [2] Luke iv. 22. [3] Matt. xiii. 54.
[4] Luke iv. 32. [5] Matt. vii. 28, 29.

6

put to Him in presence of the people. First the politicians tried Him with the question of paying tribute to Cesar; but when they got His answer, "they marvelled, and left Him, and went their way."[1] Next, the Sadducees sought to embarrass Him upon the doctrine of the resurrection, but He put them also to silence, and the multitude, hearing His reply, "were astonished at His teaching."[2] Last of all, a lawyer demanded a categorical answer to the question " Which is the great commandment," but after the reply of Jesus, followed by His own questions touching the Messiah, "no man was able to answer Him a word, neither durst any man from that day forth, ask Him any more questions."[3] When Jesus stood before Pilate, the Governor was so awed by the words and bearing of his prisoner, that he sought to escape the responsibility of condemning Him. Some such impression of the extraordinary, the marvellous, and even of the divine, was a common effect of the preaching of Jesus among all classes of hearers. So strong was this impression upon the disciples who heard Him in every kind of address—parables, proverbs, set discourses, public disputations—and also in the freedom of familiar conversation, that they said to Him, "Thou hast the words of eternal life: and we believe and are sure that thou art that Christ, the Son of the living God."[4]

What were the qualities of the preaching to which such effects were ascribed by the contemporaries of Christ we are not left to conjecture, since we can measure their impressions by our own, and by the accumulated testimony of the ages since. Of the eloquence of Pericles, who was said to carry upon his tongue the thunderbolts of Jove, not a fragment survives to certify his fame as the greatest of Athenian orators. The fragmentary remains of other orators of antiquity do not always sustain their reputation in their time. There is in the printed page so little of

1 Matt. xxii. 22.   2 Matt. xxii. 33.   3 Matt. xxii. 46.   4 John vi. 68, 69.

strength or fire that one marvels wherein lay the charm
that gave such effect to the spoken words, and feels that
much which is ascribed to the wisdom and eloquence of the
speaker lay in the feelings of the hearer, or the circumstances of the hour. A few, like Demosthenes and Cicero,
have left orations that justify their fame, and serve as
models for modern eloquence. And here and there, in the
literary history of the world, is one whose words of wisdom
and beauty have gathered fame with the ages, and are
even more appreciated now than they were in their time.
Plato and Shakespeare have a wider audience of mankind,
and a higher repute with men of thought and culture than
in their own generations;—their penetrative and comprehensive wisdom is not dimmed by contrast with any of
their successors. Now in respect of the words of Jesus
Christ, which so wrought upon the minds of His contemporaries, and have so ruled the thought and life of after-
times, it is possible to measure and weigh their significance,
to compare them with the utterances of any other teacher,
and to analyze the sources of their power. His preaching
remains upon record to testify that "never man spake like
this man."

This impression of the transcendent worth of the sayings
of Christ does not arise in any degree from the extent of
His discourses. There are authors whose works are a
library of themselves; and as we look upon the shelves
where twenty, thirty, forty volumes represent a Dickens,
a Scott, a Schiller, a Thiers, a Voltaire, an Owen, a Bacon,
we are amazed at the prolific genius, the patient industry,
or the vast erudition that such works display. But all
that is recorded of the sayings of Christ, together with
the history of His life, is contained in a duodecimo of
eighty pages;—less than one half of the New Testament
is the total of what Jesus said and did,—less than one
fourth is all that is preserved of what He himself spake.

Neither is the superiority of Jesus as a preacher due to an air of learning or of profundity in His utterances. A few names—but only the selectest few—are accepted as authorities in their several departments of literature or science, because of the accuracy of their knowledge and the solidity of their attainments; others, by an encyclopædic acquaintance with the results of science, win a more transient reputation of universal knowledge; while others —more commonly in schools of metaphysics—are taken to be wise because they seem to be profound. But this New Testament preacher makes no show of learning, and deals with no subject that calls for book-knowledge. Science, physical or metaphysical, He does not touch upon; political and social questions He alludes to only incidentally or by way of inference; but of truths that concern one's spiritual nature, and of duties between man and man and from man toward God, He speaks as never man spake, before nor since. This is true equally of the Matter of His speech, of the Manner of it, and of its Effects upon human thought, character, and society.

For the Matter of His teaching—to anticipate in part what will be fully brought out in future chapters—take for instance His doctrine of God :—a Spirit to be approached with spiritual worship and with sincerity of heart; so pure, so holy, so good, that absolute perfection is to be perfect as our Father in heaven; governing the world with a Providence so minute that the hairs of our heads are numbered, so gentle that not a sparrow falleth to the ground without our Father; so kind that one can have no cause for anxiety in temporal things, if he will but trust in God; a Moral Governor also, who makes the law of holy love the absolute rule of life and blessedness, who searches the heart by this law, who estimates character by its standard, and who will hereafter judge all men by it in their motives and their deeds;—but while thus supreme as Ruler and Judge, asserting over mankind His holy and universal authority, yet compassionate toward the guilty, seeking to save them from their sins and bring them into loving fellowship with Himself as their Father:—a God whose holiness is love and whose love would have men become perfect in holiness that they may be perfect in blessedness. Whoever will compare this Theology of Jesus, item by item, and in its grand totality, with the speculations of philosophers concerning the essence and nature of the Supreme Being and His agency in the world, and with the theories by which moralists have sought to harmonize truth, justice, love, holiness in the character of God, must confess that never man spake like this man—never man formed a conception of the divine Being so clear, so positive, so complete, so absolute in every perfection, and so beautiful in the harmony of all, so majestic in character and sovereignty yet so approachable by man, so lofty and glorious, yet so gracious and so near!

The same transcendent quality appears in the substance of Christ's doctrine of man:—a personal soul, a spiritual being, and as such worth more to himself than the whole world; a sinner whose heart is a fountain of evil, yet capable of becoming pure and holy as a child of God; an immortal spirit, who by virtue of his character, shall hereafter take his place either with spirits of darkness or with the angels that behold the face of God; a moral being created for love, and for whom the fellowship of human love would make a perfect society and loving God a present heaven. Whoever will take this anthropology of Christ and compare it with scientific theories of the origin and end of man, and metaphysical speculations touching his nature, his capacity, and his future, must confess that never man spake like this man:—never did philosopher form of Humanity a picture so true, an ideal so high, suggest a character so noble, and make this possible by living example, or open to the Race so grand and glorious a future; and never did philanthropist kindle such enthusiasm of love for Humanity itself.

This superhuman quality in the preaching of Christ is even more impressive in His doctrine of the Resurrection. A belief in the immortality of the soul—a belief that seems rooted in the soul itself—was widely, though perhaps vaguely entertained, long before the time of Christ; and the practice of mummification among the Egyptians was based upon the expectation of a return of the soul to the body; but he who will ponder Christ's assurance of a final victory over death and the grave and of a personal identity not only realized in consciousness but manifested in outward appearance, and will reflect upon the dignity that such a promise restores to our fallen nature, the consolation it imparts to grief, the hope and solace to love, must acknowledge that in the highest concernment of man—his existence and condition after death—never man spake like this man who said "I am the resurrection and the life : he that believeth in Me, though he were dead, yet shall he live." [1]

Turning from the Matter of Christ's preaching to the Manner of it—from what He said to the way in which He said it, one is impressed, first of all, with the calm spiritual depth of His sayings. With no air of profundity, the sayings of Jesus have a depth of meaning that no philosophy has yet fathomed. But this depth is not obscurity, it is simply deepness. Depth of reasoning sometimes leads to obscurity of statement; the intellectual process becomes confused, or the listener loses the clue, or language furnishes no terms for the more delicate shades of meaning. But an intuition of the spiritual life—a truth the attestation of which should be given directly by conscience or in consciousness, however deep in meaning, may be always clear in expression. Philosophers go to the bottom of

---

[1] John xi. 25.

their own thoughts, but Christ went to the bottom of
things; and one can see the truth as He states it, and feel
that it is the truth, though he may not at first measure its
whole depth, just as without diving to the bottom of the
ocean, one may see that the bottom is deep, and that pearls
are lying there.   This profound clearness in the utterances
of Christ is due to His intuitive and absolute knowledge.
Where others seek after truth by long processes of investigation, and find it only in fragments, Jesus saw truth
ensphered before Him like a crystal, and He so states the
truth that we see it and feel it, although not always able
fully to grasp it.   Thus one may read metaphysical
philosophy from Plato to Kant without gaining a clear
positive conception of that Infinite Spirit in whose existence
all such philosophy must terminate.   But when Christ
says, " God is a spirit, and they that worship Him must
worship Him in spirit and in truth," we feel that God is
a Personal Reality ; and though Christ does not define
the nature of spirit, yet when He speaks of God as thinking,
willing, loving—His Father and ours—we understand
Him better than the philosophers, though He penetrates to
the inmost depths of a nature which they had vainly
sought to define.   His depth is clear and calm because He
speaks the words of everlasting truth.

The simplicity with which He utters the profoundest
truths distinguishes Jesus from all other teachers.   It was
said of the orations of Demosthenes that they smelt of the
lamp, and the attention of the hearer was divided between
what was said and the labor bestowed in saying it well.
The elaborate finish of a Cicero, a Burke, an Everett, often
diverts the mind from the thought to the style.   On the
other hand, the apothegms of some of the most renowned
sages are uttered with an air of wisdom that offends the
taste.   But Jesus never labors to make an impression, nor
works up an effect with careful logic and rhetoric.   " His

doctrine drops as the rain, and his speech distils as the dew."

One reason of this clearness is itself a characteristic of the sayings of Christ—their adaptation to the hearts and lives of men. He is not like the chemist, who shuts himself up in his laboratory to analyze substances and form new compounds, and now and then gives to the world a new discovery—a result without process; nor like the philosopher who withdraws from common life into a region of abstractions; but His teaching is like the sunlight, for every body's eyes, like the air, for every body's lungs. The God whose infinity, spirituality, majesty, glory, holiness, He sets forth in such pregnant words, is your Father and mine; the soul whose salvation He weighs against the whole world is your soul and mine; the law of holy love, not one jot or tittle of which shall fail, though heaven and earth pass, is the rule for your life and mine; the kingdom of God is within us; His Father's house is ours; the most sublime and oppressive truths of the spiritual world, the most profound mysteries in the relations of the divine to the human through creation, incarnation and redemption, the most thrilling and exquisite discoveries of the future life are brought home as present and personal to every man. So personal are they, that to receive them into our hearts makes them our own almost as much as if we had originated them. On reading the declarations of the Sermon on the Mount, we find them so simple as to seem in a sense natural; we wonder we had not thought of them before; and yet, so deep and full are they that we can never exhaust them. For instance, the saying "Blessed are the pure in heart, for they shall see God" is so obvious, so true to the nature of things, that it appeals to every one as a direct personal summons to a holy life; and yet the most experienced Christian, the most profound theologian, has not exhausted its meaning—not Baxter nor Edwards, not John nor Paul knew all that it is to be pure in heart, nor could tell all that it will be to see God. Truth as spoken by Christ belongs to us as the sky under which we live: it is our heaven; we drink its light, we breathe its air, we grow familiar with its stars, we bathe our fancy in its clear ether, and have a home-like feeling of possession—yet we can never reach its horizon nor climb to its zenith. Never man spake like this man—bringing God and truth and heaven so near, yet making all so vast and glorious.

Another peculiarity of the sayings of Christ is the sense of fulness they carry with them, and of this fulness as proceeding from Himself. One sometimes feels that a teacher has not mastered his subject, or if at home upon one subject he is not equally learned in all; and when the most learned have told all they know, there remains something more for themselves as well as their pupils to acquire. But Jesus speaks with the composure and certainty that fulness gives; His words flow as from a fountain, and not only so, but the truth He imparts becomes in those who receive it "a well of living water, springing up into everlasting life." [1] In listening to Him one never feels that He has exhausted Himself while other truth remains to be learned, but that He knows all truth, and contains it within Himself. For truth as spoken by Christ carries with it the conviction that what He utters is part of Himself. It is not truth that He has studied and developed as an intellectual system—as Copernicus the astronomical and Cudworth the intellectual system of the universe; it is not a doctrine that He has derived from another, and teaches with His own methods and illustrations—as Plato expanded and formulated the doctrines of Socrates,—but the Truth He speaks is in and of Himself.

We make such poor work of setting forth the truth, so feeble an impression of its reality and power, because our

[1] John iv. 14.

own experience of the truth is so limited and imperfect. It does not come from the depth of our consciousness; it is not incorporated with the life of our souls, so as to give the impression that we are Truth itself; and'we take up with half-truths, or defective and distorted representations in the place of Truth. Even the wisest men sometimes put forth as profound ideas what to others seem like common-places; and most men are themselves so very common-place, of narrow views and narrow feelings, always in the same ruts of trade or politics or opinion, bigoted, prejudiced, self-willed, never rising to broad and generous views —that they give to what little of truth they do receive the complexion of their own minds, and make this common-place as themselves.

But Jesus stands before us as Himself the Truth, making upon all that hear Him the impression that He knows that of which He speaks, knows it truly, knows it deeply, knows it fully, and utters it from His inmost soul. Hence what He says is always fresh, and constant repetition cannot make it old. If He speaks of purity of heart, we know that He Himself is pure; if He commands us to love one another, we feel that He Himself is love; if He speaks of God, He produces the conviction that He knows the Father as the Father knows Him. His very words carry with them the assurance that He *is* the Truth. Never man spake like this man.

The sayings of Christ, far more than those of any other teacher, are certified by their effects, especially in the higher spheres of human thought and feeling. Since the beginning of the Christian era, how large a portion of the literature of the world has been devoted to the exposition and illustration of His words, or directly or indirectly has grown out of them. What vast libraries and sections of libraries in Europe and America are filled with books of Christian theology, commentary, and history. Down to the time

of the Reformation, how little literature was known to
Christendom that was not distinctively Christian, and since
then how largely has Christianity influenced the thought
and learning of the world. Strike out from the literature
of the Christian era all that is in any way derived from or
related to the sayings of Christ, and what would remain
in comparison worthy to influence the higher thought and
life of mankind? How little is there in the sayings of
other men that the world cherishes as life-words! How
many volumes have been made simply by commenting
upon the words of Christ!

Every one is familiar with Sir Walter Scott's dying
testimony to *the* Book—"Need you ask? There is but
one;" [1] and the great humorist of our time has left this
record of his obligations to the life of Christ—"I have
always striven in my writings to express veneration for
the life and lessons of our Saviour; because I feel it, and
because I rewrote that history for my children;" and in
his last will, he enjoined it upon his children to "try and
guide themselves by the teachings of the New Testament." [2]

The power of Christ's doctrine has been equally apparent
upon human society. A new Society, altogether peculiar,
whose foundation is faith in Christ Himself, whose bond is
love to Him and His, whose aim is moral perfection, has
come into existence through His word, and to-day exists
over half the globe. The Church of Christ founded
without political purpose or physical power, upon a Word,
an Idea, and expanding through the ages with an undying
spiritual life, witnesses that never man spake like this man.
Moreover, His words have penetrated civil society, have
infused into government the idea of justice, have redressed
social wrongs, have harmonized legislation, and lifted the
masses to a higher plane of thought and hope.

---

[1] Life by Lockhart, vol. vii. chap. xi.
[2] The will of Mr. Dickens as quoted by Dean Stanley in his funeral
discourse.

But more than all is the power of Christ's doctrine manifested in the history of the heart, under all the manifold phases of human feeling. The heart in perplexity needs not instruction so much as light, and the words of Christ are like sunlight upon a mind in spiritual darkness. The heart in trouble needs not teaching so much as sympathy, and the words of Christ come to it in sorrow with all the tenderness of the tears He wept with Martha and Mary, with all the comfort of the promise "Thy brother shall rise again!" The heart that knows the bitterness of sin wants not relief only but renewal, transformation; not merely pardon but salvation through recovery to purity and to a life in God, and the words of Christ are pardon, peace, purity, salvation, life. The heart so deceived by the world, so misled by itself, needs truth to rest upon and love to confide in; and the words of Christ invite us to lean upon Him as did John at the supper. What myriads of hearts have been swayed, molded, strengthened, comforted by His words!

The world has not yet outgrown the teachings of Christ. Great advances have been made in physical science since His day, especially within our own times; but science has discovered nothing more precious for the soul's culture than the truths that Christ brought into the world. The Philosophy of Humanity has grown to a science since Jesus taught, but this has advanced no doctrine of development or perfectibility more elevating or more encouraging than His. Science dishonors itself when it affects to ignore the teachings of Christ: for whatever else is true, His word is Truth; whatever else is brought to light, His word is both Light and Life.

Was He then who uttered these marvelous, far-reaching, unequaled words only a *Man*, of loftier genius or keener insight than the rest of His race? Will this account for those sayings of His that so distance all human wisdom

and so control the world? Must we not accept His own
explanation of this unparalleled phenomenon—"The words
that I speak unto you, I speak not of Myself, but the
Father that dwelleth in Me, He doeth the works."[1] Can
His other sayings be true, if *that* saying was false? In
view of the quality of Christ's preaching as tested by the
results of eighteen hundred years, must not we say with
even more than the confidence of the first disciples, "Thou
hast the words of eternal life; and we believe and are sure
that Thou art that Christ, the Son of the living God?"[2]

---

[1] John xiv. 10.   [2] John vi. 68, 69.

CHAPTER III.

THE whole circle of doctrines taught by Christ revolves about this central point—that He represented to men the KINGDOM OF GOD. Jesus began His public life by "preaching the Gospel of the kingdom of God;" saying, "the kingdom of God is at hand; repent ye, and believe the Gospel."[1] In the first commission that He gave to the twelve disciples, Jesus "sent them to preach the kingdom of God."[2] In His parables He spake continually of the "kingdom of God" and the "kingdom of heaven." He represented faith in Himself as the door of entrance into the kingdom of God; He promised His followers the highest honor and blessing in the kingdom of God.

What then is this kingdom of God which Jesus preached as His Gospel? and how does the knowledge of this Kingdom bring us under obligation to repent, and give us encouragement to believe? The answer to these questions must be sought in the meaning of this phrase as it required to be understood by the Jews of Christ's own time. To the men whom Christ addressed, the kingdom of God was no new idea; or rather, it was no new phrase—but it can hardly be said to have represented any definite idea to a generation that had so far lost the meaning of their own law and history. If we study closely the religion of the Old Testament we shall find that all its doctrines, laws, and institutions grow out of this fundamental thought— that God who Himself is pure and spiritual, is the true and only Redeemer of all those who desire to be no more

[1] Mark i. 14, 15.   [2] Luke ix. 2.

19

estranged from Him; that God calls men to Himself and
seeks to deliver them from bondage:—this precious truth
was sealed by the deliverance in Egypt, and the wondrous rescue at the Red Sea; and afterwards became the
foundation stone of the whole community of Israel, as
well as the sole vivifying impulse of all devotion.[1] The
grand thought that Moses brought to Israel was that
JEHOVAH, the living God, the spiritual and eternal God,
was the true Deliverer; that He desired men to come to
Him in spiritual trust and worship, and that to every one
who would so come to Him, this eternal God would be a
present help, a refuge from every trouble, care, and sorrow.

What the heathen had blindly struggled after in all the
multitude of their gods and religious forms, Jehovah had
brought to men in this Revelation of Himself; a God not
far off but nigh to every one of us; a God who is seeking
men and drawing them to Himself; a God who touches
the human spirit by His own infinite Spirit, that He may
awaken within it a childlike faith and love; a God
manifesting Himself to our consciousness as a Deliverer
from sin and evil and death.

This truth was formally embodied in the doctrine of
a Kingdom of God in this world, the nucleus of which was
His redeemed people of Israel. The political constitution
of Israel as a Nation was but a frame for this spiritual
kingdom. For a time Jehovah stood directly as the Head
of the Nation, declaring His will through the prophets,
and by extraordinary manifestations; and when the people
so far declined from this vivid spiritual conception of
Jehovah as their deliverer that they desired an earthly
king, then the kingly office was made a type of the divine
authority that yet ruled in the hearts of the true Israel:
the prophets strove to hold the people as a nation to the
original spiritual idea of this divine kingdom, and pre-

[1] Ewald, *History of Israel*, i. 533–36.

dicted a time when the kingdom of spiritual life and power, —a kingdom in which God Himself, the pure, the holy, the spiritual, the eternal, should be acknowledged and served as Redeemer and Lord—should be manifested not for Israel only but to the whole world. This was the time of promise that Jesus announced as fulfilled; this the "good news" He preached "of the kingdom of God."

The true conception of this kingdom stands out in the predictions of Jeremiah concerning the days of the Messiah. When this prophet wrote, the political kingdom had run itself down into disgrace and bankruptcy, through the vices of the kings, and the general wickedness of the people; but although the monarchy should be overthrown, and king and people be carried away captive, the Kingdom of God in the true Israel—as represented by the prophet and by all believing souls—could not be destroyed. Indeed, when armies should have failed and all earthly hopes have perished, then would stand out more clearly than ever the truth that Jehovah was the only Deliverer, that He who delivered Israel out of Egypt, must now deliver them from the oppression and captivity that threatened them and from the sins that had brought them into such disaster and perils; then too would be revived the confidence of the true Israel, through a humble, trustful submission to the will of God—faith in Jehovah as a Deliverer.

This view of the kingdom of God may be interpreted to us by our familiar conceptions of the national and historical spirit in a people, as distinguished from the form of government and the practical administration of affairs. If, for instance, one loses confidence in a President, or a Ministry, he does not abandon constitutional government as a failure, but the ideal of a good government then stands out in bold relief. When the lawful government of the United States was assailed by rebellion, and it was attempted to disintegrate the Union by violence, then the

spirit of law and·order, the essence of government embodied
in the Constitution, came forth more vividly in the *consciousness* of the people, and inspired them with new faith
and courage; and more than all, the idea of God as the
Deliverer of the Nation in its past history, and as its
present dependence and hope, came into prominence, and
His kingdom was made manifest in the signal providences
of the War, and in the overthrow of Slavery. This near
experience may help us to understand what to the true
Israelite was *the kingdom of God;*—not simply His Providential government over the world at large; nor His
universal government over this and all worlds; nor the
form of political constitution and laws given by Jehovah
to Israel; nor the King and High Priest set up in His
name; but the presence and power of God felt and
acknowledged in the hearts of those that trusted in Him
and did His commandments.

It was this spiritual conception of a kingdom *within*
Israel itself,—that did not embrace all Israel, and yet was
greater than Israel, because it did possess and should
hereafter more and more possess souls outside the pale of
the Jewish commonwealth—that Jeremiah seized so vividly
at the very moment when the national monarchy was sinking
into nothingness. "After those days, saith the Lord, I
will put my law in their inward parts, and write it in
their hearts; and will be their God, and they shall be my
people . . . . for they shall all know me, from the least
of them unto the greatest of them, saith the Lord: for I
will forgive their iniquity, and I will remember their sin
no more."[1] Where Jehovah was sought and acknowledged as the Saviour from sin, and His will was received
into the heart as its law, there was the kingdom of God.
Daniel, himself a captive, while Jerusalem lay waste and
her monarchy was overthrown, had a glorious vision of

[1] Jeremiah xxxi. 33, 34.

this spiritual kingdom, to be revived under Messiah the Prince, and he even measured off by outward events the time when His kingdom would be made manifest. Ezekiel likened the manifestation of the true Israel to a resurrection of dry bones;—"A new heart also will I give you, and a new spirit will I put within you: and I will take away the stony heart out of your flesh, and I will give you a heart of flesh. And I will put my Spirit within you, and cause you to walk in my statutes, and ye shall keep my judgments, and do them."[1] Thus underlying the whole history of Israel, and all the forms of the Jewish state and religion, was the idea of a living present God who dwelt in the hearts of all true worshipers, "as a monarch living among his subjects;"—the temple was His visible house, a representative of His sacred majesty, and its sacrifices showed how He was to be approached for the forgiveness of sin; but His true abode was in hearts delivered from sin, that honored and obeyed Him as the Redeemer-God.

With this spiritual conception of the kingdom—the presence of God as a Saviour realized to the soul—it is easy to understand how Jesus "preached the Gospel of the Kingdom of God." Coming at a time when the Jews were vassals of the Roman power; when deprived of every symbol of their nationality save their temple and its worship, they were yearning for a Deliverer; to the nominal people of God thus subjugated by military rule, yet clinging to the ancient promise of a Messiah who should restore the glory of the theocracy, He said, "I bring to you the good news of the kingdom of God; in Me Jehovah once more comes to you as a Deliverer; the time predicted by Daniel is fulfilled; the new covenant promised by Jeremiah is brought to you in my gospel; repent of the sins that have humiliated and well-nigh destroyed you; renounce your vain hopes of deliverance, and trust in Me as your

---

[1] Ezek. xxxvi. 26, 27, and Chap. xxxvii.

Saviour; repent and believe the Gospel, for the kingdom of God is at hand." The expectation of such a kingdom already existed in the minds of the more devout and spiritual among the Jews. Zacharias anticipated the advent of the Messiah as the appearing of "the Day-spring from on high," whose ways John was sent to prepare, "by giving knowledge of salvation unto His people for the remission of their sins, through the tender mercy of our God."[1] The aged Simeon waited for "the consolation of Israel," and when the child Jesus was presented in the temple, with prophetic insight he recognized in Him the promised salvation—"a light to lighten the Gentiles, and the glory of Israel."[2] Joseph of Arimathea was one who in the same spirit "waited for the kingdom of God," and he boldly identified himself with the name of Jesus, in what seemed the darkest hour of His cause.[3] But though this finer spiritual conception of the kingdom of God existed in the minds of the more devout, the body of the nation looked only for the restoration and perfection of the Davidic theocracy in perpetuity. Because of this popular expectation of the Messianic kingdom, which could easily have been kindled into the fever of a revolution, Jesus refrained from announcing Himself as the Messiah, until by His teaching and works He had gained a footing for that spiritual commonwealth which in reality He had come to establish. This commonwealth began in the little company of His personal disciples—a community brought into existence not by any supernatural intervention in the outward condition of the people, but through His own spiritual efficiency; and thus the very substance of the kingdom of God was seen to be independent of its realization in the form of the national Theocracy.[4] Yet even

---

[1] Luke i. 76-79.   [2] Luke ii. 25-33.   [3] Mark xv. 43.

[4] See a fine analysis of the doctrine of Jesus concerning the kingdom of God in Weiss' *Lehrbuch der Biblischen Theologie des N. Testaments*, pp. 49-57. For *Van Oosterzee's* view see note at the end of this Chapter.

this community, though based upon the spiritual doctrine of Christ and held together by a personal faith in Him, did not constitute the kingdom of God in the most pure and absolute sense. One of the primitive circle of twelve was a devil,[1] a confederate of Satan, the grand enemy of Christ, and of the kingdom that He had come to establish. The true kingdom commences always in the hearts of individuals, and spreads only by the communication of spiritual life. In all His parables and discourses touching the kingdom of God, Christ adhered to this spiritual conception. The kingdom consists in doing the will of the Father, and the perfection of the Theocracy will be realized when that will shall be done by men on earth as it is done by the angels in heaven—in a word, supreme love to God is the consummation of the kingdom.

Hence the kingdom of God cometh not with observation.[2] It has none of the outward pomp and circumstance of royalty, but is the development of an internal power. To find it one needs not to go to this place or that, to join this organization or that, participate in this ceremony or that;—"The kingdom of God is within you."[3] One becomes a subject of it in his own consciousness; when he, by believing, receives Christ into his heart as his Saviour, then does God as his Redeemer, take charge of him, enter into him to guide, keep, sanctify, and save him; and this coming to the realization of God in His supreme lordship over the soul is the kingdom.

This kingdom has laws for the regulation of the life through purifying and ennobling the heart. These laws, as embodied in the sermon on the mount, though in the form of simple maxims, strike down to the deepest springs of thought and motive. They revolve about two cognate ideas, Purity and Love:—"Blessed are the pure in heart, for they shall see God:"[4]—"Be ye there-

---

[1] John vi. 70. [2] Luke xvii. 20. [3] Luke xvii. 21. [4] Matt. v. 8.

fore perfect [*i. e.*, in love] even as your Father which is in heaven is perfect:"[1]—a pure and holy love toward God and man is the kingdom of heaven.

This kingdom has its privileges. Every subject is treated as a son. There are no gradations of rank, no intermediaries upon whose influence at court we must rely for favor; but the King himself comes by His Spirit to the heart of each subject and there abides: "If any man love Me, he will keep My words; and My Father will love him, and we will come unto him, and make our abode with him."[2]

This presence of Christ in the soul imparts power against all spiritual enemies; the very coming of the kingdom is deliverance from condemnation and death. The entering in of this kingdom is the casting out of Satan;—"When a strong man armed keepeth his palace, his goods are in peace: But when a stronger than he shall come upon him, and overcome him, he taketh from him all his armor wherein he trusted, and divideth his spoils."[3] Jesus spake this to illustrate His power against Satan: "If I with the finger of God cast out devils, no doubt the kingdom of God is come upon you;"[4] the overthrow of Satanic power in the world, the subjugation of the power of evil in any form, the breaking of hostile power by a power from above, marked the coming of the kingdom of God. As the advance of the Union army into the Southern States gave a sense of deliverance and safety to loyalists who had been held in durance and terror by the Confederates—the very coming of the flag of the Union into a place being the symbol of power and the pledge of emancipation —so the entering of the Gospel into a heart to possess it with its faith, its promises, and its hopes, is the signal of deliverance from the bondage of Satan, and the coming in

---

[1] Matt. v. 48, and xxii. 37–41.   [3] Luke xi. 21, 22.
[2] John xiv. 23.   [4] Luke xi. 20.

of the kingdom of God. The presence of Christ is the subjugation of His enemies.

Through this presence the soul is sanctified and ennobled; the reign of pure desires, devout affections, noble purposes is established within. The principle of holy love enthroned as the law of the mind, subjugates evil propensities, eradicates wrong habits, and every such subjection of the unholy is the dominion of the good and true.

This kingdom has its rewards, both present and prospective. There is no higher joy in kind than the free communion of the heart with one whom it thoroughly admires, respects, and loves; and the highest measure of this joy is found in that endearing fellowship with the Father into which the soul enters through its fellowship of faith and love with Christ, and which Jesus promised to His disciples as the compensation for His own withdrawal: "He that loveth Me shall be loved of My Father;"[1] "Peace I leave with you, My peace I give unto you;"[2] "These things have I spoken unto you, that My joy might remain in you, and that your joy might be full."[3]

And this present joy, so rich and satisfactory, is but the prelude to the rewards of the future of this kingdom. To be pronounced the blessed of the Father, and publicly welcomed to that sphere of light and glory where Jehovah is enthroned; to sit down with Abraham, Isaac, and Jacob in the kingdom of God; to be with Christ in person and behold His glory,—these are but items in the rich roll of blessings promised to the recipients of the Gospel. And these rewards shall be eternal. A Messianic kingdom reproducing the theocracy of David, would have been subject to the incidents of all earthly governments and all types of material organization. Limited in extent, confined to the conditions of place, exposed to the conflicts of hostile powers, it must eventually have shared the fate of other

---

[1] John xiv. 21.   [2] John xiv. 27.   [3] John xv. 11.

temporal governments, or even had it outlasted these, it
must have been circumscribed in territorial dominion and
in the number of its immediate subjects. But lying
wholly within the spiritual, which is immortal, incorporated with the very life of the soul, not only will it survive
the destruction of all outward forms and of the world
itself, but it shall endure with the duration of being.
Divine forces are in it for its perpetual conservation; it is
the kingdom of Christ and of God : the gates of hell cannot prevail against it here; in one feeble, praying, trusting
soul it is more than conqueror over death and hell; and
when Time and Death shall have essayed in vain to touch
it, " Then shall the righteous shine forth as the sun in the
kingdom of their Father;"[1] for "This is life eternal—to
know the only true God, and Jesus Christ."[2]

That this spiritual, heavenly, eternal kingdom was at
hand, and with its inestimable privileges and rewards was
open to any man to enter in, was the Gospel that Jesus
preached. Of necessity the entrance into this kingdom
must be through certain mental acts and experiences which
Christ has set forth under the terms "Repent" and
"Believe;" for, the beginning of the kingdom being
deliverance from sin, one must needs repent, to be so delivered; and the law of the kingdom being obedience to
Christ, one must have a sincere, implicit, submissive
confidence in Christ in order to such obedience; hence
faith in Jesus as the Deliverer.

The obligation to repent and believe was declared by
Jesus in express terms, and also under many parallel
forms. Thus He enjoined the renunciation of worldliness,
"How hard is it for them that trust in riches to enter into
the kingdom of God."[3] He enjoined humility as essential
to discipleship : "Whosoever shall not receive the kingdom
of God as a little child, he shall not enter therein."[4] He

---

[1] Matt. xiii. 43.   [2] John xvii. 3.   [3] Mark x. 24.   [4] Mark x. 15.

required implicit consecration, with no mental reservation, no hankering after the old manner of life; "No man having put his hand to the plough, and looking back, is fit for the kingdom of God."[1] The Head and Lord of the kingdom of God and of heaven has declared that none can be accounted within that kingdom except they repent and believe. In what sense then, can one claim to be a disciple of Christ, who does not comply with the uniform and absolute prerequisites to membership in His spiritual community?

That conception of the kingdom of God which Jesus promulgated as His Gospel and sought to embody in His Church, has been realized with increasing grandeur and power through the ages, and awaits its complete development in the perfected state of the righteous. How vast and glorious is that kingdom which to-day embraces the millions of every kindred and tongue and people and nation, who coming to the Father by Jesus Christ, worship Him in spirit and in truth; a commonwealth of believing souls owning allegiance to one Lord, and through all the diversities of race, of language, of social, civil, and ecclesiastical institutions, fraternizing in the love of Christ, their common Head, and in prayers, labors and hopes for the elevation of mankind through His gospel. And as other generations shall believe through their word, the prayer of Jesus to His Father shall be more and more fulfilled, "that they may be made perfect in one,"[2] until from the dissolving elements of this material world, unwasted by time, unhurt of death, this spiritual kingdom shall come forth in the glory of the Father and of His holy angels.

[1] Luke ix. 62.   [2] John xvii. 23.

NOTE: VAN OOSTERZEE ON THE KINGDOM OF GOD.

[3] Dr. *van Oosterzee* in his before-cited work, *Die Theologie des Neuen Testaments*, has seized upon the idea of the kingdom of God as fundamental in the Theology of Christ, but though his delineation of that kingdom is in most points admirable, he seems to have missed the primary spiritual conception of the kingdom in the Old Testament, so finely brought out by Ewald. Van Oosterzee's characterization of the kingdom, (translated by Rev. J. P. Westervelt, in the *American Presbyterian Review* for July, 1870), is as follows: "The Gospel that Jesus preached is a gospel of the kingdom, and that kingdom itself is a moral-religious institution, which, unlimited in extent, and eternal in duration, in its tendency to unite, sanctify and save mankind, embraces heaven and earth. . . . .That kingdom is (a) something *new*. "Since it had first come nigh in the fullness of time (Mat. iv. 17) it did not before exist on earth." It is thus not merely the continuation of the old line, but the beginning of an order of things not previously seen (Luke x. 23, 24: comp. Mat. xxvi. 28). It is, however, now (b) something really *present*. Where He comes, there it also appears with Him; it is already in the midst of those who ask when it shall appear (Luke xvii. 20, 21). It is by no means the same as eternal bliss: *there* consummated, it exists here in principle, and though not of the earth, yet established on earth, though it came not with external noise or parade. It is truly (c) something *spiritual*, that pertains to a higher domain of life than this visible creation. Though not exclusively yet preëminently spiritual are the privileges, duties and expectations of its subjects. What takes place here is diametrically opposite to what usually occurs in other kingdoms (Mat. xx. 25, 28; comp. Luke xxii. 24–27), and the King declines all needless interference with the civil jurisdiction (Luke xii. 13, 14). Even with the idea of the Christian church that of the kingdom of God must not be confounded. The church is only the external form in which the kingdom of God appears (Mat. xiii. 24–30; 47–50); that kingdom itself a spiritual society, personal membership with which is absolutely impossible without a renewing of the mind (Mat. xviii. 3). As such, it is also, as to its extent, (d) something *unlimited*. The Lord is even much more than the old prophets (comp. Isaiah ii. 2–4), raised above all contracted particularism, and not only at the end, but also in the midst, and at the beginning of His course preached the universality of the kingdom of God (Mat. v. 13, 14; viii. 11, 12.) Single utterances which seem to breathe another spirit (Mat. x. 5; xv. 24) must be explained by particular circumstances, and are abundantly outweighed by others (Mat. xxviii. 19; Luke xxiv. 47; Acts i. 8.) Nor is this surprising, since the kingdom of God is (e) something *unending*, bounded as little by time as by space. Did Moses and the prophets constantly point to better days, Jesus knows nothing higher than the kingdom which He comes to found, and predicts the complete triumph of His cause (Mat. xxiv. 14; xxvi. 13), and promises to remain forever with His disciples (xxviii.) What is thus destined for eternity is, however, developed in time. The kingdom of God is therefore (f) something *growing*, which, in accordance with its spiritual nature, gradually works from within to its ex-

ternal manifestation, from small beginnings and with the most surprising results (Mat. xiii. 31–33; Mark iv. 26–29). Therefore its servants must pray
(Mat. vi. 9), and work (Mat. ix. 37, 38). It is indeed possible that it be taken
away from those who ungratefully despise it (Mat. xxi. 43). Where it is, however, sought and found, there it is (*g*) something inestimably *glorious* and
blessed (Mat. xiii. 44–46; xxii. 2); a blessedness the want of which cannot be
made good (Luke xiii. 25–30) but the possession of which is to be desired above
all things, as pledge of every other blessing (Mat. vi. 33)."

The points at which this otherwise complete synthesis of Christ's doctrine of
the Kingdom might be amended are *a* and *c*—so far as relates to the Church.
That the Kingdom of God as preached by Christ was *new* in respect of the
clearness, fulness, and intensity of spiritual manifestation, is undoubtedly true;
but that the devout recognition of God as the only Lord and Deliverer, and a
loyal devotion to Him in faith and love, were primary elements in the conception of that kingdom in the Old Testament, has been shown in pp. 20–23 of the
foregoing chapter. This view is necessary both to the unity of Biblical truth
and to the clear understanding of Christ's teaching. He used the phrase
"kingdom of God" without defining it; the language was familiar to every
Jew, but Jesus sought to revive and restore its true meaning, and this was the
tone of His parables and similes showing that the kingdom was not of this
world. He did not claim to set up a new kingdom—"Think not that I am
come to destroy the law or the prophets: I am not come to destroy, but to ful-
fil," πληρῶσαι, to fill up, to fill out, in their true meaning.

The very germ of the kingdom of God given in the covenant with Abraham,
contained this doctrine of Christ: not only should one "great and mighty nation" spring from Abraham—thus giving to the covenant an outward symboli-
cal form—but "*all* the nations of the earth should be blessed in Him:" and for
the fulfilment of this, Abraham was required to walk before the Lord in per-
fectness or uprightness of soul, and to "command his children and his household after him, to keep the way of the Lord" (Gen. xvii. 1; xviii. 18, 19).
The coming of God as a Saviour to be received in trust and obedience, was
from the first the essential idea of the kingdom of God: and Christ's doctrine
of the kingdom was not "new" as to the conception of it. Dr. van Oosterzee
is nearer the truth when he says, "The word of Moses and the prophets is
taken up by Jesus, continued, supplemented, completed in such a manner, that
the old in His hand acquires a new aspect, and the new, rightly viewed, appears to be nothing else than the ripened fruit of the old."

Moreover, the true Church of Christ, one in Himself and in His Father, *is*
identical with the true kingdom of God. The external visible Church, like the
Jewish theocracy, may shadow forth that kingdom, yet representing it only imperfectly and in part: but the true Church of Christ is that "spiritual society
personal membership with which is absolutely impossible without a renewing
of the mind:" it is the kingdom as Jeremiah and Ezekiel saw it, the members
of which all "know the Lord," and have His law "in their inward parts." This
primary conception of the kingdom is the key to the whole theology of Christ.

CHAPTER IV.

For entering the kingdom of God, that which is wanted is "not learning but *life ;* and life must begin by *birth.*"[1] This was the doctrine of Jesus in His reply to Nicodemus, emphasized with a marked solemnity and authority of utterance, "Verily, verily, I say unto thee, except a man be born again, he cannot see the kingdom of God."[2] An earnest, devout Israelite, expecting the Messiah, and impressed with the divine attestation of Jesus through the miracles that He wrought, Nicodemus sought instruction of this marvellous prophet, whom he acknowledged as "a teacher come from God." Jesus, anticipating his question concerning the signs and requirements of the Messiah's kingdom, went directly to the topic that was in the mind of his visitor, though in a way as startling as it was decisive. Nicodemus had said, "Thou art a teacher come from God," and stood expecting some new doctrine. Jesus said to him, "My teaching is not of doing and leaving undone, but of becoming; so that it is not new works to be done, but a new man to do them, not simply the living otherwise, but the being new-born."[3] Here plainly was a doctrine of regeneration taught by the founder of Christianity as fundamental to His system. What does it signify? What did Christ Himself intend by being born again? The doctrine lies in the exegesis of this single phrase.

At the outset Nicodemus mistook its meaning, and

---

[1] Alford *in loc.* [2] John iii. 3. [3] Luther, *Comm. in loc.*

halted at the words in their literal physical sense. If his reply to Jesus is to be taken seriously, one is amazed at his dulness; if he meant to cavil about the matter, one is no less amazed at his frivolity. But neither stupidity nor caviling can be fairly inferred from his question, "How can a man be born when he is old? can he enter the second time into his mother's womb, and be born?"[1] Nicodemus was a "master in Israel," a man of intelligence and education, at least upon questions of religion, and therefore could not have put such a question literally. At the same time, his whole manner in coming to Jesus, and the tone of his conversation, showed that he was not a caviler but a sincere seeker after truth. Not only did he testify his respect for Jesus in coming to Him in this manner for instruction, and addressing Him as a prophet, but on subsequent occasions he used his official position for His protection, and even exhibited the devotion of a disciple.[2] His perplexity arose from his conceiving of himself as already in the kingdom of God, by virtue of his birth in the lineage of Abraham; while, in common with the body of his people, he looked to the coming of the Messiah for a higher assertion of that kingdom and its privileges for their benefit. How then could a son of Abraham be born a second time into the kingdom of God?

A Gentile who embraced the Jewish faith was admitted into the Jewish commonwealth by baptism, and was said to be born again. It was a phrase common among the Rabbis, "The Gentile that is made a proselyte, and the servant that is made free, behold he is like a child newborn." The one explains the other; the servant made free began a new kind of life, could use his powers and time in a new way, was master of himself; and a heathen brought to the knowledge of the true God and received

---

[1] John iii. 4.   [2] John vii. 50; xix. 39.

3

into the commonwealth of His worshipers, began a new life, had new thoughts, new feelings, new principles, new aims, new associations, new hopes, was like one born into a new world. Such was the theory of the school of doctors to which Nicodemus belonged, concerning the receiving a Gentile into the household of Israel; but for themselves, they had so far lost the spiritual essence and life of their religion as to have taken up the conceit that, " it was enough for them to have been of the seed of Abraham, or the stock of Israel, to make them fit subjects for the kingdom of heaven." Nicodemus not only considered himself a member of that kingdom, but felt his consequence as one of its chief men, a ruler and teacher, a member of the Sanhedrim, the high court in the Jewish kingdom of heaven. He had hoped to gain from Jesus some new light touching the coming glories of that kingdom under the reign of the Messiah. But when Jesus laid down the broad proposition, that a new birth was indispensable for every one, in order to enter the kingdom, Nicodemus was utterly confounded. He a proud master in that kingdom could understand how a poor, ignorant, unholy dog of a Gentile would require to be made over before he could aspire to the privileges of the Messiah's kingdom; but for himself this seemed as incredible, almost as impossible, as for an old man to be born a second time. "How can I, who was born of the seed of Abraham, and hence born into the kingdom of God, put myself outside of that kingdom, into the position of a Gentile, and be born again in order to get within the kingdom?" So ignorant was he of that spiritual life which constitutes the kingdom of God within the soul, that the requirements of Jesus seemed to him as difficult to imagine as the physical impossibility of a second birth. In this respect Nicodemus was a type of those who place the seat of religion in the physical nature—making it a quality or condition of the brain, the senses, the temperament, a result of inheritance, dispositions and tastes, or a product of material forms and observances. Such notions of religion are completely dispelled by the answer of Christ, showing that His meaning was not to be looked for in the region of the physical. It is not man as a physiological subject that requires to be born anew, but man in his spiritual nature, his psychological frames and feelings;—the new birth is not of the flesh but of the Spirit.

Nevertheless this is a *birth;* for though the change is neither in the organic constitution of the man, nor in the substance and powers of the soul, it is yet a change as thorough and radical as if one were made over or born again. In respect of that spiritual life, that life of obedience, faith and love which is the inner experience of the kingdom of God, one must become altogether a new man. This is the strict import of the phrase "born again." To be literally born a second time would not fill out all its meaning; it denotes the complete renovation of the inner man, and must be understood either as being renewed from the very beginning, or as being born "from above," by that influence from on high which is afterwards described as being "born of the Spirit:"—rather, both these ideas are combined in the one phrase, the former being prominent in the first instance, and the latter brought in for explanation. One must begin his life as altogether a new thing, and this he will do only under an influence "from above."

If the kingdom of heaven is realized through the coming of God to the soul as its Deliverer, if the humble, willing, grateful receiving of Christ by the soul as its Saviour from sin and the Lord of its affections and desires be the kingdom of heaven within that soul, then is it no marvel that Jesus said "Ye must be born again;" for before the consciousness of God's presence as its Saviour and

the acceptance of God as its Sovereign can spring up
within a heart which has been the home of evil thoughts
and the nursery of evil deeds, it must undergo a transformation as wondrous and complete as a new birth. If
also the kingdom of heaven be that community of loving
souls which, with no worldly marks of distinction—blood,
wealth, race, rank—are joined in one through faith in
Christ as Saviour and obedience to Him as Lord, then is it
no marvel that for being registered in that kingdom, Jesus
said "Ye must be born again." The proud, self-willed,
self-righteous heart must be converted,—made over, as it
were—and become in submission, love, and obedience,
even as a little child. If, moreover, the kingdom of heav-
en in its final consummation, denotes the visible presence
and glory of Christ enthroned in the midst of those He has
recovered unto God, then can it be no marvel that, for
admission to that innumerable company of angels and
the spirits of just men made perfect, Jesus said "Ye
must be born again:" and, "Except your righteousness
shall exceed the righteousness of the Scribes and Pharisees, ye shall in no case enter into the kingdom of
heaven."[1]

In view of the coming of that Kingdom by and
through Himself, of its spiritual nature as a process or experience within the soul by which God is seen in Christ as
a present Saviour, and accepted as Lord of the conscience,
the will, and the affections, in view of the holy character
of this kingdom in its laws of purity and love, in its privileges of fellowship with God, and the coming of the
Father and the Son to take up their abode with its true
subjects, Jesus called upon men to repent and believe the
gospel. And it was this same conception of the kingdom
as inward, spiritual, pure,—a holy kingdom in a holy
heart—that led Jesus to declare to Nicodemus, as the start-

1 Matt. v. 20.

ing point of His religious system, " Except a man be born again, he cannot see the kingdom of God!"

This requirement answers to the personal wishes of every man in his better moods. Could one live his life over again in the light of his own experience, he would guard against mistakes, improve opportunities, get advantages, now all past beyond recall! Every one sees how he could make a better thing of life, if it were given him to begin anew. In most cases, however, such fancied improvements would affect only the outward conditions and circumstances of life;—one would obtain a better education, another would improve his chances in business, or make some lucrative speculation in real estate, another would form a more advantageous or congenial alliance; and so, in one particular or other, most men would like to live their lives over for the sake of bettering their condition; would like to be " born again " with different surroundings of culture, means, opportunities, so as to start in life at a different level, with better light and guidance or better prospects of success. Here and there some humble, honest soul longs to live life over upon grounds of character—that he might make himself a better man.

Now what Christ requires as the condition of entering into the kingdom of God is that we shall do thoroughly this very thing for which we vaguely long; that we begin new lives, not in respect of circumstances, but of character; that we make earnest work of this—not changing our place and condition, nor simply changing our manners or morals in the way of an outward reformation—but that in this change we go to the very bottom of things, and in the principles, motives, and aims that make up life become altogether new, starting upon this new idea of living from the very beginning, just as though we were born into another state of existence. This it is to be born again—there is an inward, deep, radical change in the whole conception and spirit of life as toward both God and man.

Christ based His requirement of the new birth upon the wickedness of the human heart. Had condition and circumstances alone stood in the way of admission into the kingdom of heaven, this teacher sent from God would doubtless have shown how the difficulty could be removed by education or the progress of society. Were admission into that kingdom a question of morals alone—as these affect society and the outer life—Christ would have preached a reformation in manners. But as John the Baptist had foretold of Him, He "laid the axe unto the root of the trees, and every tree which bringeth not forth good fruit must be hewn down and cast into the fire."[1] To Him who knew what was in man, bad fruit was a sign of a corrupt tree, bad morals or an evil life of a wicked heart; and therefore, as He Himself preached, the tree must be made good that the fruit may be good, the heart must be made good that it may bring forth good things;[2] and so because of the wickedness of the heart, men must be born unto a new life before they can see the kingdom of God.

The preaching of Christ dealt with men not simply as ignorant and needing light, as erring and needing guidance, but as sinful, and requiring to be made over anew from the very foundation of character. "They that be whole need not a physician, but they that are sick. . . I am not come to call the righteous but sinners to repentance;"[3] that is, to such as deemed themselves good enough by nature, or able to develop a righteous character by methods of their own, Jesus had no mission; He could be of service only to those who were conscious that they were sinners, and as such had need of salvation. The starting-point in His whole work was the recognition of sin as seated in the heart, and hence demanding a new beginning

---

[1] Matt. iii. 10.   [2] Matt. xii. 33, 35.   [3] Matt. ix. 12, 13.

in respect of all that constitutes moral character. In the externals of religion the Scribes and Pharisees were the most religious of the Jews,—strict and scrupulous in prayers, tithes and alms, and in all the services that the law of Moses required of subjects of the kingdom of God; yet Jesus did not recognize them as within that kingdom or as having any sort of claim upon it. He charged them with a corruption of heart for which no ceremonial righteousness could atone: "Ye are like unto whited sepulchres, which indeed appear beautiful outward, but are within full of dead men's bones, and of all uncleanness:—ye outwardly appear righteous unto men, but within ye are full of hypocrisy and iniquity."[1] These were men of fair outward morality and apparent righteousness—the best average specimens of character among the Jews—yet because of the wickedness of their hearts they needed to be born again. And the charge of inward depravity was by no means confined to those whom Christ accused of hypocrisy in religion. He brought this accusation against all alike.

The Jews, for instance, despised the Galileans as hardly capable of being included within the theocratic family— their very name was a term of opprobrium—and some of this class having been put to death for crime or killed in a riot near the temple, so that their blood was mingled with the sacrifices, the people told Jesus of this as proof of a divine judgment for their awful depravity. But He answered, "Suppose ye that these Galileans were sinners above all the Galileans because they suffered such things? I tell you Nay; but except ye repent, ye shall all likewise perish."[2] A tower near the pool of Siloam fell and killed eighteen persons, and the Jews interpreted this as a judgment upon the victims for some extraordinary wickedness; but Jesus said as before, "Think ye that they were sinners above all men that dwelt in Jerusalem? I tell you

[1] Matt. xxiii. 27, 28.　　　[2] Luke xiii. 2, 3.

Nay: but except ye repent, ye shall *all* likewise perish."[1]
He thus taught that, although particular calamities are not
to be taken as proof of special criminality on the part of
the sufferers, yet suffering stands so closely related to sin,
that all men are equally liable to suffer, because all are
alike involved in the habit of sinning, and are substantially upon an equality with respect to that sinfulness of
heart which calls for repentance.   To the Jews who boast-
ed that as the seed of Abraham they were the children of
God, Jesus said, "Ye are of your Father the devil, and
the lusts of your Father ye will do;"[2] thus charging them
with complete alienation of heart from God, and alliance
with the spirit of darkness and evil.   And again, He declared the source of all evil in the world to be the sinful
heart that is in man; "for from within, out of the heart of
men, proceed evil thoughts, adulteries, fornications, mur-
ders, thefts, covetousness, wickedness, deceit, lasciviousness,
an evil eye, blasphemy, pride, foolishness; all these evil
things come from within, and defile the man."[3]   Not only
do overt deeds of vice and crime proceed from an evil
heart, but together with the grossest outward acts, and as
included in the same condemnation, are enumerated pride,
envy, covetousness, evil thoughts; all these are hidden
within the heart, and these "defile the man" before God.
Manifold as are the forms of evil in the world, there is but
one common fountain of evil, and that is the heart of man.

There is no mistaking the judgment of Jesus Christ
upon that point:—the doctrine of the universal sinfulness
of mankind lay at the basis of His scheme of renovation,
and His doctrine of the necessity of a new birth grew logically out of that:—both are fundamental in His theology.
The terms of admission into the kingdom of heaven are
the same for all; the reformation that is demanded is not
renouncing one's more flagrant or conspicuous sins, lop-

¹ Luke xiii. 4.   ² John viii. 44.   ³ Mark vii. 21-23.

ping off individual vices or habits, but transforming the sinful heart into a new and holy heart. "Now do ye Pharisees make clean the outside of the cup and the platter; but your inward part is full of ravening and wickedness." [1]

It is not with sins alone that the gospel of Christ has to do, but with Sin, and directly with the seat and source of sin, the Heart of Man.[2]

Keeping in mind that the kingdom of God consists in recognizing God as the Saviour and receiving Him into the heart as its Lord, one can no longer marvel that whoever would attain unto the consciousness of that kingdom within himself must be born again; so changed in heart—changed from an evil, sinful heart to a heart that loves God and seeks after holiness—so changed in his fundamental conceptions and principles of life, and in all his several purposes, motives, and actions, that he shall be throughout another man. Such was the doctrine of Jesus; the fair interpretation of His sayings teaches nothing less than this. To have the fruit good, the tree must first be made good.

Practically, as matter of experience, the new birth includes and requires *repentance* and the *renunciation* of sin. John the Baptist proclaimed the coming of Jesus by preaching "Repent ye: for the kingdom of heaven is at hand: and many were baptized of him in Jordan, confessing their sins." [3] When Jesus began to preach He gave the same exhortation: "Repent, for the kingdom of heaven is at hand." The repenting enjoined by the gospel is literally to change one's mind—μετανοεῖτε, review your course and turn from it;—it implies reflection, compunction, and regret in the review of the past, but these frames and experiences do not constitute the fact of repentance; the essence of that is the change of mind to which reflection and compunction lead—a change of *the*

---

[1] Luke xi. 39.   [2] Matt. xii. 33.   [3] Matt. iii. 2, 6.

whole mind, in desire, feeling, thought, purpose, action, a
change in the whole spirit and intent of life as toward
God and His truth, and all that affects character; and inasmuch as the heart has yielded itself to carnal, selfish,
worldly desires and aims—in a word, is sinful—it must
repent of this, renounce this way of life as the first step
toward the kingdom of God. Hence Christ insisted so
much that if any man would become His disciple, he
must begin by denying himself—must put self down in
order to set up Christ as his king. " No man can serve
two masters : ye cannot serve God and mammon." [1]   In
being born again one is not passive ; but in becoming
spiritually a new man, every one has this to do for himself—to repent of and renounce his own sin.

But the new birth is more than repenting. One may
have contrition for sin, be ashamed of it, resolve truly to
forsake it, and yet through habit or weakness return to it
again and again; to be born anew implies that repentance is
confirmed and the renunciation of sin made sure by bringing into the soul a new life-power from the Spirit of God.
To purify the heart from evil is the vital principle of the
new life, and its effectual operation will constitute the perfection of that life ;—" Blessed are the pure in heart, for
they shall see God." [2]   Repentance alone does not purify.
To be sorry for sin is not in itself the same thing as to become holy ; and since sinful desires have ruled the heart,
and sin has gained possession of the imagination, the
reason, the inclinations, the will,—of the whole man as a
thinking, feeling, acting soul—one's own resolution, however sincere, one's own decision, however earnest, proves
too weak to eradicate the propensity to evil. Therefore
must we be re-enforced from above ; we should never suc-
ceed in purifying ourselves—" for that which is born of the
flesh is flesh"—and our best purposes of amendment would

---

[1] Luke xvi. 13.   [2] Matt. v. 8.

begin under the limitations of weakness and the taint of old carnal habits. Spiritual life within us must be born of the Spirit of God. Christ has taught us that one feature of this new birth is humility—casting away pride and self-will and taking a lowly place as a sinner before the holy God;—"Blessed are the *poor in spirit*, for theirs is the kingdom of heaven:"[1] "Except ye be converted, and become as little children, ye shall not enter into the kingdom of heaven."[2] The Jewish Rabbis had a saying, "A penitent man must be like one to-day new-born."

But Christ said further, "Blessed are the *pure in heart*, for they shall see God."[3] Now the humbling is our proper act; we can and must abase ourselves before God, confessing our sins; but for the purifying we need help from the Spirit of all purity, the Holy Spirit. This Jesus taught specifically as the being born *from above,*—the normal signification of ἄνωθεν, which is veiled under the idea of a new birth. The two ideas are strictly correlative.

John had said, "I baptize you with water unto repentance"[4]—the baptism being a symbol of the washing away of sins, which they who came to be baptized professed to have repented of and forsaken. Yet so far was John from ascribing to baptism a regenerative virtue, that he spoke of the repentance which it signified as but preparatory to a work of divine purification within the soul, and added that in order to the full realization of the kingdom, through its power and majesty possessing the entire intellectual and moral nature, Jesus must "baptize them with the Holy Ghost and with fire"[5]— truly and effectually cleanse them by an inward process of purifying. And so Christ Himself taught, "Except a man be born of water AND OF THE SPIRIT, he cannot enter into the kingdom of God." By the act of baptism one professes himself new-born as to the purpose of his heart, in renouncing

[1] Matt. v. 3. [2] Matt. xviii. 3. [3] Matt. v. 8. [4] Matt. iii. 11. [5] Matt. iii. 11.

his sins; but unless that purpose has itself sprung from
the quickening power of the Holy Spirit, and is sustained
and energized by that, it will prove as evanescent as the
water applied in the outward rite. The real birth is of
the Spirit.

The complete doctrine of the Holy Spirit as taught by
Christ will be unfolded in a subsequent chapter.[1] Just here
we are concerned simply with His declaration of the necessity of the Holy Spirit to the effective regeneration of the
soul. And the point of inquiry is not the mode of the Spirit's
operation in the new birth, which Christ did not explain,
and which philosophy can but conjecture; but the necessity
of this supernatural work, which Jesus made fundamental
in His scheme of salvation. That necessity arises from the
fact that sin, having gained control over the moral powers
and affections of the man, holds him in subjection, like
"a strong man armed;" conscience is dormant, religious
sensibility is sluggish, the will itself is chained by habit
to a course of evil, and paralyzed in its movements toward
the good; but the Spirit of God convincing of sin,
awakening the sense of guilt in view of the righteousness
of God, and of condemnation in view of the coming judgment, breaks the spell of evil, restores to their normal
action the moral faculties whose service of evil had become
a second nature, and by the power of truth renews and
sanctifies the soul.[2] This action of the divine Spirit upon
the human Christ likened to the wind, which is marked
by its effects. "The wind is the emblem of concealed"
power, perceptible to observation, but inscrutable to the
understanding:"[3] "The wind bloweth where it listeth,
and thou hearest the sound thereof, but canst not tell
whence it cometh, and whither it goeth: so is every one
that is born of the Spirit."[4] Nicodemus, again perplexed

---

[1] See Chap. XII. [2] John xvi. 8, 13; xvii. 17. [3] Stier, " *Words of Jesus,*"
in loc. [4] John iii. 8.

and confounded, exclaimed, "*How* can these things be?" But Jesus maintained a reserve that not even the eager questioning of His own disciples could penetrate, concerning those "heavenly things" that lie beyond human discovery, and that philosophy of the supernatural which the highest intellects have essayed in vain.[1] He held up the fact of the new birth as proof of the working of a divine power within the soul, which like the wind, is invisible as a cause, yet recognized by the force, the suddenness, or the magnitude of its effects. "So is every one that is born of the Spirit."

The doctrine of Jesus was that "the experience of the new birth is suggestive of a supernatural cause. Take, for example, the conversion of the Apostle Paul. Look at it as a fact in the history of mind. Set aside, as irrelevant to the object before us, whatever was miraculous in the events of that journey to Damascus. Make no account of the supernatural light, the voice from heaven, the shock of blindness. Consider not the means, but the manner of that change in the man. Mark its impetuosity. Note the instantaneousness of that arrest of passion. It is like a torrent frozen in mid-air. Observe the revulsion of feeling. Threatening and slaughter give place to conviction of sin. Malignity is supplanted by prayer. Perceive the revolution of character in that instant of trembling and astonishment. Call it regeneration, conversion, new birth, or by titles more comely to philosophic taste; call it what you will, it is a change of character. The Pharisee becomes a penitent. The persecutor becomes a Christian. The murderer becomes a saint. For aught that appears in the narrative, the change is almost like a flash of lightning. How brief the colloquy which proclaims the whole of it! "Who art thou, Lord?" "I am Jesus." "Lord, what wilt thou have me to do?" We

---

[1] John iii. 12, Acts i. 7.

do not know that mind can move more rapidly than this
in such a juncture of its history, and yet move intelligently. Then put together the two lives of the man—
his life before, and his life after this convulsive crisis.
Saul and Paul join hands over this invisible gulf, as over
the river of death—the same being, yet two different men.
His character has experienced a change like the transmu-
tation of metals. Take these as facts of sober mental
history, and do they not seem to speak the presence of a
supernatural power? If the world could come to that
ninth chapter of the Acts as to a modern discovery in
psychology, philosophic systems would grow out of it;
all futile in explanation of the process, but all confessing
the reality and the divinity of the thing. . . . . . . The
world, from the beginning until now, has inferred the
presence of supernal agencies in the mental changes of
men, from less conclusive evidences than those furnished
by such a conversion. Socrates believed—and philosophy
has revered him for the faith—that an invisible spirit
swayed his thought, and he believed it on less evidence
than this. Napoleon believed and poetry has discovered
piety in the faith—that supernatural power intervened in
his destiny; and he believed it on less evidence than this.
It has passed into the cant of literature to ascribe inspiration, even divinity, to great minds on infinitely less
evidence than this." [1]

That one must be born of the Spirit as Christ taught
this necessity, is a doctrine full of encouragement, since
what is presented is not a metaphysical abstraction, but
the fact of help, present help, efficient help, divine help in
·becoming a new man. One who has been long becalmed
at sea, or driven by contrary winds, when at last a favor-

[1] *The New Birth, or the Work of the Holy Spirit*, by Austin Phelps, D.D., Professor in Andover Theological Seminary. The whole subject of regeneration
is here discussed in a masterly manner.

ing gale springs up, makes haste to catch it, puts his helm to the course indicated by the breeze and spreads his canvass so as to secure the full benefit of the wind, without once troubling himself with theories of meteorology, or demanding *how* the wind is brought to act upon him. So one driven to and fro by the passions of life, longing and sighing for peace, may be suddenly conscious that some heavenly breeze is floating over him, and if he will but spread the wings of faith and prayer he shall catch its gracious influence and be wafted into rest. What matters it that he does not know how this strange new feeling has come over him, nor why it so excites him to hope and zeal? There are realities in the spiritual world whose certainty is not impaired for lack of our philosophy, and it is enough to know that the Holy Spirit comes from God, and comes to him. Yielding his repentant, willing soul to the renewing, sanctifying power of the truth, he is "born of the Spirit," and that is salvation from sin and death.

There was no need that Jesus should come from heaven to teach us that we have sinned; that, alas, we know, and sometimes feel with bitter upbraiding. There was no need that He should come from heaven to teach us that we must repent; this we know by the judgment and reproof of our own moral sense. But when one as in the anguish of despair cries out, How shall I change my will, break off from sin, and truly become a better man?—to answer that question, it was needful that Jesus the Christ should come from God and say, "Believe on Me; receive the Holy Ghost." The Spirit convinces of sin, and the very conviction that prompts that almost despairing cry may be the beginning of His work of renewal—that cry, the birthcry of that soul. The Spirit sanctifies through the truth; and this very truth of His own presence to convince, renew, and help, He may be pressing upon the soul as its hope in the dark struggle with guilt and fear. If the heart will but open to this higher influence, it shall be lifted up to God, and sustained where all its own resolves would fail. How shall one become a new man? How find God and heaven as a reality, a possession? Let him do his known duty; do that which he himself, and only he, can do; let him repent of his sins, and give up the purpose of sinning! Then in the spirit of a little child, let him look to Christ for grace to help, to sanctify, and save. In that moment of penitence and faith, casting away his old self that he may cast himself wholly upon Christ, he is born of the Spirit, and enters into the kingdom of God.

CHAPTER V.

ONE can certify himself of his repentance; can he also
be certified that his repentance is accepted of God? One
may be conscious of his dependence upon divine power to
strengthen him against the evil that is within him and
around him; but how shall he make sure that this aid will
be given him in his extremity? Has God manifested a
concern for our salvation?—promised anything, done anything, to assure us that sin repented of shall be forgiven,
that the new life shall be inwrought and sustained in our
souls? Upon the answer to these questions all hope and
courage for reformation must depend. The answer is
given in that thrilling, that sublime announcement: "God
so loved the world that He gave His only begotten Son,
that whosoever believeth in Him should not perish, but
have everlasting life." [1] For this very purpose Jesus
Christ came into the world; for this very purpose He lived
in the flesh; for this very purpose He died upon the cross
—that through faith in the sinless man there lifted up in
triumph over sin and death, we might receive not new life
only, but life everlasting. All this did Christ Himself include in that saying to Nicodemus which linked the symbolism of the Old Testament with His personal history:
" As Moses lifted up the serpent in the wilderness, even so
must the Son of Man be lifted up, that whosoever believ-

---

[1] John iii. 16. For a critical discussion of this text see Chap. vi.

4   49

eth in Him should not perish, but have eternal life."¹
"Should not *perish !*"   "*Must* be lifted up!"   There was,
then, upon the whole race a liability to perish, which could
be averted only by the death of the Son of Man.   Surely
these words of Jesus cannot mean less than this—that His
death upon the cross sustained a necessary and vital relation to the deliverance of men from a doom that is here
contrasted with everlasting life.   The question is not one
of philosophy, but solely one of interpretation.

What, then, did Jesus intend by the "lifting up" of the
Son of Man ?   Upon two other occasions He used the same
expression, and a comparison of these will furnish a key to
its meaning.   In a dispute with the Pharisees concerning His divine mission, Jesus, knowing their murderous intent towards Him, said unto them, "When ye have *lifted
up* the Son of Man, then shall ye know that I am He."²
This could not have referred to the glorification of Christ,
His being received up into heaven after death, for the verb
is not passive, but denotes the act of the Jews in lifting
Him up—ὑψώσητε.   Hence it can only refer to His being
crucified by their hands.   That purpose to have His life,
which He knew was raging in their hearts, and which He
more than once referred to in this same discussion, would
be accomplished in lifting Him up upon the cross.

Again, as He drew near the close of life, in setting forth
the destined triumph of His gospel, He said : "And I, if I
be lifted up from the earth, will draw all men unto Me."³
The evangelist adds the comment, "This He said, signify-
ing what death He should die."   That the interpretation
given by John was the true one is clear from the whole
argument of the context.   Jesus had likened Himself to
the corn of wheat cast into the ground, "which *if it die,*

---

¹ John iii. 14, 15.   ² John viii. 28: compare v. 37: "Ye seek to kill me."
³ John xii. 32.

bringeth forth much fruit;" [1] in like manner would the Son of Man be glorified in the multitude of disciples that His being lifted up would draw unto Him. The Jews clearly understood Him by this to refer to His death, for they answered with evident surprise, "We have heard out of the law that Christ abideth forever"—their notion of the Messiah was that He would live and reign uninterruptedly in this world :—"how sayest Thou then, 'The Son of Man must be lifted up?'" The being lifted up is clearly opposed to the idea of abiding forever, and hence it signifies death as contrasted with an uninterrupted life.

The very manner of Christ's death is hinted by this phrase: "If I be lifted up from the earth." There is much plausibility in the suggestion that, as our Lord spoke in the Aramæan tongue—then the dialect of the common people in Israel—he used the Chaldee term *z'kaph* (Ezra vi. 11) or *tah-lâh* (Esther vii. 9, 10, ix. 13) which the Jews would understand to mean *to hang up a criminal on a post*, or adapting this to the Roman custom—to *crucify*. [2] Dr. E. Riggs, in his manual of the Chaldee language, defines *z'kaph*, "*to suspend*, as a malefactor on a gallows or cross." Fuerst gives the meaning—"to raise up, as a cross, to hang up;" and *tah-lâh* to hang up on a stake, for capital punishment. Thus Haman was "lifted up" upon the gallows; and the same penalty was threatened by Darius for mutilating a royal edict: "Whosoever shall alter this decree, let timber be pulled down from his house, and being 'set up' let him be hanged thereon." [3]

The Chaldee, which belonged to one of the three grand divisions of the Shemitish languages, [4] was the language of Babylonia in the time of the Jewish captivity. That the Jews there acquired it, is evident from remains of the

[1] John xii. 24.   [2] Olshausen, *Com. John*, iii. 14.
[3] Ezra vi. 11.   [4] Aramæan, Hebrew, and Arabic; the Chaldee and the Syriac were sub-divisions of *Aramæan,—East* and *West*.

dialect in the books of Ezra and Daniel;[1] and on their return to Palestine they brought this with them as their vernacular tongue. By degrees the name *Hebrew* was transferred to this Babylonish dialect: but "in the time of Christ, the popular speech of the Jews in Palestine was not pure Hebrew, but Syro-Chaldaic. Accordingly, imitations and literal translations of numerous ordinary expressions of that language must have been introduced into Jewish Greek."[2] The Greek language which, from the time of Alexander the Great, gradually won its way in the provinces of Asia and Africa that were subjected to Macedonian rule, so far as it was used by the Jews of Palestine, was affected both in its idioms and in the meaning of particular words by the Chaldee dialect. That Christ habitually used this dialect is highly probable; at least, the fact that in His death-agony upon the cross He cried out in this tongue,[3] shows that it was most natural to Him. Spoken in that tongue, the expression "to be lifted up" could have no doubtful reference to the manner of His death.

But this interpretation of the phrase does not depend upon the supposition that it was originally uttered in the Chaldee tongue. Both the Jews at large and the particular disciples of Jesus understood it in this sense: and their enthusiastic dream of an immortal reign of the Messiah upon earth was confounded by the declaration that the Son of Man must *be lifted up from the earth*. And as this lifting up would be compassed by the malicious machinations of the Pharisees, who sought to kill Him, it could only refer to the lifting up on the cross.[4] Thus from the very opening of His ministry, Jesus knew not only that He

---

[1] Ezra iv. 8; vi. 18; vii. 12, 26; Daniel ii. 4; vii. 28.   [2] Winer, *Grammar of the New Testament Diction*, Sec. III; also, Riggs, *Manual of the Chaldee Language*, Sec. II. Bleek, *Einleitung in das N. T.* § 21–36.

[3] Matthew xxvii. 46.   *Eli, Eli, lama sabachthani.*   [4] John viii. 28, 37.

should die, but that He should be CRUCIFIED; that His death would not take place in the course of nature, but by violence; and this not by stoning, as Stephen afterwards was stoned by the mob, nor by beheading, as John the Baptist suffered, but by being lifted up upon the cross. That Jesus distinctly foreknew the manner of His death is plain from His sayings to the disciples recorded by Matthew:[1] "From that time forth began Jesus to show unto His disciples how that He must go unto Jerusalem, and suffer many things of the elders, and chief priests and scribes, and *be killed*, and raised again the third day." "Behold, we go up to Jerusalem; and the Son of Man shall be betrayed unto the chief priests, and unto the scribes, and they shall condemn Him to death, and shall deliver Him to the Gentiles to mock, and to scourge, and *to crucify* Him."

But this death would possess a virtue that can be affirmed of none other. Christ announced to Nicodemus a mystery greater even than that of the new birth, when He said that His crucifixion was appointed as necessary to the salvation of mankind:—"The Son of Man must be lifted up, that whosoever believeth in Him should not perish, but have eternal life."[2] The provision of salvation was directly connected with, and vitally dependent upon the crucifixion.

That salvation comes through believing in Christ, that faith in the Son of Man is the condition of life, was taught by Jesus under every possible form of expression. "He that believeth on Me hath everlasting life."[3] "If ye believe not that I am He"—the Messiah, the sent of God, "ye shall die in your sins."[4] "He that believeth and is baptized shall be saved; but he that believeth not shall be damned."[5] But the text under consideration goes beyond the fact of believing to its ground, and connects the act of

[1] Matthew xvi. 21; xx. 18.   [2] John iii. 15.   [3] John vi. 47.   [4] John viii. 24.
[5] Mark xvi. 16.

faith directly with the death of Christ as a necessary provision for the salvation that comes by faith :—" The Son
of Man *must* be lifted up, *that* whosoever believeth in
Him should not perish ;"—ὅτι has here the force of a moral
necessity ;—to meet the requirements of the case and to
fulfill the purpose of God, it was necessary that the Son
of Man be lifted up : the ἵνα has the telic sense, in *order
that*, to *the end that*,—so that this result might be secured.
Hence the death of Jesus upon the cross sustained a
necessary and vital relation to the salvation of mankind.

How else can we account for the emphasis that Christ
gave to His dying as the condition precedent to salvation
by faith ?   One might believe that Jesus was the eternal
Son of God, that He became incarnate, that He lived a
holy life, that He did the works of God, that He taught
divine truth, that His teachings if followed would make
men wise and holy and happy—one might believe all
this irrespective of the question how this Jesus died, or
whether He died at all.   Had the Son of Man been translated like Enoch and Elijah, without tasting death, or had
He died in the ordinary course of nature, one might still
to a certain extent have believed in His mission, His life,
and His teachings.   But simply to believe in His supernatural advent, His perfect character, His true and wise
sayings, does not reach the measure and quality of the
faith that Jesus Himself prescribed.   Faith to that extent
was avowed by Nicodemus at the opening of his interview
with Christ :—" Rabbi, we know that thou art a teacher
come from God ; for no man can do these miracles that
thou doest, except God be with him."   This was a confession of the divine mission of Jesus, of His divine
works, and the divine authority of His teachings : a
faith so strong that it gave the conviction of certainty ; a
faith so sincere that he came to Jesus with a declaration
of confidence, and in the spirit of a disciple, to learn from

Him the higher signs and privileges of the kingdom of God. Yet to this very master in Israel, who was thus forward to acknowledge Him as a divine teacher, Jesus prescribed quite another element of faith, and another ground upon which faith in Himself should rest, a faith conditioned upon His crucifixion, and to arise out of that:—" As Moses lifted up the serpent in the wilderness, even so must the Son of Man be lifted up, that whoso-ever believeth in Him should not perish." Believing unto salvation, faith that would lead to eternal life, this must arise from looking unto Christ as "lifted up" upon the cross.

Christ taught this same doctrine when a little before His death, with explicit reference to the salvation of the world, He said,-" I, *if I be lifted up* from the earth, will draw all men unto me." [1] Certain Greek proselytes had expressed a desire to "see Jesus;" His disciples, who looked upon Him as the Messiah to the Jews alone, hesitated to present them, but brought the request to their Lord. The answer of Jesus, instead of pronouncing categorically upon the case presented, made this the occa-sion of proclaiming the universality of His grace and the cosmopolitan nature of His kingdom.

Hitherto He had seemed to limit His personal ministry to the Jews. When He sent forth the twelve to announce the kingdom of heaven, He commanded them saying, " Go not into the way of the Gentiles, and into any city of the Samaritans enter ye not: but go rather to the lost sheep of the house of Israel;" [2] and to the woman of Syrophe-nicia who besought Him to heal her daughter, He said, " I am not sent but unto the lost sheep of the house of Israel." [3] But now He announces that all men shall be drawn unto Him, and this as consequent upon His death. The productive effect of His dying He sets forth under

[1] John xii. 32.   [2] Matt. x. 5, 6.   [3] Matt. xv. 24.

the analogy of the fructifying seed: "The hour is come that the Son of Man should be glorified. Except a corn of wheat fall into the ground and die, it abideth alone; but if it die, it bringeth forth much fruit." [1] Then as if struggling in His own spirit with the impending sacrifice, yet implicitly subjecting His own will to the will of His Father, He said, "Now is my soul troubled; and what shall I say? Father, save me from this hour? but for this cause came I unto this hour. Father, glorify Thy name." [2] What was the *hour* that hung over Him with such painful but momentous issues, but the hour appointed for His sacrifice upon the cross? "Now is the judgment of this world; now shall the prince of this world be cast out;" [3]—the kingdom of darkness shall be broken down, "and I, if I be lifted up from the earth, will draw all men unto Me." His death would be the seed-corn that should bring forth a new life for all mankind—the Gentile world as well as the people of Israel.

In the light of this usage in the phrase "to be lifted up," it is most significant that, in His conversation with Nicodemus, Jesus did not speak of death simply as an event to be accepted by Him in the spirit of submission. He did not merely avow His willingness to die—His readiness, if need be, to suffer martyrdom, if by so doing, He could benefit mankind; nor did He simply prophesy that after His death, His life and doctrine would be illuminated by that event, and by the natural and progressive influence of truth, light, and love, would become a means of salvation to the world;—much more than this lay in His thought. From the first He looked forward to His crucifixion, His being "lifted up" as the appointed termination of His life and ministry. His going out of the world in that manner was included in the purpose of His coming into the world. His dying upon the cross was no thing of acci-

dent, His being lifted up no mere incident of priestly hate
or popular excitement,—this was in the PLAN of His mission as truly as were His advent, His preaching, His
miracles, His life of truth and love. He announced to
Nicodemus as one of the truths He had brought down
from heaven, *the necessary and vital relation of His death to
the salvation of mankind;* and for the key to this doctrine,
referred him to a memorable incident of Jewish history as
a type of the saving benefit to be derived from His crucifixion. " As Moses lifted up the serpent in the wilderness,
even so must the Son of Man be lifted up, that whosoever
believeth in Him should not perish, but have eternal life."

That was a day of terror and agony in the wilderness
when fire-serpents[1] swarmed in the camp of Israel. This
venomous reptile, a mottled snake with fiery red spots upon
its head, abounds at certain seasons in the sandy wilderness of Arabah, that skirts the western side of the mountains of Edom, from the foot of the Dead Sea to the Gulf
of Akabah. It is the terror of fishermen along the Gulf,
and of the Bedouins when encamped in the neighboring
desert.[2] So inflammable is its bite that it is likened to fire
coursing through the veins; so intense is its venom, and so
rapid in its action, that the bite is fatal within a few hours.
The body swells with a fiery eruption, the tongue is con-

---

[1] Numbers xxi. 6, 8; Deut. viii. 15: the term *Nahash*, the generic name for
serpent, is here qualified by the term *Saraph*, burning; which, by some, is
supposed to describe a fiery, inflammable bite, but by others the fiery-red appearance of the serpent itself, especially about the head.

[2] *Burckhardt*, (Vol. II. p. 814) says, " The sand on the shore showed traces
of snakes on every hand. My guide told me that snakes were very common in
these regions, and that the fishermen were very much afraid of them, and put
out their fires at night before going to sleep, because the light was known to
attract them." *Schubert, Journey from Akabah to the Hor* (ii. 406) states that
" in the afternoon a large and very mottled snake was brought to us, marked
with *fiery* spots and spiral lines, which evidently belonged, from the formation
of its teeth, to one of the most poisonous species. The Bedouins say that these
snakes, of which they have great dread, are very numerous in this locality."

sumed with thirst, and the poor wretch writhes in agony till death brings relief.

This pest suddenly appeared in the camp of Israel in prodigious numbers; from crevices in the rocks, from holes in the sand, swarmed these fiery-headed demons into every tent. There was no running away from them, and killing seemed hardly to diminish their numbers. On every side there was a cry of anguish—men, women, children racked with this fiery torture, none able to save or even help another—"and much people of Israel died."

In this extremity the people came to Moses, and besought him to pray the Lord to take away the serpents. They came confessing their sin, and acknowledging that the plague was a just retribution; for they had reviled Moses as the cause of their disappointments and fatigues in the desert, and had even reproached the name of God for their lack of bread and water. Helpless, self-condemned, in danger of perishing, they now felt that deliverance must come from God, and could come from God only. "And Moses prayed for the people."[1] The manner in which this prayer was answered showed the hand of God even more distinctly than had the appearance of the plague. For if Jehovah were about to interfere, it would seem probable that He would act upon the physical cause of the suffering, either directly, by destroying or scattering the serpents, or indirectly, by guiding Moses to some healing herb or other means of cure—thus providing a physical remedy for a physical evil. But He chose to employ a moral remedy, which by summoning the people to an act of faith, would bring Jehovah Himself before them as the direct author of their healing. "The Lord said unto Moses, Make thee a fiery serpent and set it upon a pole; and it shall come to pass, that every one that is bitten, when he looketh upon it shall live:"[2]—and presently there was lifted up in the

[1] Numbers xxi. 7.   [2] v. 8.

camp, high over all the tents, the image in brass of the fiery destroyer; and from every tent crawled forth the bitten, dying men, or were carried forth by hands that now had faith to *minister—and they looked; those eyes whose life was burning out in the fire of fever, looked where the great brazen serpent was all ablaze in the sun, (as if the myriad fire-serpents were compressed into one burning symbol)—looked, to behold the fierce destroyer nailed harmless as dead metal to the tree; looked, to learn that Jehovah was in the camp as a Deliverer, and would destroy death in victory; looked, and with the look came healing; looked, and the eye lost its madness, and shone again with the brightness of hope; looked, and the fiery torrent of the veins was calmed, and the pulse beat again with the even flow of health; looked, and he who just now stood a fiend of despair within the jaws of hell came forth a new man, in his right mind, and kissed his wife and children, and they together worshiped God; "For it came to pass that if a serpent had bitten any man, when he beheld the serpent of brass, he lived." And as Moses lifted up that serpent in the day of death and despair for Israel, EVEN SO—in like manner, for a like purpose, with like significance, the Son of Man was lifted up, and hung there upon the cross that all Jerusalem then saw, that all the ages since have seen, that whosoever believeth in Him should not perish but have eternal life.

The force of this "EVEN SO" suggests in this symbol of the serpent a significance of doctrine concerning Christ. First of all, the plague of serpents was because of sin. Though the agent of the divine displeasure was a natural pest belonging to that locality, yet the visitation of the serpents was a judgment from God. Ewald, who does not question the authenticity or the antiquity of this narrative, admits this element in the case. "The people advancing towards the Red Sea, weary of the hardships of the tedious march, and tired of the scanty nourishment afforded by the manna of the desert, complained loudly to God and Moses of the want of bread and water. Instead, however, of obtaining relief, they thus incurred a much greater evil, being furiously pursued by a multitude of large and venomous serpents, from the bites of which many died. In this they recognized God's righteous punishment for their murmuring, and repentantly entreated Moses for his prophetical interposition."[1] In the plague of the fiery serpents, the sin of unbelief, ingratitude, rebellion against God, was visited with condemnation and penalty.

Next, the people terrified and humbled by the judgment, and cut off from all human relief, looked to Jehovah for deliverance, humbly confessing their sins. In this penitent frame they came to Moses and said, "We have sinned, for we have spoken against the Lord and against thee; pray unto the Lord, that *He* may take away the serpents from us."[2] Here was acknowledged the necessity of divine interposition to take away the penalty of sin. God alone could stay the judgment.

Again, the brazen serpent was appointed by God expressly for a sign of His merciful interposition. This was no device of human ingenuity; no experiment on the part of Moses and the elders upon the imagination of the people; between this and the cure there could be no relation of cause and effect; simply as an exhibition or demonstration it could have no efficacy;—but it was God's appointed sign of mercy. Here again Ewald is true to the conception of the narrative: "Moses by divine command fixed a serpent of brass upon an elevated banner, that, gazing on it, those who were bitten might be healed; and this actually occurred. The meaning of the story is certainly not that Moses set up the image of the serpent as an object of adoration; it was obviously only a sign that,

<hr>

[1] Ewald, Hist. of Israel, 1, 599, English edition.　　[2] Num. xxi. 7.

as by the command of Jahve this serpent was waved on
high, bound and harmless, so every one that looked upon
it with faith in the redeeming power of Jahve would be
preserved from evil. It was therefore a symbolic sign,
like that of St. George and the Dragon among ourselves,
or the Serpent itself among the heathen. As that creature,
by nature the most noxious, and yet supposed capable of
being tamed, became the image of remediable bodily ill,
and consequently the symbol of Æsculapius, so here we
have something of the same import, but with an element
of reality and practical necessity." [1]

But the point of supreme moment in the case is that
men looked to God for healing mercy *through that sign;*
not only did they look to God as the source whence
healing must come, but they looked through this particular sign, as representing the fact of healing—and none
in all the camp were healed except they looked upon the
serpent of brass.

Thus far the analogy is simple, obvious, perfect. It
was to counteract an evil consequence of sin, to remove
the penalty of a moral transgression, that the serpent
was lifted up; and it was for men perishing in sin that
the Son of Man was lifted up; for men condemned
because of sin that He came with that healing of the soul
which is eternal life. The cure for the bite of the serpent
was appointed of God expressly for that end; and so, in
His counsels of wisdom and mercy it was provided that
the Son of Man be lifted up—His crucifixion was appointed for our salvation.

The case of the bitten Israelite was hopeless without
the special intervention of Jehovah; and the case of the
soul smitten with the plague of sin, stung with remorse
of conscience, condemned by the righteous law, doomed
to "perish" in its iniquities, were hopeless, had not God
sent His Son to be lifted up upon the cross.

[1] Ewald, Hist. of Israel, 1, 509.

The brazen serpent, though displayed in sight of all the camp as the divine provision of healing, was made efficacious to any individual sufferer only by his *looking*, which was the personal act of faith; and even so the Son of Man was lifted up "that whosoever *believeth* in Him should not perish, but have eternal life."[1] As deliverance from the condemnation of sin was possible only through the love of God in giving His Son to be crucified, so there is no actual deliverance to any sinner save through his own act of faith in the Son of Man as lifted up. "He that believeth on Him is not condemned; but He that believeth not is condemned already, because He hath not believed in the name of the only-begotten Son of God."[2]

There is yet another point in this analogy that comes, if possible, still closer to the root both of the evil and its remedy. As Alford describes it:[3] "The brazen serpent was made *in the likeness of the serpents* which had bitten them. It represented to them the poison which had gone through their frames, and it was hung up there, on the banner staff as a trophy, to show them that for the poison there was healing,—that the plague had been overcome. In *it* there was *no* poison, only the likeness of it. And was not He who knew no sin made sin for us? Were not sin and Death and Satan crucified when He was crucified?" In a word, did not the dying of the Son of Man upon the cross strike at the root of all human misery, and destroy the destroyer? Nothing less than this surely could He have meant when He said, "My flesh will I give for the life of the world;" "The good shepherd giveth his life for the sheep;"[4] and in that most emphatic declaration, "The Son of Man came not to be ministered unto, but to minister, and to give His life a ransom for many."[5]

[1] John iii. 15.   [3] *Comm. in loc.*   [5] Mark x. 45.
[2] John iii. 18.   [4] John vi. 51; x. 11.

This word λύτρον, *Ransom*, admits of no ambiguity : it means "purchase-money," the price paid for the release of any one from captivity, from prison, or from peril. The Septuagint uses it for אַיָּלָה and כֹּפֶר—compensation, redemption, satisfaction by a price. Thus, by the Levitical law, the owner of an unruly ox was responsible in various penalties for the mischief done by the animal. When liable to the penalty of death, he might redeem his life by a fine, and this was the λύτρον; "if there be laid on him a sum of money, then he shall give for the *ransom of his life* whatsoever is laid upon him." [1] A universal ransom-money was levied upon the people to avert a judgment from Jehovah. "When thou takest the sum of the children of Israel after their number, then shall they give every man *a ransom for his soul* unto the Lord, when thou numberest them; that there be no plague among them when thou numberest them." [2] This same redemption-tax is afterward spoken of as the "atonement money." [3]

This same term λύτρον is employed by the Septuagint for the price of the redemption of a slave, and also of land that had been alienated. "In all the land of your possession ye shall grant a *redemption* for the land." [4] The poor debtor who had sold himself into servitude could be redeemed by his kinsman; "according unto his years" [of the unexpired term of his service] shall be "*the price of his redemption.*" [5]

On the other hand, it was forbidden to accept a ransom for a murderer : "Ye shall take no *satisfaction* (λύτρον) for the life of a murderer, which is guilty of death." [6]

The verb-form of the same word is used for redeeming *by a substitute.* "Every firstling of an ass thou shalt redeem with a lamb; and if thou wilt not redeem it, then

---

[1] Ex. xxi. 30. [2] Ex. xxx. 12. [3] v. 16.
[4] Lev. xxv. 24. [5] Lev. xxv. 52. [6] Num. xxxv. 31.

thou shalt break his neck ; and all the first-born of man among thy children shalt thou redeem." [1]

The same word, chiefly in the plural form λύτρα, is common in classic Greek in the sense of ransom—a price paid for redemption. Plato uses it in describing the rich presents that Chryses brought to the Greeks for the *ransom* of his daughter. [2] Thucydides speaks of Hippocrates, tyrant of Gela, having received the territory of Camarina as a *ransom* for some Syracusan prisoners. [3] Herodotus, describing the victory of the Athenians over the Chalcideans and the Bœotians, says, "All the Chalcidean prisoners whom they took were put in irons, and kept for a long time in close confinement, as likewise were the Bœotians, until the ransom asked for them was paid. . . The Athenians made an offering of a tenth part of the *ransom-money—τῶν λύτρων*." [4] Demosthenes [5] and Xenophon [6] used λύτρον in the same sense of a price paid for a ransom. In the great tragic poet Æschylus is a striking instance of λύτρον in the sense of an expiation or atonement for murder. The chorus of mourning women bewailing the untimely end of Agamemnon, exclaim, "What *atonement* is there for blood that has fallen on the ground? [7] . . . . . All the rivers moving in one channel would flow in vain to purify murder." How admirably comes in here the New Testament doctrine of an expiation, a ransom, sufficient to atone for every crime. The Son of Man gave His life "a *ransom*, λύτρον, for many."

A ransom from what? He did not give His life to deliver the Jewish nation from the Roman yoke, for He was never concerned in an insurrection, nor a political

---

[1] Ex. xiii. 13. All these references are to the Septuagint version.
[2] Rep. 39, 3 D. ὅτι ἦλθεν ὁ Χρύσης τῆς τε θυγατρός λύτρα φέρων.
[3] Thuc. vi. 5. λύτρα ἀνδρῶν Συρακοσίων αἰχμαλωτῶν λαβὼν τὴν γῆν τὴν καμαριναίων.

[4] Herod v. 77.   [5] 1248, 25, 1250, 1.   [6] Hell. 7, 2, 16.

[7] Æsch. Cho. 42. τί γὰρ λύτρον πεσόντος αἵματος πέδῳ ;

movement of any sort, and He was put to death at the instigation of His own countrymen. He refused to place Himself at the head of the populace when they sought to make Him a king, and He declared that His kingdom was not of this world. It was not simply to deliver the poor and degraded from servitude, nor the ignorant and lowly from their condition of debasement, that Jesus gave His life a ransom; for though He foresaw that such deliverances would result from His doctrines, the social emancipation of the poor was not the work to which He devoted His life. "The Son of Man is come to save that which is lost;"[1] and it was in fulfillment of that purpose that "He gave His life a ransom for many." He might have shunned death at the time and in the mode it came to Him; but He put Himself in the way of it, and against the remonstrance of His disciples went to Jerusalem, knowing what would there befall Him—not calculating chances, nor simply incurring a risk—but deliberately accepting death. As He said to Pilate, He *laid* down His life; He came to do this; it was in His plan to die upon the cross as a ransom. He "*must* be lifted up" in order that men "should not perish, but have eternal life:"—to "perish," therefore, would be the opposite of eternal life—the loss of that blessedness in God which is the life of the soul. From that destruction Jesus has ransomed us by giving His own life.

Here then from the lips of Christ Himself is the doctrine that He came into the world to die for the salvation of the world; and deliverance from that death spiritual and eternal which is the consequence of sin, and the securing eternal life to the soul, come by faith in the Son of Man as lifted up to be a Saviour,—thus giving His life for the redemption of mankind. This is the Gospel of the kingdom. It goes through the plague-

[1] Matt. xviii. 11.

stricken world crying, O sin-smitten soul! wouldst thou be healed? look to Jesus lifted up for thy salvation. O tormenting conscience! wouldst thou be stilled? look to Jesus on the cross, lifted up for thy healing! O soul condemned and dying! wouldst find again thy life? look to Jesus, and the condemnation shall be cancelled, thy ransom accomplished, and the warrant given thee of life purchased and sealed by His death. And whosoever would not perish, let him look to Jesus and be saved!

CHAPTER VI.

SALVATION LIMITED ONLY BY UNBELIEF.

THAT the death of Christ had a remedial virtue and intent, a pre-ordained and necessary relation to the life-healing of the soul; that it was a price paid for our redemption, having therefore a proper vicarious import in respect of the salvation of the world, has been established from His own words. As in a day of dire extremity to Israel, when the sin of the people was visited upon them by a fearful and destructive plague, Moses, by command of God, lifted up the serpent in the wilderness to show that Jehovah was present as a Saviour for every one that would look to Him in faith; in like manner, by appointment of God, and for the manifestation of His present grace and succor, the Son of Man was lifted up to the hope and faith of a perishing world, "that whosoever believeth in Him should not perish, but have eternal life."[1] This last declaration announces, by authority of Christ, the practical reach and application of the saving benefits of His death. And this was followed by an utterance, if possible, still more emphatic, setting forth the Salvation as provided in the gift of God, and as realized through its acceptance among men: "For God so loved the world that He gave His only-begotten Son, that whosoever believeth in Him should not perish, but have everlasting life. For God sent not His Son into the world to condemn the world, but that the world through Him might be saved."[2] Here the *Whosoever* points to an unlimited provision, the sufficiency

---

[1] John iii. 15.   [2] John iii. 16, 17.

of the gift of God for the whole world; but the *Believing*, which is the necessary and invariable condition, suggests that the breadth of result in the numbers actually saved may not equal the breadth of provision for salvation in the death of Jesus upon the cross; universality on the part of God, the provider, limitation only by the act of Man, the receiver.

Critical authorities are pretty evenly divided upon the question whether these words were a part of our Lord's discourse to Nicodemus, or an explanatory addition by the Evangelist.[1] Though the change to the past tense[2]— " God *gave* or *sent* His Son "—may give countenance to the latter view, there is here no sign of a break in the discourse; and the statement of the origin and extent of the redemptive mission of Christ follows naturally the declaration that the Son of Man " must be lifted up." The purpose and reach of the divine sacrifice are logically connected with the fact of the sacrifice and its necessity. Whatever was the ground of the necessity that Jesus should die for our salvation, His coming into the world was projected in the love of God, for that very end; and that love is pictured as self-sacrificing, wide-reaching, all-embracing.

But inasmuch as the present line of discussion limits us to the very words of Jesus, even should this particular form of expression be doubtful, its sentiment is confirmed by words of the same import that did certainly fall from His lips. " Verily, verily, I say unto you, He that heareth my word, and believeth on Him that sent Me, hath everlasting life."[3] " This is the will of Him that sent Me, that *every one* which seeth the Son, and believeth on Him,

---

[1] Among recent commentators, Tholuck, Olshausen and others take the former view; the latter is maintained by Knapp, Meyer, Ilug, Alford.

[2] The Aorist ἔδωκε, contemplates the action in the mind of the speaker, as *brought to pass*.   [3] John v. 24.

may have everlasting life."[1] Add to these such declarations as the following: "He that believeth shall be saved,"[2] "Him that cometh to Me I will in no wise cast out,"[3] and the testimony of Christ is clear, positive, and ample to the point that through His death salvation is provided for all mankind.

There are, however, other sayings of Christ that seem in some sort to put a limitation upon the application of this provision of grace, or at least upon its result in actual experience. In answer to the question "Lord, are there few that be saved?" Jesus said, "Strive to enter in at the strait gate; for many, I say unto you, will seek to enter in, and shall not be able."[4] "Wide is the gate, and broad is the way that leadeth to destruction, and many there be that go in thereat; because strait is the gate, and narrow is the way which leadeth unto life, and *few there be that find it.*"[5] Summing up these several sayings, we find that the doctrine of Christ concerning salvation embraces the following points:

(*a.*) The fullness and freeness of the provision of salvation for all mankind, upon just and simple conditions.

(*b.*) That none do really come to Christ for salvation, except as they are influenced from the Father; and

(*c.*) That by reason of unbelief or of misdirected endeavors, many will really fail of salvation at the last.

That there is a limitation somewhere upon the practical working of the divine plan of salvation, or rather in the actual results of that plan, is the obvious teaching of Christ, in some of the passages cited above. But is this limitation *in the plan* itself? or does it in any way detract from the sufficiency of the atonement, or the fullness and freeness of the offer of salvation on the part of God? Is such an inference warranted by the declaration of Christ

<hr />

[1] John vi. 40. [2] Mark xvi. 16. [3] John vi. 37.
[4] Luke xiii. 24. [5] Matt. vii. 13, 14.

"No man can come to Me, except the Father which hath
sent Me draw him."[1] There is much to the same purport
in our Lord's discourse recorded in the sixth chapter of
John:—"All that the Father *giveth* Me, shall come to
Me." " This is the Father's will which hath sent Me, that
of all which He hath given Me, I should lose nothing, but
should raise it up again at the last day."[2] If these words
fairly imply that God has made an arbitrary selection of
the subjects of Redemption, so that salvation is provided
for only a limited number to the purposed exclusion of all
others, then how can one fulfill the commission of Christ,
that authorizes and requires His disciples to "go into all the
world, and preach the gospel to *every* creature," upon the unqualified assurance that " *he* that believeth shall be saved?"[3]

The sayings of Christ touching the "drawing" of His
Father, the "giving" by His Father, must be interpreted
in accordance with these broad terms in which He himself
first announced the gospel, and at the last commissioned
His disciples to proclaim it to the world. "God so loved
the world"—not alone the Jewish people, nor any other
people of the world; not a certain chosen portion of human
society; not some one favored age of the world, but the
world of mankind, the human race in its totality:—God so
loved the world, that He gave His only begotten Son, that
whosoever believeth—not whoever is selected and set apart
from the rest of his species, not those belonging to a favored
class,—but " whosoever *believeth* in Him should not perish."
The love is equal toward all; the salvation is open to all
upon the same simple and impartial condition; and the
result in each and every case, hinges upon the *Believing*.
This declaration, so absolute and unequivocal, is borne out
by the uniform tenor of the invitations and commands of the
gospel, and is neither contradicted nor qualified by the statement; " All that the Father giveth Me shall come to Me."

Who are the "All" here spoken of, but simply

¹ John vi. 44.   ² vv. 37–39.   ³ Mark xvi. 16.

believers? The Father gave to His Son the whole world of mankind as the field of His redemptive work, to the intent that through Him the world *might* be saved; the provision, in its own nature, renders the salvation practicable for all and possible to every man. But the very object of this salvation, that which constitutes it a salvation in reality, is *deliverance from sin;* and for this there must be repentance, and faith in the Saviour whom God hath sent; therefore, it was not certified that by the lifting up of the Son of Man the whole world would in fact be saved; but that there should be gathered to Christ a multititude of believing souls, was made sure by the promise of the Father. The discourse recorded in the sixth chapter of John was addressed to a group of cavilers, who met the sayings of Jesus concerning His Father with the demand, "What sign shewest thou, that we may see and believe Thee?"

Jesus announced Himself as the true sign—the bread of life come down from heaven,—and added, "He that cometh to Me shall never hunger, and he that believeth on Me shall never thirst." Here was the same breadth of promise to a sincere faith. "But," He continued, "ye also have seen Me, and believed not;" therefore they did not come; therefore they did not eat of the bread of life; and therefore, practically, they were not saved. Yet He comforted Himself with the thought that His mission should not everywhere and always be frustrated by the unbelief of men. Some will believe; many will believe; and all these the Father has promised to Him as His own; and these coming, one by one, with the expression of a personal faith, would be thus made manifest as of the All that are "given by the Father." Hence He added (v. 40), "This is the will of Him that sent Me, that *every* one which seeth the Son and *believeth* on Him, may have everlasting life." The believing is the coming, and the fact of believing indicates each as one of the grand total given to Christ. Hence the statement in v. 44 does not teach that God has made an arbitrary selection of certain persons to be saved, and given these to Christ, but that He has given to Christ *all* who believe, that these may be His peculiar people—and the believing is open to all. The giving is not for the purpose of excluding any, but of making sure the fruits of redemption; not for narrowing the basis, but for securing a result upon the basis and by means of it.

What, then, is meant by that "drawing" of the Father, without which Jesus declared that no man can come to Him? This also is interpreted by the act of faith, as He described it at the conclusion of this same discourse, (verses 64, 65.) Having defined the spiritual significance of partaking of His own flesh and blood, and the consequent need of a spiritual frame of mind in order to receive that "hard saying," He charged some of His own disciples with the want of this sincere spiritual faith:—"For Jesus knew from the beginning who they were that believed not, and who should betray Him. And He said, Therefore, said I unto you, that no man can come unto Me except it were given unto him of my Father;"—which is neither more nor less than the doctrine "that which is born of the Spirit is spirit," and therefore must every one be born of the Spirit, regenerated by a divine illumination. This, then, is the drawing of the Father—a gracious influence quickening the soul, and persuading it to believe.

Can any honest interpretation derive from this the notion of an arbitrary selection on the part of God, limiting the design and the application of the death of His Son, selecting some and excluding others as the heirs of life, by a bare determination of His own will?

None, indeed, come to Christ, except the Father draw them; but how many does the Father draw, who yet refuse to come! For what is the manner and the purpose of this drawing? And whence arises the necessity that the Father should draw men to Christ? Our Lord has given the answer in that sentence of condemnation which lies against the unbelieving world of to-day as justly and forcibly as against the Jews who rejected Him to His face: "Ye will not come to Me, that ye might have life."[1] The coming is believing; it is repenting, turning, trusting; and this is an act of will. The will of the man himself must move, if ever he shall come to Christ, and if his will does not move spontaneously, cordially, to accept Christ when offered as a Saviour, then nothing further can be done for his salvation except to draw him by some influence directed to incite the will. Coercion is impossible, for the will cannot be forced;—to force it by sheer power were to destroy its very nature as the choosing, willing faculty of the soul. Hardly can the will be reasoned with; for the fault commonly does not lie with the understanding and the judgment, but in the choice being fixed already upon the wrong—"Light has come into the world;" the truth is clear enough, the way is plain enough, the light is sufficient for the understanding and the conscience; but "men love darkness rather than light because their deeds are evil. For every one that doeth evil hateth the light; neither cometh to the light, lest his deeds should be reproved."[2]

In this state of facts—the salvation provided for all and freely offered to all; this salvation rendered availing as a deliverance from sin only through a personal repentance and faith; this again requiring a free act of will, and yet the will halting, not accepting, not moving toward acceptance, not "*coming*"—the only thing that can be done further is to influence the will by some power of persuasion that shall incite it to right action. That influence is what our Lord has described as the operation of the Holy Spirit upon the mind—no more to be defined than the coming

---

[1] John v. 40. [2] John iii. 19, 20.

and going of the wind, yet stirring the soul to its depths, "convincing it of sin, of righteousnesss, and of judgment," and so arousing and drawing it that the will *does* move, does choose, does decide, does come. YET NOT ALWAYS! —for the will is an agent of such fearful, such stubborn power, that it may even resist the Holy Ghost, resist the drawing of the Father, as it does resist the invitations of the Son. Hence while it is true that all who come to Christ are drawn of the Father, it is still true that others perish, not because they are hindered or neglected of God, nor because they are not solicited by the Gospel and wrought upon by the Holy Ghost, but because they *will not* come.

The argument leads to this conclusion; that the drawing of the soul to Christ by a special influence from the Father, is directed solely to this end—to overcome the reluctance, the indifference, or (to put it in the strongest terms) the inertness and stagnation of the human will; that the necessity for this divine influence in regeneration does not arise from any limitation in the normal powers of the human soul, nor any limitation in the provision of salvation through Christ, nor any limitation nor discrimination in the love· of God in planning· for the salvation of lost men;—in a word, this "drawing" of the Father does not proceed upon the basis of limitation or restriction, in the provision of redemption or in the desire of God for the recovery of sinners; it cannot create, it does not imply a hindrance to the salvation of any, nor the rejection or any, but is the reaching forth of the same love and mercy that provided the redemption, to make sure, by all means, of some actual fruit. There is nothing in any act or purpose of God that limits salvation in respect either of its adequacy as a provision or its amplitude as an offer: neither has God imposed upon any mind any kind or degree of restraint in respect to its accepting the salvation provided by Christ, and profiting to the full by its benefits. When He commands all men to repent, He does not command an impossibility: when He requires them to believe upon Christ, He means that every man should believe; when He promises salvation upon these simple and uniform terms, there are no drawbacks nor exceptions whatever.[1]

And yet the final results of Redemption will not be commensurate with the provision. The whole world *might* be saved, but alas, not all the world will be saved! Jesus Christ, the Saviour of the world, has pictured the dread and final separation of mankind into two classes at the last judgment, and has declared that the wicked "shall go away into everlasting punishment, but the righteous into life eternal."[2]

Here is a limitation in the actual results of salvation:— but whence does this arise? What is the turning-point, the dividing line? Does Christ Himself desire to save only one-tenth of the human race? or one-fourth? or one-half? Did He not die for all? Has not He invited all?

Whence comes the difference? We are brought back for an answer to that pivot of human character, the will, as the turning-point of destiny. It is just the question of believing or not believing. Believing on the Lord Jesus Christ as the Saviour from sin is the beginning of that new life which is salvation. Without this free committal of his soul to Christ one cannot so much as start in the new life; and therefore, if the man himself, under the light of the gospel, the invitations of Christ, the drawing of the Father, does not turn and believe, his deliverance from sin is an impossibility. This is no arbitrary ruling of the Creator; it is the law under which the soul exists by the

[1] For a full discussion of the relations of the Holy Spirit to human volition see the author's volume on "the Holy Comforter."

[2] Matt. xxv. 46.

necessity of its moral constitution. It is not that God created any soul with the intent that it should perish; nor that He either dooms or leaves any to perish by limiting or withholding on His part the provision of salvation; for "God sent not His Son into the world to condemn the world, but that the world through Him might be saved." Why then is not the whole world *ipso facto* saved? How comes it that any are condemned? The evangelist has answered this question in terms which, if they be not the very words of Christ, are the logical complement to His own statement of the condition of salvation: "He that believeth on Him is not condemned; but he that believeth not is condemned already, because he hath not believed in the name of the only-begotten Son of God."[1] His non-acceptance of the only possible deliverance from sin leaves him to the consequences of sin, in condemnation and death.

The requirement of faith as a condition of salvation is not arbitrary, but is necessary upon the highest moral grounds. One cannot be saved except through being freed from sin; and he cannot be freed from sin except by repenting, and by forsaking sin through that divine help which is brought him in the cross of Christ and by the coming of the Holy Ghost. Believing on Christ is a condition with which every one can comply; it is a just, necessary, and simple requirement, compliance with which is salvation and life in the very act; the one sole limitation upon the final results of Christ's redeeming sacrifice arises from the unbelief of men, which even the drawing of the Father often fails to overcome. We come back, therefore, to the doctrine of a full and free salvation as declared by Christ without limitation—no limitation on the part of God, neither in the magnitude of the provision itself, nor in the scope of the offer of salvation, nor in the intent with which that offer is made; no limi-

[1] John iii. 18.

tation upon the result save what the will of man imposes, through unbelief. It is a full salvation, adequate to the wants of the whole world; it is a free salvation, offered equally and impartially to whoever will accept it.

The gift of God proclaims this. "God so loved the world that He gave His only-begotten Son:"—that single fact carries with it the whole argument. He who sends his only son to fight for his country could add nothing to that proof of his devotion to the country in all its interests —to its material prosperity, to its moral unity, to its government and laws, to the whole nation. The sending is the final argument; and when He who sends is the Almighty Father, whose one only Son represents the infinitude of His love, and that sending is grounded in His love and pity for the world, that fact alone determines the conclusion that He would have all men to be saved.

The sacrifice itself proclaims this; necessary in all its fulness for one, adequate in its oneness for all. It was not against sins numerically that Christ testified by His cross, nor was it a certain form or number of transgressions that called for His mediation; but it was *Sin* that He testified against as treason to the government of God, and that required an expiation which by its virtue in redeeming one could equally avail for all.

The word of Christ proclaims this universal sufficiency of His sacrifice both in scope and in availability: "Him that cometh I will in no wise cast out"[1]—"that the world through Him might be saved."[2]

The testimony of myriads confirms this declaration. In all the ages since, whosoever has applied by faith for this salvation has found that it awaited him upon his simply coming, and that it sufficed for his personal necessity as if provided for him alone; nor has any one ever failed of salvation who would only believe.

[1] John vi. 37.   [2] John iii. 17.

He, therefore, who refuses to come to Christ, does all that lies in his power to hinder the consummation of the world's deliverance. A universal deliverance from sin, a universal consecration to a holy life in God, would render this world as pure and blessed as heaven; but every man that will not come to Christ for personal deliverance from sin, so far as in him lies, delays and frustrates that blessed consummation. The angels ushering in the Son of Man sang, "Peace on earth, good-will toward men;" but unbelief breaks in upon that song with the discord and strife of sin.

He that refuses to believe in Christ sets himself against all the forces of love in the universe that are seeking his good. God the Father has bent upon him His infinite compassion; the Son of God has given for him His life upon the cross; the Holy Spirit has convinced, admonished, entreated, drawn him; heaven and its holy inhabitants have sought to welcome him to their joys; but all this potency of love fails to save him because of his unbelief!

CHAPTER VII.

RELIGION in its broad acceptation—the obligation of the Soul toward God, as the object of worship and obedience—is the subject of supreme moment to mankind, and that upon which in all ages mankind have bestowed their chiefest care and thought. "Man is born with two needs, at once distinct and inseparable, the *moral* and the *religious* instinct. Free, he yet feels that there exists a law which should regulate his will. Capable of intelligence and of love, his mind and his heart require an infinite object. Every man possesses the instinct of the Good, and the instinct of the Infinite, in a word, the instinct of the Divine. He who can live without faith in the Divine, or who has smothered that sublime faith within him, does not belong to humanity."[1] Where this instinct has developed itself normally, the outward manifestation of Religion has taken almost as many varieties as there are differences of race, in mental characteristics, in domestic habits, and in social and civil customs. And so comprehensive is the obligation of the religious feeling, that it takes as many types as there are faculties and sentiments of the soul, and modes of moral expression and action—now the *Reason* giving to Religion its particular cast; now the *Imagination;* now the *Senses* and now the *Tastes;* now the *beautiful* in Nature, now the *hopeful* in Fancy, the *pleasurable* in Feeling; and now the *gloomy*, the *grotesque*, the *horrible;*—yet these diversified and even

[1] Emile Saisset. *Essais sur la Philosophie et la Religion au xix. Siecle*, p. 287.

79

contradictory manifestations of the religious idea or the religious feeling, are, for the most part, but exaggerations of some one element or feature which the religious idea properly includes, or which has a real basis in the religious feeling.

Difficult as it is to discriminate each and every phase of Religion by a note or sign peculiar to itself, we may distribute the various types of Religion that have been developed among mankind apart from Christianity, into five general classes ;—(a) the intellectual or speculative ; (b) the formal or ceremonial; (c) the humanitary, or religions of good works; (d) the imaginative, or religions of superstition ; (e) and the spiritual or pietistic, in which the meditative and emotional piety of the inner life is exalted above all modes of intellectual statement, all outward forms of worship, all practical works of beneficence.

In the time of Christ, these leading types of Religion had all found expression in the world's history. Plato had elaborated his monotheistic conception of God as the all-comprehensive Idea ; while at the same time he had exalted Virtue, Truth, and Beauty into a sort of intellectual Triad—a Trinity not of hypostases but of predicates—allegiance to which was the very essence of morality. With him Religion is the realization of the idea of the good, through the Reason bringing all the principles and actions of the soul into a perfect unison, and so to an intellectual harmony with God. The highest virtue is wisdom or absolute knowledge; yet he said of God, " It is hard to investigate and find the Framer and Father of the universe ; and if one did find him, it were impossible to express him in terms comprehensible by all." [1]

Aristotle, who lacked the mystic, poetic temperament of his great master, by the severity of his critical method

[1] Tim. p. 28.

reduced the Deity to pure Intelligence, absorbed in self-contemplation, subject and object in one, the final cause of the world,[1] as the end of all its aspirations. To this almost impersonal, self-quiescent, incorporeal substance, Aristotle ascribed neither creative power nor moral quality. With his disciples, Aristotle's conception of a self-immanent Intelligence, dissociated from the world, degenerated into bald materialism, under the two-fold form of Atheism and Pantheism; and so the Divinity that to Plato was the highest intellectual conception, through being contemplated solely with relation to the intellectual system of the universe, was either retired to an infinite distance and a state of absolute repose, or reduced to a mere potency or energy in the kingdom of Nature. Religion as pure intellectuality reached its highest development in Plato, only to be marred and materialized when handled by minds less delicate and pure than his own.

The boast of modern Rationalism that in matters of belief it has emancipated the human intellect by admitting only that which is originated or established by Reason itself, may well be confronted with the fact that the highest product of Reason in the sphere of Religion was wrought out, and had well-nigh run out, before Christ came, and can be compared impartially with His teachings. It pushed one factor in Religion to an extreme that well-nigh destroyed the thing; for Religion and God as its object were reasoned into nothingness.

While certain philosophers had thus refined Religion into a speculative nonentity, the actual religions of the pagan world at the time of Christ were full of superstition

---

[1] His thinking is upon Thought; ἔστιν ἡ νόησις νοήσεως νόησις (*Metaphys.* xi. ix. 4) and since He is the highest and best, His thinking is upon Himself. He moves the world not by an energy proceeding from Himself, but by the attraction that is in Himself, the power of the Beautiful or the Good. (*De Coel*). ii. 10-12.

6

and sensuality—appealing to the Imagination by mystery, by the fascinations of pleasure and the torments of pain, and addressing the senses through forms of beauty, as in Greece, or by objects of terror, as in Egypt, [1] and in the remoter East.

The three remaining types of Religion were fully illustrated among the Jews of the time of Christ. Some made the virtue of religion consist in the close adherence to forms. To pay tithes of all that they possessed, even of the farthing herbs in their gardens, to fast twice in the week, to be careful even to scrupulosity in keeping the Sabbath, to offer all the sacrifices and observe all the sacred days prescribed by the law—such rigid Formalism constituted their religion. Others laid stress upon their good works; giving alms before men, and counting their charities for piety. And there were various sects of Jews—such as the Essenes and Therapeutæ—who formed themselves into communities or brotherhoods, like later orders of monks, for cultivating piety by seclusion from the world, rigorous self-denial, and devout secret meditation.

Thus all the leading forms under which the religious idea or the religious feeling has found expression in the history of mankind, were in full development before the time of Christ. And these characteristic types, the speculative, the ceremonial, the superstitious, the humanitary, the pietistic have continued to reproduce themselves in new countries and among new peoples, and have even attempted to run Christianity itself into their several modes. Yet the Religion of Christ, Religion as taught by Him in its principles and exemplified by Him in its spirit, is something apart from each and every one of these religious types,—sublime in its simplicity, profound in its origin,

[1] Some of the Egyptian divinities were spiritual in their nature and beneficent in their attributes; but others were grossly animal in their aspect, or formidable, with the flail and scourge; and the Egyptian Hades was a region of darkness and horrors.

springing from the inmost depths of the soul, and universal in its reach and application. From His teachings one obtains quite another view of religion, in its nature, its spirit, and its power.

First of all, Christ referred true religion to the heart as the seat of its vitality. If we inquire after the nature of Religion as Jesus presented it, we find that it was not a something which a man took upon him from without—a set of opinions that he espoused, a set of customs that he adopted, a set of regulations that he conformed to; nor was it a something which a man performed outside of himself—a round of ceremonies that he fulfilled, a course of devotions or of charities that he went through with: but while it covered all these—beliefs, devotions, observances, charities,—and used them all as evidences of its presence, Religion itself as to its essence, was within the soul, and proceeded thence to the outer life.

This fundamental conception of religion Christ presented under a variety of aspects. In the sermon on the mount, he traced *sin* to the inmost recesses of the heart. Murder is being angry with a brother without cause; adultery is the unchaste look, imagination, desire; swearing is the profane thought, the irreverent feeling; and so every sin is traced to the heart, and if a sinful act is conceived and purposed in the heart the man is guilty, even though he does not commit the act in its outward form. " A corrupt tree bringeth forth evil fruit;" [1] and " an evil man, out of the evil treasure of his heart, bringeth forth that which is evil." [2] Hence Religion, which is to rectify the mischief of sin, must dispossess sin of the heart, and install itself there, at the centre of the moral life. The process by which this is effected is an interior spiritual work;—repentance is a sorrow of the heart, and a turning of the will away from the sin ; to be " born again," is to be inwardly

---

[1] Matt. vii. 17.   [2] Luke vi. 45.

renewed, so changed in heart as to be a new man in respect of spiritual things; to believe upon Christ is for the heart to trust itself to Him ; " Blessed are the poor in spirit,"— they that are humble and broken in heart—" for theirs is the kingdom of heaven." And as with the beginning of religious experience, so of its consummation : it is through-out a spiritual work; the process of renovation and sancti-fication, in the perfecting of the religious life, is to go on within the soul. " Blessed are the pure in heart"—those made inwardly and spiritually pure—" for they shall see God."[1]

Nor is it in essence alone that Religion is thus intensely spiritual and inward;—religious acts, to have reality and value, must proceed from the heart, and fairly represent its spiritual frames. " When thou doest thine alms do not sound a trumpet before thee, as the hypocrites do, in the synagogues, and in the streets, that they may have glory of men ; but when thou doest alms, let not thy left hand know what thy right hand doeth, that thine alms may be in secret." [2] In deeds of charity, one must not court the observation and applause of men, but act from pure, unselfish motives, as under the eye of his Father, which seeth in secret.

Like precepts are laid down concerning prayer. One must not be ostentatious in his personal devotions :— " When thou prayest, enter into thy closet, and when thou hast shut thy door, pray to thy Father, which is in secret." [3] Prayer is the communion of the heart with God. It does not consist of words ; much less is it to be valued by the multitude of words.[4] In Thibet, the Buddhists make use of a prayer-cylinder, in which yards of petitions, written upon narrow strips of paper, are wound like ribbon around a wire that passes through the centre, and each revolution of the cylinder upon this axis counts for a repetition of all

[1] Matt. v. 3, 9.   [2] Matt. vi. 1-4.   [3] Matt. vi. 6.   [4] Matt. vi. 7.

these prayers; so that one needs only to keep twirling his cylinder at intervals, and he will secure the benefit of whole hours, and even miles of prayer! Some economize time by setting the cylinder at work by water-power, or other mechanical contrivance, while their hands and feet are busy in other matters. And this tendency to mechanicizing prayers is always found where the efficacy of prayer is sought in the *opus operatum*. But the doctrine of Christ drives one back from all modes and forms, from the surroundings and accessories of devotion, into the citadel of the soul, to find if he there possesses true religion. The alms, the prayers, the offices of charity and devotion, that are turned out upon dress parade, give no evidence of true loyalty to God, or of real strength in religious character. This must be found within where it exists at all, and when prayers and almsgiving take a public form, publicity must never be the end in view. As a matter of *consciousness*, or of self-congratulation, the left hand must not know what the right hand doeth;[1] yet he who has this inner spirit of devotion toward God and beneficence toward man, is commanded to let his light so shine before men that they may see his good works, and *glorify his Father*, which is in heaven.[2]

Christ declared that no amount of praying and prophesying in His name, nor the multitude of wonderful and practically useful works done in His name, will avail to certify one as His disciple, nor commend him to favor at the judgment, where the inward spirit of love and devotion is wanting.[3] Thus by every form of presentation, for the essence of Religion He sends us back to the inmost centre of the soul. Religion is, first of all, a thing of the heart, internal and spiritual—" a good man, out of the good treasure of his heart, bringeth forth that which is good."

What then is this good treasure of the heart—this inner

1 Matt. vi. 3.   2 Matt. v. 16.   3 Matt. vii. 22, 23.

essence of Religion? Is the heart mere feeling—the seat
of emotion only? Modern physiology so distinguishes it
from the brain as the seat of thought; but in the language
of the Hebrews the heart was also the seat of intelligence
and of the moral faculties and affections; a man thought
in his heart,[1] he purposed in his heart;[2] he turned his
heart this way and that;[3] and so the Understanding and
the Will, as well as susceptibilities and emotions, were com-
prised in the heart; this was the center of self-determina-
tion, and hence of moral character and spiritual life. In
the same sense the heart was spoken of by Christ as embodying all the constituents of moral life; and therefore,
the Religion that is in and of the heart must be conceived
of as a matter of intelligent principle, of voluntary determination, and of devout feeling. These together constitute the heart—the moral substance of the man—answering to the stock and sap of the tree. An analysis of
His teaching on this point gives the following results:

True Religion is an inward *principle* of holy living,
through consecration to a holy God. This was the root-
idea of the law given at Sinai, underlying each particular
precept; for the commandments that refer to specific outward actions—enjoining particular duties and forbidding
particular sins—are all founded in and governed by the
preamble " I am the Lord thy God," and the first declaration " Thou shalt have no other gods before Me." The
acknowledgment of this one only God—the Lord Jehovah,
the living one, *thy* God—the personal Spirit who is the
Creator and Lord of the human spirit, who has a right of
possession in every living soul, and who only should be
confessed as God and Lord; who is set forth as the maker
of heaven and earth, and the giver of the earth to man for
his abode; who is a holy and jealous God, visiting ini-

---

[1] Is. x. 7; 1 Chron. xxix. 18; Is. xxxii. 4; Gen. xvii. 1–17; Job xii. 3.
[2] 1 Sam. xiv. 7; Is. x. 7; lxiii. 4.   [3] Job xv. 12; Is. xliv. 20.

quity, yet multiplying mercies to them that love Him, a God whose very name must be had in reverence and never lightly spoken—the acknowledgment of this one spiritual, holy, supreme Lord, allegiance to His majesty, obedience to His authority as holy, just and true—this principle lay at the foundation of the decalogue, and of the whole system of religion set forth in the Old Testament. The Eternal, Almighty Holy Spirit, the Creator and Lord of all, is here set before man not simply as an object .of contemplation, to be admired as the highest conception of the Divinity that the intellect can attain to—but as having direct personal relations with the human spirit as His own image, as having a claim upon mankind severally for worship and allegiance, and as seeking to draw each individual soul into the conscious, loving, faithful relationship of a child of God. To recognize this spiritual and Holy Being not simply as existing but existing in *that* relation, to acknowledge His rightful authority, to accept His law, and to devote the soul to Him in a holy, loving obedience —this inner principle of serving God is the sum and substance of the Decalogue, and of the Religion of the Old Testament. All offerings and sacrifices, all prayers and alms, all Sabbaths and ceremonies were worse than worthless without this.

This fundamental principle of the Jewish theocracy had become well nigh obsolete under the mass of forms and traditions that men had heaped upon it; but Christ restored this as the first commandment in the code of the kingdom of God as His spiritual commonwealth. He did not abrogate nor in any wise modify this original conception of Religion. To suppose that Christ relaxed the obligation of this principle of spiritual consecration in favor of some easier, lower type of piety expressed through faith as mere *feeling*, is a spiritual conceit and doctrinal error of most dangerous tendency. In the Christian system faith does not displace nor qualify the principle of holy obedience; it encourages us to trust in Christ for the forgiveness of sins, thus atoning for our lack of obedience in the past, and to look to Christ for help in obedience for the future. Perfect faith will conduce to perfect obedience; for the rule and standard of Religion as presented in the words of Jesus, is identical with that which underlies the Decalogue—an inward principle of holy living through consecration to the will of a holy God.

This was His own rule of life as the perfect man : " I seek not Mine own will, but the will of the Father which hath sent Me." [1] " I came down from heaven, not to do Mine own will, but the will of Him that sent Me." [2] " My meat is to do the will of Him that sent Me, and to finish His work." [3] This was the deep, constant, controlling principle in the active obedience of Jesus Christ, and on the side of passive obedience it was the same: " Not My will but Thine be done." And though He covers our disobedience by His righteousness, and takes away our sins by His cross, and offers to our weakness the helping-hand of faith, He accords to His disciples no lower type of Religion than that which He illustrated, no lower rule of life than that which He observed. Nay rather did He put new life and emphasis into the fundamental principle of the decalogue as the law of His own kingdom: for He compressed the ten commandments into that one rule of holy obedience and consecration, and crowded this home upon the heart, saying : " Thou shalt love the Lord thy God with all thy heart, and with all thy soul, and with all thy mind." [4] We cannot go deeper than this for a foundation of Religion, we cannot rise higher than this for a standard of life, we can have nothing broader, fuller, more complete and final as a spirit of consecration. It is the most spiritual conception of Religion that the philosopher

[1] Matt. xxii. 37.   [2] John vi. 38.   [3] John iv. 34.   [4] Matt. xxii. 37.

can form, and at the same time the most simple and practical rule of piety that can be given to a child. This principle settled within the soul as the one aim and law of its life is the "good treasure of the heart," out of which all good things are brought forth.

This principle supposes the free, intelligent choice of God and His service as the soul's supreme delight: its choice as an abiding state of preference, in distinction from particular acts of volition, yet including these and imparting to them a decisive character as acts of holy love.

Where true Religion is, there the soul has elected God as its supreme good; has accepted God as its ideal of excellence; has enthroned God as the Sovereign of its acts, its thoughts, and its desires; and it abides in this its supreme choice as its satisfying rest and portion. As a state of preference this is the permanent choice of the soul, that underlies, and with more or less of conscious determination influences, all the choices and actions of the mind, and so gives character to the whole man.

This elective principle carries along with it the feelings of the heart. It is not a dry intellectual state, though it may seem dry when analyzed for purposes of definition; neither is it a cold, stiff purpose of the will, though its value and durability as a principle require that it shall take the form of fixed rigid resolution; but feeling enters into the choice, animates the purpose, keeps the resolution all aglow. For the choice which the soul makes in Religion is not simply a choice of opinions, nor a choice of systems, nor a choice of ends personal to itself, but the choice of an object of affection, even of its highest love: the choice is itself *affection* going forth in the act of will, as the dominant love of the heart. Not duty, nor fear as toward God in His Majesty, nor simply approbation in the contemplation of the divine excellence; but *love* it is that inspires the deep principle, the fixed purpose of the soul to serve and honor God in holy living. Thus Religion absorbs all the powers and affections of the soul.

But that which gains this complete possession of the man spiritually also controls him practically. This deep inward principle, this sublime spiritual conception, this supreme absorbing purpose, this one dominant engrossing affection, is also a life-power. The soul does not shut itself up within itself, as in a temple, to worship the Unseen, the Absolute, and keep its Religion as a thing separate and sacred from the life ; but that which is rooted so deep within and nourished with such warmth of love, blossoms forth upon the world, sheds abroad its fragrance, and drops upon every side its golden fruit. The good tree, by the law of its nature—all the forces of its constitution and its life conjoining—brings forth good fruit; and so the good man, out of the good treasure of his heart, bringeth forth good things ; and as the quality of the fruit speaks for the tree, so the good deeds testify of the character. " By their fruits ye shall know them." [1]

This doctrine of good fruits does not at all conflict with Christ's condemnation of ostentation in religion, in Matt. vi. 1-7. What He there objected to was not the bare publicity of the act, but publicity as a *motive* to the act;—praying " to be seen of men," giving alms " to be seen of men "—performing the most sacred duties in a way to attract attention, personating piety with a view to get a reputation for piety—this it was that Jesus condemned. But the opposite of religious ostentation is not hiding one's light under a bushel, concealing religious principle and feeling so as not even to be suspected of it, avoiding religious conversation and whatever might bring the repute of godliness. The command of Christ to His disciples is ; " Let your light so shine before men, that they may see your good works, and glorify your Father which is in

[1] Matt. vii. 16.

heaven." The shining is the beauty of a translucent character: the light shines through because it is within; and it shines simply because it is there. It is not a calcium light hung out now and then to dazzle passers by—but pure sunlight, which shines because it is. The religious principle being seated within, and having control of the understanding, the will, and the affections, is the life of the whole man. The tree being of good stock, sound, healthy, and well-nourished with sap, brings forth good fruit; and the true Religion is known, not by the professions it makes, nor the forms it adopts, but by the influence it has upon the spirit and conduct of the man, upon his habits and actions, and by the positively good things that he does, under its living inspiration, as naturally and as regularly as the tree brings forth fruit—" his own fruit," the fruit natural and proper to itself. "The good man out of the good treasure of his heart bringeth forth that which is good."

The test that Christ applied to the religious professions of individuals, may be applied with equal fairness to his own system of Religion:—this also may be tested by its fruits. We have seen how, under the power of the religious idea and the impulse of religious feeling, mankind distorted and exaggerated particular elements and features of Religion, and produced a cold intellectual abstraction, an ideal worship of fancy or taste, a pretentious self-righteous charity, an elaborate and cumbersome ritualism, a monstrosity of the imagination and the senses, a monastic and ascetic pietism; and how utterly human wisdom failed of realizing to itself the conception of a spiritual and holy God, and a spiritual and holy consecration, so as to render this a controlling power in the life. But Religion as interpreted by Christ fills the highest reach of Reason in respect of the nature of God; strips Imagination of uncouth images and morbid fears, and adorns it with new beauties

and glories in the realm of the spiritual; purifies the Affections, consecrates the Will; puts soul and unction into
every Form of worship, puts life and love into every
Charity; makes the whole man, body, soul, and spirit, a
consecrated vessel of the divine grace, a consecrated dwelling of the divine Spirit, a consecrated channel of the
divine will; and this by bringing the man into such near
and loving relations with God, that this limited, dependent, and imperfect human spirit is in accord with that
infinite, absolute, and perfect Spirit who fills immensity
with His presence, and makes heaven glorious and blessed
with His holy love. The Religion that so leads man up
to God, and so brings God into fellowship with man, must
have come down from heaven. By its fruits we know it
to be divine.

CHAPTER VIII.

THE SPIRITUALITY OF WORSHIP.

FROM the interior essence of religion as a life we pass to its outward expression in acts of reverence toward God. Christ laid down a formula of worship based upon the true conception of the divine being:—"The hour cometh, and now is, when the true worshipers shall worship the Father in spirit and in truth; for the Father seeketh such to worship Him. God is a spirit; and they that would worship Him must worship Him in spirit and in truth." [1] It is an axiom of the Christian faith that the mode of worship must correspond with the essence of God, which is spiritual, and the feeling of the worshiper must correspond with the character of God, which is paternal. What that essential nature of God is which is declared by the term spirit, must be defined largely by negatives. A spirit is not physical, not corporeal, not tangible, not visible, as these properties are attributed to forms of matter; nevertheless, we conceive of a spirit as a living substance, and as possessing both intelligence and personality. The term πνεῦμα was applied to the Father by Christ in the most absolute sense. The Septuagint had made this word familiar to Jewish readers as descriptive of the Spirit of God acting in creation and prophecy. But Jesus said God is *spirit*, pure spirit, thus defining His essence in respect of its immateriality; and the argument is, "God being pure spirit cannot dwell in particular spots or temples; cannot require, nor be pleased with, earthly material offering, nor ceremonies as such; on the

[1] John iv. 23, 24.

other hand, is only to be approached in that part of our being which is spirit,—and even there, inasmuch as He is pure and holy, with no by-ends nor hypocritical regards, but in truth and earnestness." [1]   In the ever-memorable words of Augustine, "If thou wouldst pray in the temple pray within thyself: but first be thou the temple of God." [2]

God is spirit. Jesus announced this sublimest conception of the nature of God, without defining it; announced it to a plain woman without simplifying it to her comprehension; left it to go upon record without solving the mystery that it contains. Yet as He was stating the fundamental principle of religious worship, to govern His followers for all time, it is fair to assume that He used the term spirit in a sense sufficiently intelligible to His hearers for the practical application of His rule. He would hardly have laid down for universal guidance in a matter of universal obligation, a proposition that could not be translated into the common ideas of men.

Our notion of spirit arises from our consciousness of understanding, of personality, and of power—conceptions that we attach to the *Ego*, the conscious self, in distinction from the material body with which this is invested. The Jewish scriptures had made familiar to the common mind this conception of spirit as an immaterial substance, possessing consciousness, understanding, personality, will, energy—for they ascribe to the πνεῦμα all spiritual functions, and distinguish it alike from the body, and from the soul, the animating principle of the body. It is the spirit in man that has understanding, that is capable of moral affections, that is the image of God, the inspiration of the Almighty, and this shall return unto the God who gave it,

---

[1] Alford on John iv. 23.

[2] In templo vis orare, in te ora. Sed prius esto templum Dei, quia illo in templo suo exaudiet orantem.

when the dust shall return to the earth as it was.[1] The same scriptures speak likewise of spirits as existing in a higher condition than man, and possessing higher capacities than are given to man in his present state. These are incorporeal, so far as cognizance of the senses goes; yet they are described under human modes of conception, as possessing powers of vision, of motion, and of action, vastly superior to any attainable by man. This idea of a spirit as a higher order of being was common among the Jews in the time of Christ. Philo believed in good and evil angels, and that these were identical in substance with the souls of men, though disconnected from bodies.[2] Jesus recognized the common belief in an order of spirits, when He said to His disciples after his crucifixion,—" A spirit hath not flesh and bones as ye see me have."[3]

In declaring that God was pure spirit Christ gave no countenance to the pantheistic notion of the divinity as diffused in space or as the soul of the universe. On the contrary, He at the same time defined both the individuality and the personality of God, in the formula of worship; —" they that worship *Him.*" This infinite Spirit is to be approached by the human spirit, as a personal Intelligence. Moreover the name Father ascribes to God relations and affections such as pertain only to personality.

Because God is spirit men must worship Him, and not any material representation of Him; must worship Him, and not any place where He is supposed to be; and they must not even worship Him in any one place alone, as if He were embodied or contained in that place, or were to be found only there. This was the point of His reply to the woman of Samaria :—" The hour cometh, when ye shall neither in this mountain, nor yet at Jerusalem, worship the Father:"[4]—then true worshipers will not resort to

---

[1] Ec. xii. 7.
[2] Philo Judæus on the Giants.
[3] Luke xxiv. 39.
[4] John iv. 21.

either with the feeling that the place gives validity or
sanctity to the act of worship. This did not imply that
there had been no sincere, real worship at Jerusalem or
Gerizim; for the contrast was not so much between the
true and the false, as between the perfect ideal and a
shadowy approximation. By the true worshipers are intended not only such as worship in sincerity of spirit, but
those that worship according to the true and perfect ideal.
"The worship of God in its highest conception, is that
which is most homogeneous with the divine nature. Now
God is spirit, and as such, elevated above space and time;
hence, the devotion which is in spirit, uttering itself in-
dependently of time and place, never ceasing, subject to no
external conditions, carried on in the inner sanctuary of
man, constitutes the only worship which corresponds to
its ideal." [1]

But was this saying of Christ concerning worship in
the spirit intended to disparage outward worship, and to
foreshadow its abolition under a higher purer conception of
Religion? The whole tenor of His life and doctrine forbids such an inference. Jesus Himself prayed openly and
audibly in the presence of His disciples. The prayer recorded at length in the seventeenth chapter of John's
gospel was an act of worship, and was rendered not in accordance with any Jewish form, but by Jesus as the
founder of the new dispensation about to be committed to
His disciples. He also taught His disciples to pray, and
how to pray; and the brief form of prayer that He gave
to them was adapted to be used in a collective act of worship: "*Our* Father: give *us* our daily bread." And
moreover Christ gave the assurance of a special blessing to
those who should unite in worship, and meet for that purpose in His name: "If two of you shall agree on earth as
touching any thing that they shall ask, it shall be done for

[1] Olshausen, Comm. *in loc.*

them of my Father which is in heaven: for where two or
three are gathered together in my Name, there am I in
the midst of them." [1] He also distinctly contemplated
and provided for the association of His disciples as a
Church, for worship and communion, and ordained sacraments to be therein observed. After His resurrection, He
met with His disciples in what appears to have been a
stated assembly for religious worship upon the first day
of the week.

If outward worship is made an end in itself, if all
thought and care are concentrated upon the manner of the
outward act, with the feeling that when this is regularly
performed the worship is accomplished—this is wholly at
variance with Christ's doctrine of true spiritual worship.

If again, the outward worship is regarded as a means to
an end, if by the law of association, and by the suggestion
of spiritual truth through appropriate symbols, it serves to
educate the mind in religious thought and feeling—as was
the design of the Jewish ritual—these ends are legitimate
and valuable, though such a conception of worship falls
below the ideal enunciated by Christ.

In its highest and best relations, outward worship is the
expression and exponent of the inward frame and feeling
of the worshiper. The feeling of devotion gives to worship
an unlimited universality of utterance, and renders natural
and fit the outward form.

This feeling should lead one to approach God as a
Father. This name presents to the heart the moral and
sympathetic aspect of the divine Being, as the term spirit
presents to the understanding the conception of His essential
nature. This Spirit, though infinite in His own nature, is
not at an infinite remove from us in space nor in feeling,
but is a loving Father, who thinks upon us, cares for us,
and seeks us, desiring the communion of our spirits with

1 Matt. xviii. 19.

7

Himself. This enunciation meets the longing of the more devout and spiritual minds of pagan antiquity for a near and conscious intercourse with God. Said Dio Chrysostom, "There exists in all men an eager longing to adore and worship the gods as nigh. For as children, torn from father and mother, feel a powerful and affectionate longing, often stretch out their hands after their absent parents, and often dream of them; so the man who heartily loves the gods for their benevolence towards us and their relationship with us, desires to be continually near them and to have intercourse with them; so that many barbarians, ignorant of the arts, have called the very mountains and trees gods, that they might recognize them as nearer to themselves." [1]

But Christ would bring God nearer than the mountain, nearer than the temple, in the spiritual, living, reciprocal intercourse of the father and the child. In its longing to localize the Deity, Paganism materialized Him—first personifying the powers and effects of nature as representatives of the Divinity, and finally transferring to these its whole conception of God. There is the same tendency in the materialistic Pantheism of modern times—to resolve the Divinity into a law, a force, a principle, an essence, or at best a soul resident in nature; but this while bringing God nigh, in a sense, yet takes away the value of the nearness by robbing Him of personality, which alone renders worship reasonable and communion possible. True worship must be founded upon the spirituality of God. "His being a spirit declares *what* He is; his other perfections declare what kind of spirit He is. All God's perfections suppose Him a spirit: all center in this: His wisdom does not suppose Him merciful, or His mercy suppose Him omniscient; there may be distinct notions of those attributes, but all suppose Him to be of a spiritual nature. If we do not render to God that spiritual worship which corresponds

[1] Dio Chrysost. Orationes, xii.

to His own nature, a statue upon a tomb with eyes and hands lifted up, offers as good and true a service as we." [1]

In its conception of worship as a spiritual act addressed to a spiritual being, Christianity puts into a simple and universal formula the deepest conclusions of philosophy. It assumes the great truth embodied in the organization of matter under existing forms of order and beauty, and in the arrangement of diverse and conflicting physical laws to effect one common purpose—that a supreme intelligence, a spiritual power, gave to the universe its existence and its laws. What natural theology thus argues, Christ declared as a first axiom of religion ;—God is Spirit. Whence it follows, since God is the Creator of the Universe, it is absurd to suppose that His own essence can be bounded by a temple, or ministered unto by material offerings; and since God is the Father of all existing intelligences, it is absurd to represent Him by any material image, or to worship Him in any other way than by an intelligent homage, obedience and love. "They that worship Him must worship Him in spirit and in truth."

The nature of man requires this spiritual homage to the Father of spirits. Reason and self-respect demand that man, who is essentially a spiritual and not an animal being, shall recognize the spirituality of his Creator, and worship God with his rational and voluntary powers.

He degrades himself when he represents his Creator by anything lower in the scale of existence than his own soul, or renders to God a mere service of form. Worship is the homage, the adoration, the reverent and loving devotion of man as a free spiritual intelligence toward God as the Father of Spirits, infinite in His nature and perfect in His holiness. Such worship recognizes God's absolute independence, His rightful sovereignty, His glorious moral perfection ; and is rendered by one spiritual nature unto

[1] Charnock on the Divine Attributes.

another spiritual nature that infinitely transcends it in power and majesty, that infinitely excels it in purity and virtue. Not hands but hearts must worship God; not wood and stone but living souls must furnish His abode. This doctrine, however, must be taken in connection with the doctrine of the new birth which underlies the whole conception of the kingdom of God; for "man is not born as a temple of God, nor can he make himself one, but can only be restored to that eminence by the Spirit, whom the Son of God communicates to his soul." [1]

The formula of Jesus touching worship is a distinct protest against *Ritualism* as claiming to represent the Christian idea of worship. I would not question the sincerity of a worship rendered through elaborate forms; but the *Ritual* does not constitute either Christianity or worship, and the bowings and genuflexions, the attitudes and crossings, the vestments and candles, are not properly Christian worship. True worship may use forms for its expression, and indeed will naturally appropriate forms of some kind as its language; but by just as much as the place and the form of worship come to be looked upon as essential to the genuineness and acceptableness of the worship, by so much does the form overlay and hinder the free action of the soul toward God. If the form of worship appeals to the senses more powerfully than the truth itself appeals to the soul, if the studied artistic effect of the worship diverts the feeling from spiritual emotion to æsthetic sentiment, then is the form set above the spirit, and there is danger that the living essence of worship will be wanting. The eye may be charmed with the architecture of the cathedral, the ear entranced with the music of the organ and the choir, the very soul suffused with the perfume of incense, and yet while every sense is thus wrapped in the outward similitude of worship, there may be no true spirit of worship in the

[1] Neander.

heart. And if once the mind is imbued with the notion that salvation depends upon the place or the form of worship, it will exaggerate the most insignificant incident of that form into an essential of its own life.

But on the other hand the spirituality of worship must be distinguished from mere sentimentality in religion. The poetry of Byron abounds in apostrophes to nature in the vein of worship. Novelists of the worst school of French license, will pause in a tale of infamy to utter some pious feeling touching the stars, the trees, the flowers; to invoke the sea, the breeze, the mountain, the cloud, the moon—Nature in whole or in detail—as the personification of the religious sentiment; and after this ebullition of devotion, will proceed to deform virtue and to glorify vice. Confucius teaches that by meditating in the seclusion of the mountains and water-falls, man returns to the primitive goodness of his nature; and thus the magnificent growths of the forests and the delicate beauties of the garden and field become moral tonics to the soul. Now no moralist has excelled Christ in lessons of wisdom derived from nature, and no poet has surpassed Him in delicacy of perception for the beauty of flowers, the waters, the sky, and for the traits and habits of sentient creatures: and therefore it is foreign to the genius of Christianity to disparage a taste for the beautiful in the physical creation, or to undervalue this as tributary to the religious sentiment. But that enthusiasm for nature which never speaks the name of God, which expends itself upon effects without thought of the First Cause of all, which even substitutes an effect for the cause as an object of religious emotion, has no one element in common with the spiritual devotion that Christ declared to be the only true worship. It is at best but a more refined idolatry, reproducing in the mysticism of the pantheist and the dream-talk of the poet, the homage of the ancient Greek and Roman, or of the

modern Hindoo and Chinaman to material forms as representing some beneficent property or power in nature.

The spirituality of worship set forth by Christ is a
feature of His religion that adapts it for universal diffu-
sion. Like the light Christianity can go anywhere; like
the air men need only to breathe it. Its worship requires
but these two factors:—a spiritual and holy God revealed
as a loving Father, and an humble, loving. trusting mind,
that looks up to Him in reverence and obedience. The
Jew coming like Simeon in faith and holy expectation, to
sacrifice amid the splendor of the temple and the pomp of
its ritual; the Gentile who, like the devout Cornelius,
amid the distractions of military life, without temple or
altar, yet feared God with all his house and prayed to
Him always; the prisoner Paul in the guard-room of
Nero's palace; the exile John in the rocky solitudes of
Patmos; the missionary apostle, a solitary witness for the
living God in face of the temples, shrines and divinities
of Athens; the throng gathered at Troas to hear his fare-
well words, and break the bread of Christian fellowship;
the martyrs who entered the arena to be devoured of wild
beasts, praying as they went; the saints who hid themselves in the catacombs of Rome and worshiped by the
light of the sacred lamp; Luther, in his monk-cell crying
to God from the depths of an awakened spirit; Tauler, in
the grand cathedral of Strasbourg, in the midst of altars,
pictures, images, incense, and the pomp of a corrupted
worship, proclaiming the true light, love, and joy of the
Holy Ghost within the soul; the Waldenses in the fast-
nesses of Piedmont; the Huguenots in the caves of the
Pyrenees; the Covenanters on the lonely heath or the
dreary shore; the Pilgrims on the houseless island, keeping the Sabbath in snow and sleet; these all, and whoever
with singleness of devotion has worshiped the Father,
have kept up through the ages the undying succession of

true worshipers. The proudest monument of pagan worship is a shattered ruin upon the Acropolis of Athens; the temple at Jerusalem with its goodly stones is buried under the Haram of the mosque of Omar; the antiquarian digs for its foundation; the Jews wail beside the traditional stones of its wall; but He with whom there is neither Greek nor Jew, who dwells in humble, believing souls, seeks and owns as true worshipers all who, in whatever tongue, cry "Abba, Father."

CHAPTER IX.

YEARS ago, when the cloud that hung over the African race in the United States was so thick that there appeared no possibility of deliverance, Mr. Frederick Douglas called for a bloody insurrection as the only hope of liberty; and even that seemed rather the frenzy of despair. Depicting the wrongs of his people with an eloquence that awed his hearers, telling tales of horror that made one's hair stand on end, he cried for the retribution of blood. Friends, counsels, measures, events had failed to further their cause, or had been linked in connivance with the wrong; patience and hope were utterly gone, and there remained only the last struggle of desperation. When he ceased speaking, there was a hush of horror and dread over the assembly, that seemed to confirm his forebodings. Directly in front of the platform sat a tall gaunt figure, black as the night that Douglas had depicted:—a woman who, had she lived in Africa, might have passed for a sorceress or a sibyl, but who had won repute among her people as a prophetess taught of God. Her very name she claimed to have received by inspiration—*Sojourner Truth*—a type of her mission : " Truth" because she was appointed to give the Lord's testimony; "Sojourner" because she was to go from place to place testifying as she went, and sojourning only long enough to testify. Fastening upon the speaker her keen black eye, now fired with a holy indignation, and raising her finger as in prophetic admonition, she cried in a voice that pierced every ear, "Frederick, *is God dead?*"

104

Like a flash of lightning that question scattered a darkness that all had felt. Faith, patience, hope, courage came back with the reviving of the thought of a living God.

The years have confirmed Sojourner's faith. When the national government had surrendered itself in every department to the intrigues or the assumptions of the slave-power; when Congress had enacted the Fugitive-Slave law, and the President had made haste to enforce it by Marshals, Commissioners and United States troops; when the Missouri Compromise was repealed, and the Supreme Court decided that slaves could be held as property in the territories of the United States, and the Chief Justice gave the sanction of his office to the stigma that "black men had no rights which white men were bound to respect;" it seemed indeed that the cause of the slave was hopeless, and that nothing remained to him but the recklessness of desperation. But God was not "dead." The very audacity that sought first to control the general government and then to subvert it, overreached itself; and we have seen slavery abolished by proclamation of the President, and the army of the United States employed for its overthrow; Congress that had been the tool of the Slave-power, dictating to the States of the Slave Confederacy measures of justice to the freedmen; those States recognizing the political equality of the blacks as the condition of their own restoration to political privileges in the Union; the Constitution that had been made a shield for slavery, amended so as to prohibit the exclusion of any citizen from the polls by reason of race, color, or former state of servitude; the President congratulating the country upon this momentous change of policy as the most important event since the foundation of the government, and taking pains to efface the stigma that the Supreme Court had affixed to the black race. [1] A retribution so thorough and particular,

---

[1] President Grant's proclamation of the ratification of the Fifteenth Amendment.

a revolution so complete and circumstantial, effected by means above human foresight or control, gives emphasis to the faith of the sable prophetess in the living God.

Yet there are those who style themselves "friends of progress," and assume even the ambitious role of the priesthood of Humanity, who would deprive the poor and oppressed of this kindling thought, this great and blessed hope, and would make God dead alike to good or evil in the world. Not content to reduce all physical phenomena to a system of fixed laws, which admit of no superintending Power, and with which no volitions, either natural or supernatural, interfere, they would bring human society and history into the same category, concluding all the phases of national growth and decay, and the actions of individuals in all the varieties of human conduct, by physical conditions that determine the development of individuals, of nations, and of races according to certain subtile, perhaps uninterpretable, but nevertheless uniform and all-controlling laws. This was the theory upon which Mr. Buckle projected his History of Civilization:—that "the actions of men, being determined solely by their antecedents, must have a character of uniformity, that is to say, must, under precisely the same circumstances, always issue in precisely the same results." So strong was his conviction that all human actions, including those that seem to be prompted by personal feelings—even marriages on the one hand, and crimes on the other—are determined by general laws, that he expressed his belief that "before another century the chain of evidence will be complete, and it will be as rare to find an historian who denies the undeviating regularity of the moral world, as it is now to find a philosopher who denies the regularity of the material world."[1] This moral order, however, in Mr. Buckle's meaning, is not the Providential ruling of the world according to a divine plan,

[1] *History of Civilization in England,* I. pp. 14, 24.

but the development of mind and of Nature, each by the
laws of its own organization, and with "a reciprocal modifi-
cation from which all events must necessarily spring." Mr.
Buckle's admirers have sought to relieve him of the charge
of Fatalism; yet when this school of Positivists speak of
"the Infinite" and "the Absolute," it is the infinite and
absolute in *Idea* or in *Law*—some vast generalization of the
phenomena of the universe under a law of correlation—and
not an infinite Spirit, who created the universe, and now
upholds and governs it through laws that are the mute expressions of His own will and power.   Either the Personality of God is denied altogether, and the Deity is only the
highest formula for the generalization of existing laws, or
if His personality is admitted, He is conceived of as
separated from the actual course of affairs, and existing if
not in the state of inactivity attributed to Buddha, at least
in the attitude of *non-intervention* by any volition or act
of His, direct or indirect, in the ongoing sequence of
events.   Thus Comte speaks of the doctrine of Providence
as a transient theory, a makeshift of ignorance, which in
the progress of science has been displaced by the discovery
and the systematizing of laws.

It is impossible to harmonize this world-scheme of the
Positivists with the teachings of Christ.   The displace-
ment of Providence from the world, the denial of God's
personal interest in His creatures and His superintendence
over them as a present reality, is directly at variance with
the doctrine of Jesus, who taught that His Father watches
over all creatures and events, and is concerned in the
affairs of men both individually and collectively.   Upon
most points it is easy to reconcile alleged differences
between science and revelation ; and it may be assumed
that there is no fact of science fairly proved that may not
be reconciled with the Scriptures fairly interpreted.   But
the denial of a divine Providence in the world, present,

personal, particular, cannot be reconciled with the teachings of Jesus; and hence if He taught herein the truth of
God, that materialistic theory which has no place for God
in the ordering of affairs, must be false. It is of the first
importance, therefore, to determine from the collation of
His own words, what Christ did teach concerning Providence.

First. Those physical phenomena which are commonly
described as *the course of nature,* Christ represented as
being under the direction and control of God, and as expressing His purpose and will. "Love your enemies,
bless them that curse you, do good to them that hate you,
and pray for them which despitefully use you and perse-
cute you, that ye may be the children of your Father
which is in heaven: for He maketh His sun to rise on the
evil and on the good, and sendeth rain on the just and on
the unjust."[1] Now the sun rises with undeviating regularity—the diurnal revolution of the earth upon its axis
causing that appearing and disappearing of the sun which
we call sunrise and sunset. These laws are fixed and as-
certained: and although the laws by which the rain falls
are less definitely understood, the showers come not by
chance, nor by miracle, but by law. And yet Jesus traced
the rising of the sun and the falling of the rain, in the
universality of their beneficence, to the purpose of God in
so ordering them for the good of His creatures; and He
pointed to the uniformity of these events as an expression
of the impartial goodness of our Heavenly Father, to be
followed by us as an example. Now there is no force in
the argument drawn from this illustration—that, by the
impartiality of love, we should be perfect in the same way
as our Father in Heaven is perfect—if the sun rises or the
rain falls by laws of its own producing, or by eternal

[1] Matt. v. 44, 45.

laws, or by purely mechanical law, from which all idea of a designing will is shut out.

In the phenomena of Nature we must be careful not to confound regularity of sequence with causation, or to mistake uniformity for efficiency. Where one event invariably follows another in the same circumstances, we say there is a law of succession; but it does not follow that the event next preceding is the efficient cause of its successor. Mere phenomena cannot be perpetually adduced to explain phenomena. The conception of causality requires an active will-power somewhere back of the apparent physical law. To Christ that will was ever present and ever active in all the ordinances of Nature.

This He assumed when He taught us to pray to our Father in heaven, saying "Give us this day our daily bread." Now bread is procured by processes that obey established chemical, vital, and mechanical laws, both separately and in combination—the growth of the wheat, the harvesting, threshing, and winnowing, the grinding of the flour, the mixing of the dough, the baking of the bread— the agency of Nature uniting throughout with the agency of Man; and there is nothing apparent in the process of bread-making that cannot be referred to one or the other of these visible agents. But whence comes the power of heat and moisture, acting upon the soil and the seed to produce the living growth? whence the principle of fermentation? and whence the power of heat to convert the paste into bread?

In looking at a grist-mill, the wheels, the gearing, the hopper, the stones, the bolter, one remarks the ingenuity of man in this machinery for grinding his flour; but the wood and iron of which the water-wheel is made, the water that turns it, the stones that grind the meal, these are no more of man's providing than are his own mind and muscle that appropriate such materials to his use. And after all,

that which grinds his flour is the sun: for the sun perpetually gathers the moisture that forms the clouds, whose
showers feed the stream that turns the mill.   And so, back
of all the ingenuity of man, and of all visible agencies of
Nature, the doctrine of Christ refers us to our Heavenly
Father as the giver of our bread, and bids us ask Him for
it day by day.   But one could not thus *ask* Nature for
daily bread; since Nature has no intelligence nor will, nor
conscious power of adaptation, in the processes by which
she ministers to the sustenance of man.   One can not pray
to a law of physics or of chemistry as to a Father! The
laws of Nature remove further back the point at which
the will of God touches the whole process of providing
our food, but these do not disconnect that process from the
divine will and reduce it to a function of Nature.   A father
who grows his own grain and grinds his own wheat, literally provides bread for his children; but one who does
other business, is a merchant, a banker, a doctor, a lawyer,
and buys all his bread of the baker, is none the less the
giver of the daily bread of his household.   A little boy
lost in the streets of New York, and unable to tell where
he lived, gave his father's name and said that he made
bread.   After a fruitless search among the bakers, it was
discovered that the child's father was a merchant, but was
accustomed on leaving home for his business to say play-
fully to the little fellow, "Now I must go and make some
more bread for you."   Yet he did make bread for his child
as truly as if he had baked it.   When a father goes away
from home and leaves an order with the baker to supply
the family during his absence, he still provides their daily
bread; and if he should prolong his absence for years, and
simply send remittances to meet the necessities of his family,
these intervening processes would not sever nor even suspend his personal agency as the provider.

    Now God is our Father; and the far-reaching arrangements He has made through which we obtain our daily bread, cannot dissociate the provision for our wants from His loving thought and care. Both the constitution of man and the circumstances in which he acts are fairly included within the providential purposes of God. Man acts either from his own nature, or from the influence of circumstances, or from a combination of these two factors; and He who created both man and nature with their mutual adaptations, can also bring them together in special adaptations, through His familiar and constant supervision of their several laws. And the fact of this personal divine agency in and through the ordinary phenomena of life, is fundamental in the doctrine of Christ concerning Providence.

Christ also taught the *universality* of this Providence over the kingdoms of Nature and of life. It is God who clothes the grass of the field, and gives to the lilies their beauty, though they toil not, neither do they spin. It is our heavenly Father who feedeth the ravens and the fowls of the air, though they sow not, neither do they reap nor gather into barns. [1] God gave to the birds their free un-caring nature, and the instinct by which they seek their food; and in the diversities of food made ready for the diversities of creatures are manifested a forethought and plan that argue an intelligent providence. The uniformity of this adaptation cannot account for the fact of the adaptation; and when we inquire why each bird and each beast seeks always and finds its own kind of food, there can be no better answer than that which Christ has given, "Your heavenly Father feedeth them."

In discoursing of Providence, Jesus instanced the *particular care* of God toward those that love Him and trust in His will. His argument from the universal care of God for the lower orders of creatures, the raven, the spar-

[1] Matt. vi. 26-31.

row, was that the children of God should so much the more trust in Him for all the wants of the body, and devote themselves spiritually to His holy kingdom and will. "Are ye not much better than they? shall He not much more clothe you, O ye of little faith?"[1] The argument is from the less to the greater:—"therefore take no thought"—be not anxious about the necessaries of life,—"saying What shall we eat? or What shall we drink? or Wherewithal shall we be clothed? for your heavenly Father knoweth that ye have need of all these things."[2] To have any validity in logic, to give any encouragement to faith, this argument must proceed on the assumption that God takes immediate cognizance of the condition and wants of those who look to Him in trust, and arranges outward circumstances for their advantage: for the counsel "Seek ye first the kingdom of God and His righteousness," is followed with the unqualified assurance "and all these things shall be added to you;"[3]—an assurance grounded in the fact that "your heavenly Father *knoweth* that ye have need of all these things"—"*therefore* take no thought for the morrow."

The counsel that Jesus gave His disciples touching their deportment under danger, was based upon the same doctrine of God's personal care over His children. They were charged not to fear human enemies who could do them no real harm, and whose apparent power of mischief was under the restraint of their heavenly Father:—not even a sparrow is forgotten before God; and "the very hairs of your head are all numbered."[4] This same argument Christ applied to Himself. When tempted of the devil, in the extremity of hunger, He refused to turn stones into bread, and confided in the loving care of His

---

[1] Mat. vi. 30.   [2] Mat. vi. 31, 32.
[3] Mat. vi. 32, 33.   [4] Luke xii. 6, 7.

Father for the relief of His necessities.[1] Again, when Pilate sought to intimidate Him, saying, "Knowest thou not that I have power to crucify thee," Jesus answered, "Thou couldst have no power at all against me, except it were given thee from above."[2] By this He meant not simply that the power of earthly rulers is derived from God as the supreme disposer of events; but that Pilate had no present power of proceeding against Himself, except by the permission of His heavenly Father. His meaning was precisely the same as in that saying to Peter a few hours before, "Thinkest thou that I cannot now pray to my Father, and He shall presently give Me more than twelve legions of angels? But how then shall the Scriptures be fulfilled that thus it must be?"[3] Jesus believed in the constant superintendence of His heavenly Father over all the events of His life:—constant, as operating through the common established order of things, and particular, as adapting events to occasions, means to ends.

What is sometimes called "special providence" may be special only in our recognition of it—special because the importance of the event to ourselves leads us to notice it as something extraordinary; but Christ taught that the Providence of God is not something occasional and exceptional, but is as constant and particular as the care of a Father over his children:—special, therefore, only as being personal and particular.

But Jesus did also include in His doctrine of Providence the fact that, to accomplish particular ends, God does sometimes put forth *direct acts of control or intervention in human affairs.* In view of the small number of preachers of the Gospel as compared with the work of evangelization, He instructed His disciples to "pray the Lord of the harvest that He would send forth laborers into the har-

[1] Matt. iv. 3, 4, 11.   [2] John xix. 10, 11.
[3] Matt. xxvi. 53, 54.

8

vest." [1] Now such a prayer could have force only upon
the assumption that God does act directly in the affairs of
this world, for particular interests, and shape men and
means toward given ends.   Again, in predicting the
destruction of Jerusalem, Christ announced that as His
own coming to judgment, and indicated to His disciples
what would be the signs of that coming—directly connect-
ing the war, famine and pestilence that did actually
attend that terrible siege, with a divine retribution for the
sins of the nation.   He promised also safety and protection to His own disciples, and declared that for their sakes
the days of tribulation should be shortened. [2]   All this
came to pass by means apparently natural, but under the
guidance of a supernatural power.

The whole doctrine of Christ concerning the Providence
of God teaches that this is a living reality, present, constant,
universal, and particular, both mediate and immediate.

This doctrine accords with the highest Reason, and gives
a key to the course of Nature itself.   For either we must
believe in a Providence over the world that extends to the
particular while it controls the universal, or allow the athe-
istic notion of chance, or say that events can come to pass
by laws or agencies beyond His knowledge or control, and
therefore that His whole purpose of wisdom and beneficence
in the creation is liable to be frustrated through causes out
of sight or out of reach—that a broken rail may throw the
train off the track, or a tiny borer under the keel may sink
the ship.   But in face of the evidence of final causes,
strengthening the native belief in an intelligent Creator, it
is impossible to refer the origin of the world to chance;
and if chance did not produce the world, it cannot come in
at this late day to divide its events with the Supreme
Intelligence that shaped these at the first.   To withdraw
any class of events from the knowledge or the power of

[1] Matt. ix. 37, 38.   [2] Matt. xxiv. 22.

God, and declare these absolutely independent of His control, would be to say that He had made a world He could not manage; and moreover, such is the inter-dependence of events, both great and small, and, on the broad scale of things, adverse and hostile events, permitted for awhile, are so often made to contribute to the very end they threatened to frustrate, or are overridden by some sublime and comprehensive movement—that the logical principles involved in creation, and the course of affairs in human history, shut us up to a belief in the providence of God as extending to all actual events.

It does not relieve this necessity to deny a personal Providence, and fall back upon a system of general laws. These laws, incapable of originating themselves, can find the reason of their own existence only in the will of the all-wise and almighty Creator, who set them in order foreseeing and including their working and results. Climb we never so high the ladder of second causes, at the top we find the Infinite stretching above and around us: the ladder is supported not by its own strength nor by the solidity of its foundation, but by an invisible hand from above; it is only by looking up that we can climb with safety, and if we take out a pin here and a rung there as insignificant or unnecessary, we shall break through and fall over into the abyss of Atheism. The doctrine of Providence as taught by Christ differs equally from Fatalism and from Pantheism. It recognizes the personal care of our Heavenly Father, acting both through the laws that He has impressed upon Nature and apart from these, and thus it keeps Him in a constant connection of thought, feeling and will with the creatures of His hand.

This doctrine of Providence harmonizes perfectly with our consciousness of free-will. Free-will is a fact of consciousness, and we can neither go back of the testimony of consciousness nor explain that away. We know that we

have the power of choice, and that in moral action we
might choose otherwise than as we do. Yet our free choice
and action in any given case do not exclude this from the
divine prevision as an event, since the certainty of an event
as matter-of-fact to the mind of God cannot conflict with
the free-agency of man in bringing to pass that event.
Certainty and Freedom are not irreconcilable factors in the
problem of life. The time and place of my birth, for instance, were determined in the Providence of God without
my agency or even my consciousness. It was by His will
that I began to live. But when I began to move by my
own volition did I cease to sustain any relation to the will
of God? Were the boundaries of His Providence limited
by the nursery?—and did I pass out from under the Providential government of God the moment I began to act by
my own will? That were absurd. But on the other hand,
did God compel my actions, and above all compel my sinful actions? I know better; since consciousness assures me
of my freedom, while common-sense instructs me as to His
Providence. It is equally true that I am free and that
God reigns.

The doctrine of Providence taught by Christ harmonizes also with the general laws of the physical world. The
laws under which we generalize the orderly sequences of
phenomena are thoughts or purposes of the Creator wrought
into permanent links of succession ;—a stereotyped edition
of certain divine ideas, continually renewed from the same
plates. But is the whole of the divine nature bound up in
these, and imprisoned by them ? These laws are the permanent base for the operations of His Providence : as
proofs of divine forethought for our welfare, they tend to
give stability and confidence to our dependence upon
Providence. To lay in fuel for the winter in the summer
is to provide for the daily wants of one's family as really as
by marketing every day ;—the one form of Providence does

not preclude the other. Because God ministers to our necessities so largely through a system of general laws, He is
not thereby cut off from a living sympathy and care for us.
It is still our Father in Heaven who gives us day by day
our daily bread, and who delivers us from evil.

The doctrine of Christ concerning the Providence of
God furnishes a rational ground and motive for prayer.
Under stress of want or danger it is an instinct of the soul
to pray. But prayer is the merest superstition if there is
no personal, acting, guiding Providence. Only in the belief that we have a Father who knows our wants and can
relieve them, who thinks upon us, and will hear us, can
we pray in faith.

This doctrine encourages us to trust in God with child-
like confidence and affection. Such a faith will lift the
soul to the sublimity of absolute repose : not the repose of
inaction or of indifference, but of that confidence in God's
presence, power, wisdom, love, that frees the mind from
all uneasiness or concern in respect to either the wants of
the body or its own future. " Fear ye not, ye are of more
value than many sparrows." This very confidence begets
its own triumph. The faith of Sojourner Truth was as
ready for her own necessities as for the sorrows of her people. Her child had been stolen and sold into slavery ; and
she knew only in a vague, general way, that she must seek
redress at the Court-house, and that for this money was
required. She thought within herself, " God has money,"
and she made her application directly to Him. In her
own graphic and pathetic story, " I didn't rightly know
which way to turn ; but I went to the Lord, and I said to
Him, ' O Lord, ef I was as rich as you be, an' you was as
poor as I be, I'd help you, you know I would ; an' oh ! do
help *me*.' An' I felt *sure* that He would, an' He did."

A man seeing her writhing in agony before the Court
House, asked what was the matter, and directed her to

friends who took up her case and pressed it until her child was recovered. This child-like simplicity of trust in the providence of God is authorized by the teachings of Christ. One may be too wise to admit a ground for it in his philosophy, too proud to admit a place for it in his own spirit; one may love the world too much to be willing to relinquish that, and making the kingdom of God his supreme desire, to trust his heavenly Father for his daily bread; one may be so bent upon plans of his own that he cares nothing for Providence unless that can be enlisted in these; but he that really believes what Christ has taught concerning our Father in heaven, he that exercises a true Christian faith, will so trust in the Lord at all times, as to live without solicitude, in the constant exercise of gratitude and devotion. And how little should we know of grief if we had more of gratitude! how little should we know of despondency, if we had more of devotion! When we shall fully love, then only will we fully trust.

CHAPTER X.

As the instinct of prayer is an argument for a Providence—since every aptitude of man's nature finds some corresponding adaptation in the system of things with which he is connected—so also is the fact of Providence the decisive warrant for prayer. The spontaneous impulse of the soul in peril, want, or fear, to invoke the aid of an unseen Power—that is to pray—encourages the belief that, distinct from physical laws and phenomena, there is a spiritual Power, able to modify or shape the course of things for our advantage, or to interpose His will in some direct counteraction to apparent evil. Why is man so constituted that in his helplessness he flies to the Infinite for succor, if all things move forward by inexorable law, and God has abandoned the world to fate? Then prayer were but a mockery of human misery—the wounded, terrified bird, seeing the serpent about to spring upon it, and beating its breast wildly against the bars that shut it in. That very principle of relation by which science links events to their antecedents, and means to ends, should find in this normal tendency of the soul to look to a higher Power, a law of interaction by which prayer links the soul to God by the feeling of dependence, and brings God to the soul in the bestowal of help.

That devout philosopher, *Schleiermacher*, defined religion as *the feeling of dependence upon the Absolute.* When physical science has formulated all the known phenomena of Nature under invariable laws, and metaphysical science

119

has systematized all the known phenomena of mind under categories of its own, and materialists have sought, by a process of mental physiology, to reduce the manifestations of intelligence to mere functions of the brain, there yet remains within the consciousness—to be called out upon emergencies of ignorance, of danger, of trouble, of want— the feeling of dependence upon a Something somewhere that is Absolute, that is above want, danger, or necessity, that is dependent upon nothing outside of itself, but can take upon itself the support of needy, dependent creatures. That feeling prompts to prayer, and prayer points to Providence.

And so, upon the other hand, the fact of a Providence— the active guidance and superintendence of persons and events by a Spirit of infinite wisdom, power and beneficence,—gives a perfect warrant for prayer, makes it reasonable to pray, makes it hopeful to pray, makes prayer a reality, as the address of one conscious spirit to another conscious spirit, who knows the needs of the suppliant; makes prayer a power, as the appeal of a dependent spirit to the Almighty Spirit who will help the needy when he crieth. Such was the doctrine of prayer that Christ taught to His disciples, and that He himself put in practice upon memorable occasions of His earthly life.

At the foundation of His teaching on this subject was the conception of prayer as *the direct address of the soul to God as its Father.* " After this manner pray ye: Our *Father* which art in heaven." [1] ."Enter into thy closet and pray to thy *Father* which is in secret." [2] As an encouragement to prayer Christ referred to the readiness with which parents regard the requests of their children, and said, " If ye then being evil know how to give good gifts unto your children, how much more shall your *Father*

---

[1] Matt. vi. 9.   [2] Matt. vi. 6.

which is in heaven give good things to them that ask Him." [1]

The prayers of Jesus Himself were direct addresses to His Father. " I thank Thee, O Father, Lord of heaven and earth, because Thou hast hid these things from the wise and prudent, and hast revealed them unto babes." [2] "What shall I say? Father, save me from this hour? Father, glorify Thy name." [3]

The last prayer of Jesus for His disciples, was the audible communion of His soul with His Father, whom He invoked by name, at each petition: [4] " Father, the hour is come:" "O Father, glorify Thou Me with Thine own self." " Holy Father, keep through Thine own name those whom Thou hast given Me." "O righteous Father, the world hath not known Thee." In the extremity of His anguish in the garden, He prayed, " O my Father, if it be possible let this cup pass from Me:" [5] and from the cross He cried, "Father, forgive them." [6] This direct address to God as Father is a striking characteristic of Christian prayer. Human language cannot express all that this mode of address implies.

"The Father" is a living person; the Father of our spirits a living Spirit; the Father of all, the living possessor of all, who as the Creator has control over all beings and events. Therefore to pray to God as a Father is to recognize Him as in immediate relations to us personally, and to all that concerns us. One loses sight for the moment of all calculation of means and agencies, of secondary causes and intermediate laws, and sees only the great preponderating truth of the living Spirit, infinite in presence and power, who is above every law and nigh to every soul.

But the mind does not rest in this conception. Prayer is more than imagining what God is; more than meditating

<hr>

[1] Matt. vii. 11. [2] Matt. xi. 25. [3] John xii. 27, 28. [4] John xvii.
[5] Matt. xxvi. 39. [6] Luke xxiii. 34.

upon God; more than any subjective state or feeling produced in us as the reflex influence of divine contemplation.
In prayer the soul goes out to God; it addresses God as
one that can be reached by its supplications. The *Father*
being not a principle nor a law, not an abstraction nor a
poetic name, but a living person, is one who can be spoken
to—yes, this Infinite Spirit, this Maker and Lord of all
things can be *spoken to* by you and me, for He is our
Father; and in teaching us to open our petitions with this
endearing name, Christ taught us to come to God through
no intervening agency, but making as it were our consciousness directly audible to His.

Moreover, the name by which we address God in prayer
implies that He has personal relations to our interests, and
is personally interested in whatever affects our welfare.
"The Father" concerns Himself personally, directly, constantly, in and for the happiness of His children. The
name signifies a mutual relationship, an endearing sympathy; it warrants us in appropriating to ourselves the divine
personality by a filial affection that identifies this with our
very life: "When thou hast entered into thy closet, and
hast shut to the door"—shutting out the while even the
nearest of earthly friends—then canst thou, for the moment
as it were, have God unto thyself, and "pray to *thy* Father
who seeth in secret."

Still further, the name by which Jesus taught us to address God in prayer is a name that pledges to us His presence and His love. The instinct of prayer was not given
to mock us with vain aspirations and unsatisfied longings;
neither has God required us to pray simply in acknowledgment of our own dependence, and of His power and
majesty. He is our Father; and the one Father who loves
us with a love that is always wise, pure, unselfish, perfect.
"What man is there of you, whom if his son ask bread,
will he give him a stone? or if he ask a fish, will he give

him a serpent? If ye, then, being evil, know how to give good gifts unto your children, how much more shall your Father which is in heaven give good things to them that ask Him."[1] The conception that underlies all true prayer is that of a direct address to God as a Father.

The teaching and example of Christ authorize us to *include in the subject matter of prayer, our physical necessities and our temporal interests in general.* Some would restrict prayer to themes and objects purely spiritual—thinking thus to avoid the speculative difficulties of the Christian doctrine of Providence, and yet keep up a living connection between God and the human soul. But the essential difficulty in expounding Providence is not got rid of by transferring it from the sphere of matter to that of mind, since the mind also has laws of its own. Many of the phenomena of thought, memory, association, feeling, can be reduced to that observed regularity of sequence which indicates a *law* of action or manifestation, and it is no easier to conceive or explain how a distinct personal Power could move harmoniously amid the laws of such a sphere than amid the laws of matter. Indeed, seeing that mind possesses the faculty of free will, and therefore can oppose itself to the will of God, it may even be more difficult to give a philosophy of divine action within the sphere of mind than in that of matter.

The validity of prayer is given in the argument heretofore adduced for a personal Providence. That argument rests substantially upon the same grounds with the argument for a personal God—the apparent ordering or purposing of events with reference to foreseen ends ; the combination of different and even opposite laws or phenomena so as to produce some special and beneficial result ; the manifold adaptations of things to persons and of persons to things—. all this, wherever discerned, gives intuitively the convic-

[1] Matt. vii. 9, 12.

tion of a planning and over-ruling mind; and that conviction utters itself in the spontaneousness of prayer for
what lies beyond the compass of our own will. A French
philosopher at dinner with the keen-witted Sidney Smith
declaimed against the notion of Providence as contrary to
the laws of things. The beautiful workings of cause and
effect in Nature he used to illustrate the glory of Science,
while denying the existence of God. Changing the subject
Smith observed : " How skilfully this pastry has been prepared." " Admirable," rejoined the philosopher, " it
could not have been better made in France." "Well,
then," said Smith, " from the skill shown in compounding
this dish to our taste, we must infer *the non-existence of
the cook.*"

The logic that denies a Providence in a world so full of
the wise and careful adaptation of means to ends, must
land at last in this absurdity. The mind intuitively asserts an intelligent cause wherever it perceives such adaptation. And the universality and particularity of Providence in the affairs of life was used by Christ as the argument for making our temporal concerns the subject-mat-
ter of prayer. The petition " Give us this day our daily
bread," is not to be reserved for some extremity when one
is in danger of starving, but is a daily prayer for God's
blessing upon our industry, for the means of temporal support; and while we thus look to God for daily food, we
are encouraged not to suffer temporalities to become too
engrossing, since our Heavenly Father knows what we
have need of, and Himself will care for us.

Christ taught that *prayer has a positive influence with
God.* With some truly devout persons it is a notion that
" God's end in requiring prayer is solely that it may be a
means to work in the petitioner a suitable frame of mind;"
that its influence is wholly subjective ; that the feelings of
veneration, dependence, humility, gratitude, trust, which it

calls into exercise are the substantial benefits of prayer,
its real efficacy; while its true answer is found in the
frame of submission and peace that it induces in the suppliant. A familiar illustration of this view likens prayer
to "a man in a small boat laying hold of a large ship :
who, if he does not move the large vessel, at least moves
the small vessel towards the large one."

That the frames and feelings proper to prayer form no
small part of its beneficial influence, and contribute much
to the spiritual growth of one who rightly cultivates them,
all must agree. But could one cultivate these, would it be
possible to cherish such frames and feelings for any length
of time, if he regarded prayer simply as a kind of spiritual
gymnastics to be practised upon himself for the sake of
these effects? Suppose him to say, 'I cannot see how there
can be a Providence, for every thing moves on by fixed
laws : I do not imagine that prayer has any influence upon
God, that my asking for a thing has any connection whatever with my receiving it; indeed, I believe that every
thing comes to me or befalls me in the regular course of
nature ; nevertheless, I will pray for the sake of cultivating
the feelings of dependence and gratitude, and of improving
my own spiritual state ;'—how long would one holding such
a philosophy be likely to keep up his unmeaning and ino-
perative petitions for the sake of their reflex influence upon
himself? or how long could he cherish a lively interest in
that which at heart he did not believe in? Those spiritual
frames which are most important to the soul's culture, are
best developed through faith in the efficacy of prayer as a
direct address to our Father in heaven ; and Christ constantly declared the prevailing influence of prayer with
God Himself as the incentive to its exercise. "*Ask* and it
shall be given you;"—the asking precedes and influences
the giving—" seek, and ye shall find; knock, and it shall
be opened unto you: for every one that asketh, receiveth:

and he that secketh, findeth: and to him that knocketh, it shall be opened." [1]

The effect of united, consentaneous prayer to secure some specific object of faith, in the sphere of spiritual influences, is set forth in the declaration, "If two of you shall agree on earth, as touching anything that they shall ask, it shall be done for them of my Father which is in heaven." [2] After Jesus had confounded His disciples by His power in withering the barren fig tree, He made this an argument with them for faith in prayer: "Have faith in God—for verily I say unto you, that whosoever shall say unto this mountain, Be thou removed, and be thou cast into the sea, and shall not doubt in his heart, but shall believe that those things which he saith shall come to pass, he shall have whatsoever he saith. Therefore I say unto you, What things soever ye desire when ye pray, believe that ye receive them, and ye shall have them." [3] Though this may not be construed as a literal promise of power to work miracles, yet under the figure of removing a mountain, it sets forth this substantial truth—that earnest, believing prayer is directly efficacious with God for removing great difficulties and achieving great works in connection with His cause.

Luke records the parable of the unjust judge, to show that "men ought always to pray, and not to faint" [4]—that favors are granted to persistent importunity which might be withheld from a weaker petition; and the same thing is taught by the parable of the man who went to his friend at midnight, and importuned him for bread. [5] Where there is a Will to be influenced, a Heart to be affected by entreaty, one can understand how perseverance in prayer may be an element of success; but of what use were importunity in a world from which the personal superinten-

---

[1] Mat. vii. 7.   [2] Mat. xviii. 19.   [3] Mark xi. 22, 25.
[4] Luke xviii. 1-9.   [5] Luke xi. 5-9.

dence of God had been ruled out by inexorable laws? Our reiterated crying would avail no more than that of the priests of Baal, when they cried all day long " O Baal, hear us," and cut themselves with knives in the frenzy of their importunity. A thousand cries could not move Laws to sympathy ; Fate cannot be melted by importunity ; but belief in the personal care of God over the world warrants persistency in prayer.

The assurance that God is influenced by prayer is rendered more personal and practical through the relations of Christ to the Father on the one hand and to the disciples on the other. With a view to comfort His disciples upon the eve of His departure, He said, " Whatsoever ye shall ask in My name, that will I do, that the Father may be glorified in the Son." [1] " If ye abide in Me, and My words abide in you, ye shall ask what ye will, and it shall be done unto you :" [2]—and again, " Whatsoever ye shall ask the Father in My name He will give it you." [3] Here the efficacy of prayer is grounded in the argument of love. And all the instructions and promises concerning prayer given by Christ rest the motive and encouragement to pray, not in its effect upon our own hearts, but in its positive influence with God to procure the object of our hearts' desire. It is what our heavenly Father *engages to do* that is held up to our faith in asking.

If it be asked, How can God be influenced by our prayer ?—it is a sufficient answer, that He says He is so influenced. And if it be asked again, How can God answer a particular prayer in a world of general laws? it is a sufficient reply that He is God. Such questions lead to an enticing field of speculation ; but whatever theory we may invent to explain the manner in which God may answer prayer in harmony with the laws of matter and of mind, we should remember that this is purely a specula-

---

[1] John xiv. 13.   [2] John xv. 7.   [3] John xvi. 23.

tion, and not to be put forth as a fact, either discovered or revealed.

Since the Bible does not teach that prayer is commonly answered by miracle, we are not at liberty to introduce the miraculous to support our theory of prayer. But it is a prerogative of Spirit to direct, adapt, and combine the properties and laws of Matter for its own ends. And since this is done even under the limitations of the human spirit, much more must God—a Spirit of unlimited knowledge, wisdom and power—be able to bring His will to bear upon the laws and conditions of Matter and Mind so as to direct and develop what He desires to bring to pass, without impairing that orderly constitution of things which He has established.

Professor Tyndall has said, " The ideas of prayer and of a change in the course of natural phenomena refuse to be connected in thought ;" but this is only when thought narrows itself and narrows all the powers of the universe to the groove of physical uniformity; when thought denies the spirituality of its own parentage, and its affinity with a world of spiritual intelligences. The separate properties of nitrogen and oxygen were fixed unchangeably from the moment of their creation ; nor could it have been possible to conceive beforehand how these two alien inorganic substances could be made to support the life of organized beings ; but now that so great a marvel has been accomplished by intelligent adaptation, it is conceivable that He who has combined the deadly nitrogen and the consuming oxygen so as to produce the life-giving atmosphere, can also combine, direct, or control laws, properties, tendencies of diverse and seemingly contrary natures, so as to bring forth new results of beneficence. He is at home in the laboratory of Nature, and equally at home in the processes of Mind.

Moreover, it is a groundless assumption that the course

of things must be changed in order that prayer may be answered. No science can claim that all phenomena are included within its categories; above the laws of phenomena that we do see may be other and more subtile laws beyond our ken; and in the working of those higher spiritual laws, prayer may enter within the plane of physical phenomena like an eccentric chuck, which shifts the centre without impeding the motion or changing its general direction or area.

Illustrations of spiritual powers and operations derived from mechanical instruments, are necessarily coarse and imperfect; yet even these may serve to render abstruse subjects more intelligible. Connected with the spinning-jenny is an alarm-bell that rings a moment before the receiving spool is filled with the twist, signaling to the operator at the opposite side of the machine to come and set an empty spool in the order of succession; the next moment the machinery itself cuts the thread, drops the full spool into a basket, drops the new spool into its place, and begins to wind as before. By this contrivance the attendance of one hand is dispensed with, but the *contrivance* which lifts the mechanism one grade nearer to the plane of intelligence, does not thereby merge itself into the mechanism, nor dispense with its own superintendence and its power of occasional intervention. That signal-bell answers to prayer, invoking the great Architect of Nature to adapt His own laws and combinations to some impending necessity.

God, in His forethought of events, may have assigned to prayer the place of a condition precedent to particular results, so that this also enters into some law of phenomena higher than our sciences can reach. Or there may even be in believing prayer, some subtile power of causation over events themselves; the true odic, or odyllic force, may be centered here. But all theorizing upon the subject must

9

end at last in this bare statement; that God has declared that He is, and will be, influenced by the prayer of faith.

But though Jesus taught that prayer is influential, as a direct appeal to our Father in heaven, He also announced *certain conditions upon which prayer, to be efficacious, must proceed.* These are as follows,

a. The object prayed for must be in harmony with the divine Wisdom as seeing, and the divine Love as choosing always that which is best for the suppliant. Mere importunity ought not to procure for us anything which upon the whole is not for our good. "Thy will be done" is therefore the governing clause in every petition, and prayer should always be offered in humble submission to the will of God. "Even so, Father, for so it seemed good in Thy sight."[1] "Nevertheless, not as I will, but as Thou wilt."[2]

b. Prayer must be offered in faith; not as an experimental essay with Providence, nor for the manipulation of our own feelings; but with the earnest conviction that the thing we pray for will be bestowed, if, on the whole, this is best for us, and if, under all the circumstances, this is wisely possible. "All things, whatsoever ye shall ask in prayer, *believing,* ye shall receive."[3]

c. In order to successful prayer the tone of our desires should be supremely spiritual. In praying for temporal benefits we should have in view chiefly the spiritual benefit to be attained through freedom from earthly anxieties. "Seek ye first the kingdom of God, and His righteousness; and all these things shall be added unto you."[4]

d. Christ taught us to pray in His name. That name at once expresses the love of God to man, and denotes the nearness of our humanity to God. "Whatsoever ye shall ask the Father in My name, He will give it you."[5]

---

[1] Matt. xi. 26.   [2] Matt. xxvi. 39.   [3] Matt. xxi. 22.
[4] Matt. vi. 33.   [5] John xvi. 23.

The influence that Christ has ascribed to prayer exalts man to the dignity of a spiritual Power. Materialism would degrade man to a slave of physical laws; atheism would make him the creature of accidents and circumstances; but Christianity enthrones man as a co-worker with God in the realm of spiritual agencies. Man's feeling of dependence upon God is the avenue to his power with God. This lifts him into the line of those Providential forces that rule the world. Thus it is that "the kingdom and dominion, and the greatness of the kingdom under the whole heaven, are given to the people of the saints of the Most High."[1]

Am I truly a man of prayer? of earnest, believing prayer? Then am I more the ruler of the world than Alexander or Napoleon. Then nothing shall stand before my power. Do the wicked heap up oppression, and frame iniquity by a law? I go into my closet and cry, "Arise, O Lord," and presently the earth shakes, the heavens smoke, and Slavery goes down in a sea of fire and blood. It is I who have overthrown it, working up yonder above the clouds, where God meets my prayers. They who sit in Paris, in London, in Berlin, holding royal or diplomatic conferences to settle the future of Europe and the East, they who devise wars of dynasty, of ambition and conquest, must take the man of prayer into their counsels; for if they plot iniquity, he will go up into the King's chamber and overthrow it: he will reach forth his hands and touch the springs that are behind their armies and beneath their thrones. When the church shall fully use her prerogative of prayer the kingdom of God will come in the demonstration of the Spirit and of power.

By the virtue that is lodged in the prayer of faith, whosoever will may approximate himself to God in character. "This is the will of God, even your sanctification;" and

[1] Daniel vii. 27.

he who would be holy knows assuredly that, in every petition for a pure heart, he prays for that which God would
have him above all things to possess.   Such a longing
opens the heart to the life-forces of the divine Spirit, and
moves the soul upward toward God; yea, let one but utter
that first lisping cry "God be merciful to me a sinner," and
no mountains can shut in that cry, no clouds weigh it down,
no laws restrain it:—that yearning of the soul after God
shall bring God to the soul as its Father, its Saviour, its
Comforter.   "Lord, teach us how to pray."

CHAPTER XI.

No teacher ever set forth himself so constantly, so prominently, so imperatively as did Jesus Christ. It is offensive to taste, and savors of vanity or presumption, when a teacher continually claims the merit of originality or of discovery, and exacts of his disciples homage to his person, his wisdom, or his opinions. Yet with Christ, "I say unto you," was the preface to every discourse, sometimes to almost every sentence; "believe Me," "receive Me," the demand made upon the hearer not only as a test of discipleship, but as the evidence of love for truth and for God, and the necessary condition of eternal life. He summed up His whole teaching in that memorable saying, "I am the Way, and the Truth, and the Life:"[1]—not I *show* the way, but I Myself am the way; not I *teach* the Truth, but I am Myself the truth; not I *give* or promise life, or will lead My followers unto life, but I *am* the life:— and though God requires all men to come unto Him, and is seeking and calling them by all the methods of His providence and His grace, "no man cometh unto the Father, but by Me."

But the marvel of His character is, that with all this preaching of Himself, this constant repeating of I and Me, there is in the sayings of Jesus no tone of egotism, no air of presumption, no trace of that form of self-assertion which suggests pride or vanity in the speaker, or offends the taste or judgment of the hearer. As a psychological phe-

[1] John xiv. 6.

nomenon this calls for explanation. Why is it that we not only tolerate from the lips of Jesus, but receive with reverence, assertions and demands concerning Himself that in any other would be an offensive arrogance?

This is not simply because of the force and moment of the truth He utters; for though one who announces a new and important truth is entitled to have his name stand in honorable association with that truth, yet we could not endure that he should be always setting himself before the truth and demanding that it should be received in his name. Had Newton insisted upon the perpetual recognition of himself as the discoverer of the law of gravitation, his vanity would have detracted from his fame. Truth is greater than any man. Yet Jesus said " *I* am the Truth," and men are not staggered by even so bold a form of self-assertion.

Mr. Liddon, in his Bampton lectures, has grouped together in a striking manner these personal assertions and claims of Jesus in His teachings. " He distinctly, repeatedly, energetically preaches *Himself*. He is the Bread of life. He is the living Bread that came down from heaven: believers in Him will feed on Him and will have eternal life. He points to a living water of the Spirit, which He can give, and which will quench the thirst of souls that drink it. All who came before Him He characterizes as having been by comparison with Himself, the thieves and robbers of mankind. He is Himself the one Good Shepherd of the souls of men. He knows and He is known of His true sheep. Not only is He the Shepherd, He is the very door of the sheepfold. To enter through Him is to be safe. He is the Vine, the Life-tree of regenerate humanity. All that is truly fruitful and lovely in the human family must branch forth from Him; all spiritual life must wither and die if it be severed from His. He stands consciously between earth and heaven. He claims to be the One Means of a real approach to the invisible God: no soul of man can come to the Father but through Him. He promises that all prayers offered in His name shall be answered; if ye ask anything in my name, *I* will do it. . He claims to be the Lord of the realm of death; He will Himself awake the sleeping dead; all that are in their graves shall hear His voice. He will raise Himself from the dead. He proclaims, 'I am the Resurrection and the Life.' He encourages men to trust in Him as they trust in God: to make Him an object of faith just as they believe in God; to honor Him as they honor the Father. To love Him is a necessary mark of the children of God; if God were your Father, ye would have loved Me. It is not possible to love God, and yet to hate Himself. He that hateth Me, hateth My Father also. The proof of a true love to Him lies in doing His bidding: if ye love Me keep My commandments. ... All radiates from Himself, all converges toward Himself. .... He commands, He does not invite discipleship. ... His message is to be received upon pain of eternal loss, and in receiving it men are to give themselves up to Him simply and unreservedly. No rival claim, however strong, no natural affection, however legitimate and sacred, may interpose between Himself and the soul of His follower. He that loveth father or mother more than Me is not worthy of Me. How can Christ thus bid men live for Himself as for the very end of their existence? How can He rightly draw toward Himself the whole thought and love even of one single human being, with this imperious urgency, if He be anything else or less than the Supreme Lord of life. "[1]

This manner of Christ is an index to His doctrine concerning Himself. If He had nothing back of a human consciousness upon which to base such assertions, was He

---

[1] This same thought is admirably presented by Rev. T. Binney, of London, in his "*Sermons of Forty Years.*"

not more visionary than wise? So far from being the way and the truth, was He not either misled or misleading? Underlying His whole teaching there is a claim of personal supremacy, of absolute authority, of perfection in knowledge and truth, of lordship over the soul, of dominion over life and death—a tone of self-assertion in respect to things upon which no man has a right to be confident of his own wisdom and power, which can not be reconciled with modesty, with truth, or with soundness of judgment, if He who thus proclaimed Himself the Way, the Truth and the Life, was simply a wiser and better sort of man than His fellows. Separated from Himself His words lose their meaning. The subject of His preaching was Himself to such a degree that neither doctrine nor life remains in His words apart from His own personality. But the words of Jesus are pervaded with the consciousness of His divine Sonship which gives Him right to speak with absolute confidence and authority.

This doctrine, however, is not a mere inference from the manner in which Christ summoned the people to trust in Himself. He distinctly taught that He was the Son of God, the representative of the Father upon earth, His associate and equal in heaven. He allowed Himself to be addressed by this title without objection or qualification of any kind. At the opening of His ministry, when Jesus was calling disciples one by one, Nathanael, struck with His knowledge of the heart, exclaimed, "Rabbi, Thou art the Son of God."[1] In the hearing of the rest, Jesus suffered this title to pass unchallenged, and not only so, but He assured Nathanael, who had confessed this faith from his own inward conviction, that he should hereafter behold the outward visible confirmation of it, in the heavens opened, and the angels of God ascending and descending upon Him who there stood in the garb of the Son of Man.

[1] John i. 49.

Thus the seeming contrast of the two titles, "Son of God" and "Son of Man," points to the real unity of their subject—the true Humanity and the divine Sonship being offset in terms or titles only, as two diverse aspects of the same person. Jesus did not disclaim the title, "Son of God" which Nathanael gave, and employ the phrase "Son of Man" as a substitute for that; on the contrary, He accepted this, and virtually approved it, as a declaration of faith from His new disciple: "Because I said unto thee, I saw thee under the fig tree, believest thou?" This miraculous vision, with the attendant knowledge of his heart and life on the part of an utter stranger, had impressed Nathanael with the conviction that this new prophet was the Son of God. Nathanael may have had only the vague Jewish notion touching the Messiah as the Son of God; yet his acknowledgment being based upon the supernatural knowledge that Jesus had shown, pointed to something deeper than an official title; and the answer was, "Thou shalt see greater things than these"—shalt even have the witness of angels from heaven that I am He.

It was not, however, the plan of Jesus to proclaim His divinity openly at the first. He sought to put Himself into thorough sympathy with mankind and to draw them into confidential relations through His own hearty humanity; and He desired also to test the sincerity of men in spiritual things by opening His divinity to the discovery of their faith. He did not first approach them upon the side of wonder and awe by declaring His Godhead, nor by manifesting it through marvels addressed to the senses; but upon the side of love and compassion, through the lowliness and tenderness of a common humanity, from which by degrees He lifted them up to discern in His own works and words the tokens of His divine Sonship.*

A mode of revealing Himself so wisely adapted for testing His true character and also for educating the faith of

His followers, led Jesus at the first to speak of Himself as the " Son of Man " instead of openly proclaiming Himself the " Son of God." But if the latter title were not His by the same right as the former, how can we reconcile His accepting this from others, with the modesty of using the inferior title, and with the honesty that marks His whole speech and life ? He permitted Himself to be called the " Son of God " well knowing that this was intended to be an ascription of divinity, and under circumstances that were equivalent to His proclaiming His divinity. It is not claimed that the appellation " Son of God " is itself decisive of the divinity of Christ—for this was a Jewish title of the Messiah, the Anointed ; but it was given to Jesus and accepted by Him as a token of Divinity. The question is purely one of exegesis, to be determined by a careful annotation of the passages in which the title occurs. It is applied to Jesus twenty-five times in the four Gospels, several of these, however, being but repetitions of the same cases or incidents.

a. Jesus was accosted as " the Son of God " by Satan and by other inferior demons. [1] Perhaps in these cases the conception of the Messiah as the King of the Jews, anointed of God as His vicegerent in the world, will exhaust the meaning. In Luke iv. 41, for instance, the name Christ is given as the equivalent of this epithet ; " Devils came out of many, crying out, and saying, Thou art Christ, the Son of God. And He rebuking them, suffered them not to speak: for they knew that He was Christ." But on the other hand, the exclamation of the demons in the country of the Gergesenes, " Art thou come hither to torment us before the time ?" seems to imply a recognition of His divine power and authority. They apprehended banishment from earth to hell, from opportunities of mischief to the unmitigated endurance of punish-

[1] Matt. iv. 3, 6 ; viii. 29 ; Mark iii. 11 ; v. 7 ; Luke iv. 3, 9, 41 ; viii. 28,

ment, before the final judgment; and they ascribed to Jesus the power so to order their destiny.

b. In a few instances this title was used by the enemies of Jesus, by way of taunt or sneer;—as for instance when passers by reviled Him as He hung upon the cross, wagging their heads, and saying, " If Thou be the Son of God, come down from the cross." [1] The full force of such a taunt, and the miraculous power of self-preservation which the challenge implied, would seem to attach the notion of divinity to the epithet " Son of God."

c. The same interpretation must be put upon the exclamation of the centurion and his brother soldiers, " Truly this was the Son of God." [2] A Roman soldier accustomed to despise the Jews, could have no sympathy with their expectation of a Messiah, and if he had heard from the lips of Jews the title " Son of God," he could hardly have attached to it their peculiar theocratic signification. But a Roman of that time, and a soldier withal, would be susceptible to superstitious fears touching the gods as manifesting themselves in supernatural phenomena; and when he saw the earthquake, the resurrection of the dead, and the other marvels that attended the death of Jesus, filled with awe of these miraculous signs, he cried out, " *Truly* this was the Son of God." That title had just fallen upon his ears in the taunts of passers by; he takes it up with the emphasis of truth, and gives it not their meaning but his own; and from his point of view it would signify a divine person.

d. The High Priest used this title in the Messianic sense when he said to Jesus, " I adjure Thee by the living God, that Thou tell us whether Thou be the Christ, the Son of God." [3] This was a title of honor based upon the usage of the Old Testament touching the ideal theocratic king as the anointed Son of God. Thus the Lord promised to David concerning Solomon, " I will be his Father and he

[1] Mat. xxvii. 40, 43.   [2] Mat. xxvii. 51; Mark xv. 39.   [3] Mat. xxvi. 63.

shall be My son." [1]   And in the second Psalm the anointed
of the Lord is exalted above all kings and peoples: " I
have set My King upon My holy hill of Zion.   Thou art
My Son, this day have I begotten Thee." [2]   This usage of
the Old Testament interprets the current language of the
Jews in the time of Jesus, concerning the Christ as the
Son of God;—He was the ideal theocratic king.   Yet even
in the second Psalm, He is not declared a Son simply by
virtue of His being constituted a king, but is anointed
king because upon other grounds of divine favor He was
already the chosen Son :—the Sonship preceded the Kingship.   It is evident from the narrative as given with so
much detail by John, that the blind man to whom Jesus
gave sight had only the current Jewish conception of the
Son of God as the Christ.[3]

e.   We come now to the use of this title by the disciples
of Jesus, as an index to their conception of His character.
Though Nathanael may have used the titles " Son of God "
and "King of Israel" as equivalent, John the Baptist attached to the former a deeper meaning, when he saw and
bare record that "this is the Son of God."[4]   John acknowledged the pre-existence of Jesus as the warrant of
His pre-eminence ; "He that cometh after Me, is preferred
before Me; for He *was* before Me ;"[5] and as "the only
begotten Son, which is in the bosom of the Father, He *declared* God, whom no *man* at any time hath seen."[6]   The
title " Son of God," based upon this recognition of His
origin and functions, denotes something higher than an
honorary distinction of office—some relation to God Himself that was peculiar and pre-eminent.   The deep significance of this relation appears in that tender reference to the
" only-begotten" which closes the discourse with Nicodemus ;—"For God so loved the world that He gave His

---

[1] 2 Saml. vii. 14.   [2] Ps. ii. 6, 7.   [3] John ix. 35, 36.
[4] John i. 34.   [5] John i. 15.   [6] John i. 18.

only-begotten Son, that whosoever believeth in Him, should not perish but have everlasting life."[1]

The disciples on board the ship in the tempestuous night, when they saw Jesus walking on the sea;[2] Martha in her confidence that Jesus might have saved her brother, and her wondering hope of his resurrection;[3] Peter asserting the constancy of the twelve after the multitude of disciples had turned back;[4]—these all rested their confession of Jesus as "the Son of God" upon some token of divinity that gleamed through His words or acts;—the winds and the waves obeyed Him, He had power over diseases and death, He had the words of eternal life. Thus the disciples, Jews though they were, and imbued with the Jewish doctrine of the Messiah, appear to have attached to the name "Son of God" a meaning higher than any official title would convey.

f. It only remains that we consider the cases in which Jesus spoke of Himself as the Son of God, and of His oneness with the Father. There were undoubted instances in which He used this name not as designating His official calling, but as expressing an unparalleled personal relation with God.[5] "Verily, verily, I say unto you the hour is coming and now is, when the dead shall hear the voice of the Son of God; and they that hear shall live. For as the Father hath life in Himself, so hath He given to the Son to have life in Himself."[6] Jesus here claimed for Himself the most essential property of divinity—life in self-possession and the power and prerogative of imparting life to others. This power He put forth in raising Lazarus from the grave, when He purposely kept aloof until Lazarus was dead, saying, "This sickness is not unto death, but for the glory of God, that the Son of God might be glorified thereby."[7] Here He associated

[1] John iii. 16. [2] Matt. xiv. 33. [3] John xi. 27. [4] John vi. 69.
[5] Matt. xxi. 37. [6] John v. 25, 26. [7] John xi. 4.

Himself with the Father in the glory that would ensue from a miracle evidencing the highest property of divinity to be vested in Himself.

In the parable of the wicked husbandmen He separated Himself from all the servants of God who had been sent before, as the son and heir, who, because of this immediate relationship to the householder, was deserving of a peculiar reverence.[1] Again, in speaking of His second Advent, He contrasted the Son of God with both *men* and *angels:* "Of that day and that hour knoweth no man, no, not the angels which are in heaven, neither the Son, but the Father."[2] Whoever the Son was, He was distinct from men, and above the angels; for He was clearly and absolutely contrasted with both, not here in respect of knowledge, but in degree as a being. The gradation is, "no *man,*" no "*angel,*" not even the *Son.* Who then was He?

The Jews of that time understood Jesus to claim equality with God by His manner of speaking of His Father. After He had healed the impotent man at the pool of Bethesda, the Jews sought to slay Him, because He had done these things on the Sabbath-day. Jesus answered them "My Father worketh hitherto, and I work." God Himself, who has proclaimed the Sabbath as a hallowed rest, though He has ceased from His work of creation, continues, nevertheless, His work of beneficence, in caring for the world; and I do as my Father does. Now if Jesus were only man, this same argument would have exonerated every pious Jew from keeping the Sabbath according to the law of Moses; but as, on another occasion, He declared that "the Son of Man is Lord even of the Sabbath-day,"[3] so here He associated Himself with God in the right and reason of His action, and rested His authority to "work" upon the Sabbath-day on His prerogative as the Son of God. His accusers resented this as a claim of divinity,

---

[1] Matt. xxi. 37.   [2] Mark xiii. 32.   [3] Matt. xii. 8.

and "they sought the more to kill Him, because He not only had broken the Sabbath, but said also that God was His Father, *making Himself equal with God.*"[1]

Though in common speech they may have used the title Son of God to designate the Messiah in His official character, yet they understood Jesus to use it as denoting sonship in essence and in dignity—equality with God in being and in power. If in this charge His accusers were perverting His meaning, Jesus had every reason, personal and public, for correcting the misunderstanding. His life was in danger, and He could have pacified His enemies by denying their construction of His words : He desired a hearing for His message, and this He might have hoped for by allaying such a blind and passionate prejudice. But instead of rejecting their interpretation of His words and disclaiming the thought of equality with God, He went on to say that as the Son of God His thoughts and actions were identical with those of the Father ; that He possessed the power of the Father, even to raising the dead and judging the world; that even as the Father, He had life in Himself; and He summed up the discourse with the demand " that all men should honor the Son even as they honor the Father." The logic of this whole argument depends upon the fact that Jesus admitted and justified the claim of equality with God which the Jews had attached to His words.

For a man to put forth such a pretension was blasphemy ; and the Jews more than once accused Jesus of this crime, and sought to stone Him to death. On one occasion, at the feast of the dedication, the Jews said to Him, " If thou be the Christ, tell us plainly." To this He answered, " The works I do in my Father's name, they bear witness of Me."[2] In so far as the title "Son of God" was an equivalent for " the Christ," this answer could not

¹ John v. 18.   ² John x. 24, 25.

have exposed Him to the charge of blasphemy. That the Christ should speak of God as the Father whom He represented in His official character, and should appeal to works done in the Father's name, was legitimate, and in accordance with the Jewish notion of the Messiah. But Jesus went farther than this, and having declared His own absolute power over His sheep, even to the giving them eternal life, He rose to the sublime assertion, "*I and my Father are One.*"[1] At this the Jews took up stones to stone Him for blasphemy, "because," said they, "that Thou being a man, makest Thyself God." The *gravamen* of the offense was that "*being a man*" He made Himself God, by asserting that He and His Father were *one;* but there would have been no blasphemy in claiming a moral unity with the Father through His representative character and commission as the Christ.

Jesus might have refuted the charge of blasphemy in either of two ways:—by showing that His words did not admit of the construction that His accusers had put upon them ; or by declaring that He was truly divine, and therefore not guilty of blasphemy in making Himself God. He did not seek to parry their construction, but proceeded to justify His words by an argument from the less to the greater. Reminding them that in their Scriptures judges were called "gods" as the organs of the divine word and will, He claimed that He could literally appropriate the title "Son of God" in its full meaning, because the Father had sanctified Him and sent Him into the world. Then once more appealing to His works, He reiterated the assertion of oneness with God—"the Father in Me, and I in Him." So far were the Jews from being convinced or pacified by His answer, that they sought again to take Him, that they might visit upon Him the punishment of blasphemy.

The charge of blasphemy became a conclusive proof that

[1] John x. 22 seq.

He meant to assert His own divinity, when, at His trial, He not only suffered this charge to be revived without contradicting or explaining it, but re-affirmed His Sonship under that construction of His meaning. When Pilate declared that he found Jesus guilty of no offense against Roman law, the Jews cried out, " *We* have a law, and by our law He ought to die, because He made Himself the Son of God." [1] The law referred to was that against blasphemy. [2] A claim to be the Christ would not have been blasphemy, but only imposture or enthusiasm; to have rendered it blasphemous to assume the title " Son of God," that title must have signified divinity itself. But Jesus declined to vindicate Himself from this charge. Now there was no humility in remaining quiet under so horrible an accusation, when by a word He could have denied the intention of blasphemy in His use of the phrase Son of God; yet, when He stood before the Sanhedrim, the High Priest adjured Him by the living God to answer whether He was the Christ, the Son of God. Jesus not only answered affirmatively, " Thou hast said," but went on to proclaim His " coming in the clouds of heaven, sitting on the right hand of power." [3] Thereupon the High Priest rent his clothes, saying, " He hath spoken blasphemy," and for blasphemy they found Him " guilty of death."

Clearly the title Son of God was understood to denote participation in the divine nature, and equality of essence with God ; and Jesus, knowing that this title was so understood, consented to receive it, and used it of Himself; and when charged with blasphemy for making Himself equal with God, He did not deny that He claimed equality with God, but did deny that this was blasphemy or presumption, and insisted that He and His Father were one. Either then He had within Him the consciousness of divinity, or He was a demented enthusiast.

[1] John xix. 7.   [2] Lev. xxiv. 16.   [3] Matt. xxvi. 63–66.

10

This ONENESS with the Father which Jesus constantly affirmed as the testimony of His own consciousness, was not merely a moral unity—oneness in spirit and feeling, or unity of action, for the same object, upon the same plan—but a oneness that made it impossible for Him to act as in any way separate from God. " The Son can do nothing of Himself."[1] This, says Bengel,[2] " is a feature of glory, not of imperfection; such declarations proceeded from His intimate sense of unity, by nature and by love, with the Father." The Son can do nothing of Himself, not because He is wanting in power, or inferior and dependent in His nature, but because His Being is inseparable from that of the Father. The " can do nothing" is a moral inability based in the will of the Son.[3] Whatever the Father does, that the Son does, with the same power and the same intent. His sheep shall never perish, for none shall pluck them out of *His* hand,—no more than they would be able to pluck them out of His Father's hand. Having thus asserted His own omnipotence, in the same terms in which He declared the omnipotence of the Father, He added " I and my Father are one:"—one, not merely in agreement of will, but in unity of power, and so of nature; for omnipotence is an attribute of the nature of God.[4] It was for this that the Jews said " *Thou makest thyself God!*" The Father is in the Son; the Father worketh in the Son; and this with a unity so perfect and continuous that the Son who puts forth divine power in the view of men, is not a being extraneous to God, but in essential nature, the source of working power, is One with God. His sonship was a relation to the Father that could be shared by no other. " No man knoweth the Son, but the Father; neither knoweth any man the Father save the Son, and he to whomsoever the Son will reveal Him."[5]

---

[1] John v. 19.   [2] " Hoc gloriæ est, non imperfectionis." Bengel, *Gnomon* in loc.
[3] Tholuck, *in loc.*   [4] Bengel, *Gnomon*, John x. 30.   [5] Mat. xi. 27.

"If a man love Me, My Father will love him, and we will come unto him, and make our abode with him."[1]

In answer to Philip's desire to behold a theophany after the manner of the Old Testament, Jesus said, "He that hath seen Me hath seen the Father,"[2]—"by reason of the consummate unity which subsists between us, just as the soul, in itself invisible, is seen by what it does through the body."[3]

The prayer of Jesus, "O Father, glorify Thou Me with Thine own Self, with the glory which I had with Thee before the world was"—expresses the consciousness that Jesus had of Himself as an incarnation, and of His eternal pre-existence with the Father. He does not say, the glory that I received from Thee, by promise, at My coming into the world, but the glory which *I had*, ειχον, with Thine own Self, in a unity of participation with the Godhead, *before that the world was.* "He always was having it, *was in possession of it;* He never *began* to have it."[4] In this utterance, surely, He made Himself God.

The testimony of Jesus concerning Himself, though it nowhere gives us the doctrine of His divinity in the form of a philosophical concept, nevertheless makes it clear that the doctrine of a divine consciousness in Christ was not the invention of a later philosophy in the Church, but is given in the synoptical Gospels, as well as in the more dialectical Gospel of John, as it fell from the lips of Christ; so that we must agree with Dorner, that "all genuine historical investigation presses to the result that the founder of our religion was Himself, through His own Self-consciousness, and the utterance of that to others, the cause at once of the introduction into the minds of men of the Christian idea of the God-man, and of the attribution of that to Him."[5]

<hr />

[1] John xiv. 23.   [2] John xiv. 9.   [3] Bengel, Gnomon, John xiv. 9.
[4] Bengel, John xvii. 5.   [5] Dorner, Doctrine of the Person of Christ. Intn. p. 45.

The apostles did not invent this doctrine to magnify their Lord after His decease; they were slow at first in coming to the recognition of His divinity under the veil of His humiliation; though they confessed Him to be the Son of God, this faith was shaken for a time by His yielding Himself to death; yet it came back, after His resurrection, and then Jesus sealed it by accepting the homage of Thomas, who atoned for his momentary unbelief by the full glowing confession "My Lord and My God."[1] By consenting to receive that declaration, Jesus warranted our implicit belief in the divinity of His person.

The question here is not at all whether Thomas, by the elasticity of an enthusiastic nature, had vibrated from the extreme of skepticism to that of credulity. If Thomas was deluded into such a confession, what shall we say of Jesus, who not only did not disclaim it, but openly received it as His due, and pronounced those blessed who should come to Him with the same faith in His Sovereignty and His Divinity? Was He deluded? Or did He sanction a delusion? Or was He not both Lord and God?

This divinity of His person gives to the words of Christ supreme authority over the souls of men. He is Lord of the conscience, Lord of the affections, Lord of the will; His doctrine is Truth, His command is Law, His promise is Life. The soul that would live must obey Christ, must trust Him, must serve Him. The soul that would come to God as the Father must come by Christ.

The divinity of His person imparts to His sufferings and death a majesty and a tenderness that should draw men to Him in the most reverent and grateful devotion. That Jesus should die a witness for His principles and teachings, and in testimony of His love to man, was heroic, was pathetic, was inspiring. But when we bring into our

[1] John xx. 28.

conception of Jesus this divine Sonship, and consider of what ineffable dignity and majesty was He who thus suffered, there comes over the soul an awe and reverence which not all the martyrdoms of history could inspire; and when we reflect that this Son of God gave Himself to this shame and suffering for us, is there any tie or claim of earth that can so move our souls to gratitude and devotion? Consecration—the giving up all, body, soul and spirit to such a Saviour,—is the least to be thought of by one who believes upon the only-begotten Son of God.

CHAPTER XII.

THE COMFORTER—THE HOLY GHOST.

The Mission of Christ was begun, consecrated and ended by the intervention of the Holy Ghost. He was begotten of the Holy Ghost;[1] at His baptism the heaven was opened, and the Holy Ghost descended in bodily shape like a dove upon Him;[2] after His resurrection, Jesus met with His disciples, and having identified Himself to them as their crucified Lord, "He breathed on them, and said unto them, Receive ye the Holy Ghost;"[3] and on the eve of His ascension He bade His disciples await the baptism of the Holy Ghost,[4] whose coming into the Church He had already promised as a permanent substitute for His own withdrawal from the world.[5] Since Jesus gave such prominence and significance to the Comforter in the administration of His kingdom upon earth, it is important to fix with definiteness His doctrine of the Holy Ghost, and the place of that doctrine in His scheme of theological thought. An induction of particulars upon this question gives the following results.

First. Christ taught that the Holy Ghost was *the Revealer of Truth from God to the souls of men.* In quoting against the Scribes the prediction of David concerning Himself as the Son of God, He invested this with the authority of divine inspiration; "For David himself said *by the Holy Ghost,* The Lord said to My Lord, Sit thou on My right hand till I make Thine enemies Thy footstool."[6]

[1] Mat. i. 20; Luke i. 35.   [2] Luke iii. 21, 22; Mat. iii. 13; John i. 32.
[3] John xx. 22.   [4] Acts i. 5, 8.   [5] John xiv. 16, 26; xvi. 7.   [6] Mark xii. 36.

This prevision of the Messiah's exaltation was above the range of David's imagination as a poet, and was imparted by the Holy Ghost. Jesus constantly appealed to the Old Testament as "the word of God,"—thus recognizing in it the voice of divine inspiration. [1]

He instructed His disciples to look directly to the Holy Ghost for the suggestion of Truth adapted to their necessities. "When they shall lead you and deliver you up, take no thought beforehand what ye shall speak, neither do ye premeditate, but whatsoever shall be given you in that hour, that speak ye; for it is not ye that speak *but the Holy Ghost.*" [2] This was an assurance of immediate inspiration, to the extent certainly of guidance in vindicating their faith under circumstances of difficulty, responsibility, and danger. This special guidance of the Holy Spirit in the perception and adaptation of Truth was the compensation that Jesus promised to His disciples for the loss of His personal teaching. "When He, the Spirit of Truth is come, He will guide you into all Truth; for He shall not speak of Himself; but whatsoever He shall hear [*i. e.* from the Father] that shall He speak; and He will show you things to come." [3] The "Spirit of Truth" embodies in Himself the very principle of Truth and the knowledge of all Truth; and His power is directed to bring the human mind into harmony with that higher sphere of spiritual thought and life where Truth is the bond of unity. As the absolute possessor of Truth, He also imparts Truth in its highest, purest forms; and by both these methods, the ennobling and the illuminating, He would guide the apostles into all truth.

Christ had manifested the truth from His own consciousness, and as a teacher had opened the way into the highest domain of knowledge; but the spiritual meaning of much that He uttered was at first only imperfectly apprehended

[1] Luke iv. 4; John x. 35. [2] Mark xiii. 11. [3] John xvi. 13.

by His disciples. More than once did He reprove their slowness of heart to believe. And indeed, the disciples trained in the sensuous conceptions of the Jews touching the Messianic kingdom, could not fully comprehend the sacrificial bearing of the death of Christ, until after His resurrection and ascension. Hence it would be the office of the Holy Spirit to bring this and kindred truths, as Jesus had Himself declared them, into vivid remembrance, to give them definite form, to illuminate their meaning, to guide the apostles to a right understanding of them, and also to open new reaches and applications of the Truth—showing "things to come." "The Comforter, which is the Holy Ghost, whom the Father will send in My name, He shall teach you all things, and bring all things to your remembrance, whatsoever I have said unto you."[1] "When the Comforter is come, whom I will send unto you from the Father, which proceedeth from the Father, He shall testify of me."[2] "He shall glorify Me; for He shall receive of mine, and shall show it unto you."[3]

These several declarations set forth the Holy Spirit under every possible relation to the Truth; as revealing truth under new phases; as announcing prophetically facts to be accomplished in the kingdom of God; as interpreting truths already proclaimed by Christ; as guiding sincere minds into the clear and full knowledge of truth. But the highest function assigned to the Spirit of Truth is that of employing the truth as a power of sanctification upon the hearts of men—not a power for the intellect merely, but for the feelings and the will also. The prayer of Jesus for His disciples, "Sanctify them through Thy Truth; Thy word is truth,"[4] would have its fulfilment when the Holy Spirit should guide them into all truth. Christ announced that the Holy Spirit would exert upon the minds even of sinful men a direct power of conviction

[1] John xiv. 26.   [2] John xv. 26.   [3] John xvi. 14.   [4] John xvii. 17.

and rebuke through the doctrine of Christ: "When He is come, He will reprove the world of sin, of righteousness, and of judgment:"[1] by making manifest the innocence and holiness of Christ, the sinful unbelief that had rejected Him, and His assured triumph over all the powers of evil, and thereby working in the minds of such as had rejected Him, a humiliating and self-reproving conviction of their guilt, the Holy Spirit would vindicate the Truth embodied in the life and death of Jesus, and would secure to His Gospel a triumphant efficacy.

That which the Holy Ghost thus effectively presents to the minds of men is the truths of Religion, especially as these are embodied in the Holy Scriptures. Christ did not promise that He should enlighten us in the science of nature, of history, of government, or make new discoveries of the mysteries of creation;—but that He should convince men of sin and lead them to faith in Christ Himself —a work having immediate reference to the extension of the Kingdom of God.

A second point in Christ's doctrine of the Holy Spirit was that *He was the source of the supernatural gifts and powers imparted to the first disciples for the furtherance of the Gospel*

When Jesus commissioned the apostles to go into all the world and preach the Gospel to every creature, He promised that these signs should follow them that believe: "In My name shall they cast out devils; they shall speak with new tongues, they shall take up serpents; and if they drink any deadly thing it shall not hurt them; they shall lay hands on the sick and they shall recover."[2] The fulfilment of this promise is recorded by Luke in the following words, uttered by our Lord just before His ascension : " Ye shall be baptized with the Holy Ghost not many days hence ; and ye shall receive power after that the Holy Ghost is come upon you"[3]—or ye shall

---

[1] John xvi. 8.   [2] Mark xvi. 17.   [3] Acts i. 5, seq.

receive the power of the Holy Ghost coming upon you :— the spiritual endowment of the apostles for their work, and supernatural powers to certify their calling and to convince the world of the divine warrant of the Gospel.

Even His own miracles—though these proceeded from the power that dwelt always in Himself—Jesus referred to the Spirit of God. The Pharisees accused Him of being in league with Beelzebub, the prince of the devils; but Jesus answered them : " If I cast out devils by the *Spirit of God*, then the Kingdom of God has come unto you. "[1] Had His reply ended with these words, we might have taken the expression " Spirit of God " for an influence upon Himself, emanating from the Father ; but He added, " All manner of sin and blasphemy shall be forgiven unto men, but the blasphemy against the Holy Ghost shall not be forgiven unto them. "[2]   From this it is evident that Jesus intended by the " Spirit of God," that same " Spirit of Truth" of whom He afterwards spake as " the Comforter," for blasphemy could not be uttered against an unconscious influence, but only against a divine Person.

It was, further, the doctrine of Christ that the Holy Spirit would *abide in the hearts of believers, and with the Church, collectively, for guidance, comfort, encouragement, support.* To prepare His disciples for His departure He gave them two topics of consolation :—first His own temporary return :—" A little while, and ye shall see me . . . I will see you again, and your heart shall rejoice." [3] But His resurrection, while it would revive their hopes of His kingdom,[4] and give them the most absolute confidence in His promises, would nevertheless be followed by a second and lasting bereavement of His presence, through His ascension to the Father.   For this bereavement there was provided a second and permanent consolation, in the

---

[1] Matt. xii. 28.   [2] Matt. xii. 31.   [3] John xvi. 16, 22.   [4] Acts i. 6.

coming of the Comforter: "I will pray the Father, and He shall give you another Comforter, that He may abide with you forever"—a Helper ever within call; an Advocate always at-command. This Comforter would even be nearer to them and more constantly with them than Christ had been in His bodily presence. "He dwelleth with you and shall be in you." He would come in a manner invisible to the world, and that the worldly mind could not comprehend: come through the quickening of the consciousness to a realization of higher spiritual truths; come as a gracious, soothing, healing influence upon the mind itself in the deepest concernments of the soul; come in the experiences of the inner life in the love of Christ, in the sense of the forgiveness of sin and of fellowship with God, in the feelings of hope, comfort, peace, joy, in all that pertains to our relations with our Heavenly Father and to our final salvation. As Christ became incarnate in Humanity for its redemption, so is the Holy Spirit perpetually incarnate in the Church for its sanctification.

All the teaching of Christ concerning the Holy Ghost assumes or implies both *the divinity of the Spirit and His distinct personality*. He spake of the Spirit not as a thing, an attribute, an influence, a property, but as a person; He ascribed to the Spirit such acts and offices as can be affirmed only of a person; had He said "I will send My spirit or My Father will send His spirit," this might have meant nothing more than that He would cause them to feel an influence from Himself, or that an influence proceeding from God would bring their feelings and actions into accord with the spirit of Christ. Had He promised to His disciples specifically a spirit of wisdom or a spirit of power, this might have signified nothing more than a guidance or an efficiency imparted by divine influence. But He spake of *the* Spirit,—thus defining one distinct Spirit; the Holy Spirit, designating the Spirit by a personal and

moral characteristic; and He used the personal pronoun—
"the Holy Ghost *whom* the Father will send in My name;
whom the world cannot receive, because it seeth *Him* not,
neither knoweth *Him*."[1]   This constant use of "He" and
"Him" denotes personality; it would be a solecism thus
to speak of an unconscious influence.

Jesus said, also, of the Holy Spirit, He shall *abide* with
you; He shall *teach* you; He shall *guide* you; He shall
hear and shall *speak;* He shall *glorify* Me; He shall *testify* of Me;—all which are personal acts, which no stretch
of metaphor could predicate of an unconscious influence.

Moreover, a personality is attributed to the Holy Spirit
as distinct from the Father and the Son : "*I* will pray the
Father ;" now prayer is the act of one personal consciousness addressing itself to another: "I" and "the Father ;"
and *He*, i. e., the Father, "shall give you another Comforter"—a Helper in the stead of Jesus ;—that *He*, this
Comforter thus distinguished from both the Father and
the Son, may "abide with you forever." Leaving all metaphysical refinements about personality, in the doctrine of
Jesus, the Holy Spirit is so far distinct from the Father
and the Son that the pronouns in the first, second, and
third persons may be applied to them separately, and to
describe their relations and actions one toward another.

At the same time, His doctrine ascribes to the Holy
Spirit a true and proper divinity ;—the acts and attributes
of divinity, absolute knowledge, foresight of things to come,
power over the memory, the thoughts, and the wills of
men, and power to impart miraculous gifts.   In the formula of baptism, the sacrament by which disciples are ini-
tiated into the kingdom of Christ, the name of the Holy
Spirit is linked upon equal terms with the names of Christ
and of the Father :—"baptizing them in the name of the
Father, and of the Son, and of the Holy Ghost."[2]   Here

[1] John xiv. 17.   [2] Matt. xxviii. 19.

the "Name" denotes personality; and in the solemn consecration of a soul to its Creator and Lord, it is not credible that anything lower than Divinity would be associated
with the Name that is above every name, as worthy of like
homage and devotion. But it was in condemning the
blasphemy of the Pharisees that Jesus set forth in the
strongest terms the divine personality of the Holy Ghost.
While His own divinity was veiled under the humiliation
of the flesh, men might impugn His acts and be pardoned;
but so clear and strong is the proof of divine power in acts
performed by the Spirit of God, that to contemn Him is
an unpardonable sin. "Whosoever speaketh a word
against the Son of Man, it shall be forgiven him; but
whosoever speaketh against the Holy Ghost, it shall not
be forgiven him, neither in this world, neither in the
world to come." -

This doctrine of Jesus is a warrant for faith in the Gospels
as a divinely inspired record of Himself. Since the Holy
Spirit quickened and guided the apostles in the recollection,
the conception, and the statement of truth as uttered by
Christ Himself, the record of the words of Jesus in the
Gospels is authenticated by divine authority; and should
therefore be received with loving reverence and obedience.
Like a great poem or symphony it carries within itself the
tokens of the Master. And He who is perpetually in the
Truth, quickening the letter into life, is also in the world
convincing men of this same truth; convincing them of
their sin and their need of a Saviour; convincing them of
the righteousness of Christ, and His power as the Holy Son
of God to save them from their sin; convincing them of
judgment, the condemnation under which every sinner
lies, the condemnation that is upon the world, and the
judgment to come: and so the Spirit who is in the truth,
is also by the truth speaking to the hearts of men with
conviction.

How full of *responsibility* is the hearing of the Gospel, seeing that in it God speaks to every man, as He spake to Israel face to face! How full of *peril* is it to disobey the Gospel, seeing that he who resists this truth resists the Holy Ghost. But how full of *encouragement* also, to all who proclaim the Gospel is the assurance that the Spirit of God who inspired it at the first, still lives in it and speaks through it. To human view the conversion of a soul that is committed to selfishness by force of will, by pride and habit, or that is steeped in iniquity and hemmed round with evil associations, may appear not only difficult but hopeless. But when Jesus commanded His disciples to go into all the world and preach the Gospel to every creature, He appointed the divine word as the instrument and promised the divine Spirit as the power, and with these all things are possible to him that believeth.

The personal bearings of Christ's doctrine of the Holy Spirit are of inestimable value. His predominant thought in the promise of the Spirit to His disciples was their comfort under bereavement and their endowment for the labors and conflicts of His service. So far from promising them exemption from trials, He forewarned them of tribulations that would arise out of the very fact of their discipleship ;[1] but in the sore bereavement of His absence, the Comforter, the Helper would be ever within call. Every word of this precious promise stands good for every disciple and for all time ; to every bereaved and sorrowing but trusting heart the Comforter comes ; to every burdened, struggling, but praying and believing soul, the Helper is nigh. Men often proffer sympathy without help or help without sympathy ; but in the coming of the Holy Ghost are pledged both comfort and help, available and satisfying.

And in that coming, moreover, is our grandest incitement and hope for the endeavor of holy living. To attain

[1] John xvi. 33.

moral perfection is, at times at least, the aspiration of every true soul. No one of the beatitudes so thrills the heart with longings for its own disenthralment from evil, as this ; " Blessed are the pure in heart; for they shall see God."[1] That beatific vision has been the dream of poetry and philosophy, that likeness to God the longing of devotion. But what poetry and philosophy have depicted in the infinite distance, and devotion has sighed for with wingless and baffled desires, finding still

"Somewhat to cast off, somewhat to become,"

is brought within reach, made possible, made actual, when the Holy Spirit of God comes to dwell in our hearts, to teach us all things, to guide us into all truth and show us things to come. Renovated through the virtue of this Holy Presence, and illuminated with this inward guidance, the soul may see God.[2]

[1] Mat. v. 8.

[2] For a fuller discussion of the New Testament doctrine of the Holy Spirit, see the author's volume on "The Holy Comforter."

CHAPTER XIII.

THE Theology of Christ has always a background of Eschatology; and His doctrine of the Last Things is one of the most distinctive features of His system. All His teachings point to His second coming, and to the marvellous events which shall attend that both to the living and the dead. The Kingdom of Heaven shall then be perfected; the Son of Man shall appear in power and glory, and the issues of the present life shall be made up in the unchanging conditions of the Hereafter.

But until that great consummation what and where shall be the state of the dead? Do they sleep in unconsciousness? Do they enter at once upon their final state of award? Or do they linger in some intermediate state of uncertainty, of imperfection, possibly of purgatory?

The reticence of Jesus upon such points as these is in marked contrast with His pronounced utterances concerning the finalities of the future state, and with the eagerness of the human mind, and especially of human affection, to withdraw the veil from what directly follows death. The poet[1] has well expressed both the longing and the mystery, " when Lazarus left his charnel-cave."

> "Where wert thou, brother, those four days?"
> There lives no record of reply,
> Which, telling what it is to die,
> Had surely added praise to praise.
>
> Behold a man raised up by Christ!
> The rest remaineth unrevealed.
> He told it not; or something sealed
> The lips of that Evangelist.

[1] Tennyson, *In Memoriam*, xxxi.

160

Upon all that concerns the state of the departed Christ addressed Himself not to curiosity but to faith ; not to the speculative fancy but to the moral feelings, and this by setting up character rather than condition as the object of attainment. Unless the parable of Dives and Lazarus be understood of a scene in Hades, there is hardly anything in the teachings of Christ concerning the state of the soul between death and the judgment. Yet by one brief word uttered just as He was expiring on the cross, Jesus lifted the veil from untold possibilities of life and felicity to the soul after death. One of the malefactors at His side said unto Him, "Lord, remember me when Thou comest into Thy kingdom." "And Jesus said unto him, Verily, I say unto thee, To-day shalt thou be with Me in Paradise."[1]

What mysterious questionings start up at the reading of these words. They were the promise of the dying Saviour to the penitent transgressor. They were the answer to the prayer of a public criminal, who confessed the justice of his condemnation for his·deeds ; but who, amid the agony of a lingering death, turned to Jesus with the homage of his soul, and the prayer of adoration and trust. Most suggestive are they of the compassion and grace of the Redeemer, and of the certainty of salvation to every true penitent.

But our inquiry is now directed to the terms and contents of the promise. *Where* did Jesus promise to convey the spirit of the dying thief? To Paradise. *When ?* To-day. In what society would he there be? With Christ Himself. *To-day* shalt thou be *with Me* in *Paradise.*

What, then, and where is PARADISE? Is this only another term for heaven? Does it signify the final blessedness of the righteous? or does it apply to some state intermediate between death and the judgment, in which the soul

[1] Luke xxiii. 42, 43.

11

awaits the resurrection of the body, before entering into its final abode?

The state of departed saints directly after death has been the subject of wide speculation in the Church from the earliest times; and the most opposite theories have been broached according to the prevalence of a more sensuous or a more spiritual philosophy, of a more literal or a more fanciful interpretation of the Scriptures. *Justin Martyr*, who lived in the first half of the second century, denounced as a heresy the doctrine that souls are immediately received into heaven at death, and maintained that the souls of the righteous depart to a temporary but happy place—an intermediate state. On the other hand, *Cyprian*, bishop of Carthage about the middle of the third century, held that those dying in the Lord were taken immediately to His presence. Again: *Tertullian*, at the beginning of the third century, believed that *Martyrs* went immediately to heaven, but that for believers in general, there was a delay in some intermediate state, before arriving at the heavenly glory; whereas *Origen*, who flourished at Alexandria at about the same period, taught that immediately after death believers go first to Paradise, which he imagined to be a happy island; as they grow in knowledge and piety, they proceed on their journey from Paradise to higher regions, and having passed through various mansions which the Scriptures call heavens, they arrive at last at the kingdom of heaven, properly so called. The perfection of blessedness ensues only after the general judgment. [1]

In later times the doctrine of purgatory was added to that of the intermediate state by the Latin Church, though never accepted by the Greek Church. At the Reformation, many Protestant theologians in rejecting a purgatory, rejected also the notion of an intermediate state, while

[1] See citations in Hagenbach, *History of Doctrines*, § 77, 78.

others retained the doctrine that the souls of the righteous linger in some vestibule of the heavenly kingdom until the last judgment. The former view is well-expressed in the burial service of the Church of England for the dead: "Almighty God, with whom do live the spirits of those that depart hence in the Lord, and with whom the souls of the faithful, after they are delivered from the burden of the flesh, are in joy and felicity."

The belief in an intermediate state for the righteous, in which they await the consummation of all things before being presented at the throne of the Father, obtains especially in the Lutheran communion, but has able advocates as well in other communions; so that from the earliest times till now, this has been a subject upon which great latitude of opinion and great diversity of theory have been admitted within the range of Orthodoxy.

The notions of some of the early Fathers were influenced by the pagan philosophy in which they had been trained before their conversion, and which instead of being wholly discarded was applied, sometimes unconsciously, to the interpretation of Christian doctrines. Thus the speculations of Persia and Greece concerning the transportation of the soul through a series of abodes up toward the dwelling-place of the gods, found their way under modified forms into Christian theology. The Jewish Rabbis had long been addicted to fanciful allegories concerning the kingdom of the Messiah; in His reign the garden of Eden was to be restored, and the righteous would dwell in Paradise, with royal apparel, in palaces of gold, amid groves and fountains and flowers of wondrous fragrance and healing virtue. Such Scriptures as the thirty-fifth chapter of Isaiah were taken as a literal picture of the abundance of sensuous delights in this Messianic Paradise; and the apocryphal book of Esdras promises to the children of God a dwelling in a beautiful garden, where are streams of milk .

and honey, and mountains covered with lilies and roses. Such views tinctured the popular belief of the Jews concerning the future abode of the righteous, and we trace their influence also in some of the early Christian writings.

But the great storehouse or rather university of ideas concerning the future state was Egypt—from which the Greeks and Romans derived their most impressive notions of the experiences of the soul after death. The book of prayers and forms which the Egyptians deposited in the tomb as a sort of guide and passport for the departed spirit through the world of the dead, teaches that the soul continues conscious after death ; that it enters into Hades, a gloomy region under the earth ; that if already pure it passes safely through this dismal abode ; but if impure or defective is subjected to discipline ; that on emerging from Hades it is judged, and having passed this ordeal it advances through seven distinct halls up to as many palaces, till it arrives at last at the chief dwelling of the gods. Prominent in this conception of the Future State was the notion of a detention after death in a sort of border-land, before reaching the highest blessedness, and of a gradation through which the soul must pass in its ascent to the Elysian fields—which answered to Paradise.[1]

We trace this general conception down through the literature of later nations, and find it culminating at last in the magnificent poem of Dante. In his Paradise are ten heavens, nine of which revolve about the earth as a common center, each filling the sphere of a planet, and the tenth or highest is motionless, and encircles and contains all the rest. Each of these heavens contains spirits in different degrees of advancement toward perfection ; in the

---

[1] For a complete view of the Egyptian doctrine of a future state, see the "Book of the Dead," translated by Dr. Birch, in *Egypt's Place in Universal History*, vol. v.; also an analysis of the same by the author of this volume, in the *Bibliotheca Sacra* for 1868, pp. 69–112.

ninth are the Orders of Angels, and in the tenth is the visible presence of God.

Thus in all ages and among all people have contemplative and imaginative minds—philosophers, poets, theologians,—been exercised upon the state of the soul after death, and especially whether it is in a condition of immediate consciousness and blessedness; or for a time unconscious or asleep—to be hereafter vivified; or, if conscious, whether at once made perfect in bliss, or subjected to intermediate delays and changes in its progress towards the highest phase of its existence. Hardly any question has for the human mind such a universal power of fascination. Yet in comparison with the fundamental fact of a future state of rewards and punishments to become at some time the experience of every human soul, these details of time and mode are more curious than momentous, and are treated in the sacred Scriptures with a discreet silence. Only hints are given, where our instinct of immortality craves minute and copious information; and the best Biblical students are far from agreed in their interpretation of these hints, or in the doctrines they would base upon them. Still the field is open for ever-new inquiry, and by comparing spiritual things with spiritual we may get at least an inkling of the truth.

What did our Lord intend by Paradise? This was the only instance in which He used the word, except as John cites it from His lips, in the Apocalypse;[1] and it occurs but once besides in the New Testament.[2] It is a word of Eastern origin which the Greeks borrowed to describe an oriental park—such for instance as the Greek general Xenophon saw on his famous march into the interior of Asia—and which is described as "a wide park enclosed against injury, yet with its natural beauty unspoiled, with stately forest trees, many of them bearing fruit, watered by

[1] Rev. ii. 7.   [2] 2 Cor. xii. 4.

clear streams, on whose banks roved large herds of ante-
lopes or sheep."[1] For this feature of Easte: a scenery—re-
sembling somewhat the forest of Fontainebleau in France,
though more rich and luxuriant—the Greeks adopted from
the Sanscrit the name Paradise.

This word came into the New Testament through the
Septuagint; for the Greek translation of the Hebrew Scriptures, made three centuries before Christ, was widely in use
among the Jews in His time, and many of the quotations
from the Old Testament in the New are made from that
version. In the Septuagint *Paradise* is used for *Eden*,
wherever that word occurs in the English version, and
a's) for *garden*. Thus where Solomon says "I made me
gardens and orchards,"[2] the Septuagint reads, "Paradises."
In the prophecy of Balaam: "How goodly are thy tents,
O Jacob; as the valleys are they spread forth, as gardens
(*Paradises*) by the river side."[3] In the book of Nehemiah
is a curious instance of the same meaning that Xenophon
gave to the word. Nehemiah who lived at the court of
Babylon, says "The king gave me a letter to Asaph, the
keeper of the king's forest, that he may give me timber to
make beams for the gates of the palace."[4] The word
"forest" here the Septuagint gives Paradise—a pleasure-
forest or preserve. The first notion of Paradise to a Jew
therefore, was a royal garden like Eden; indeed the garden in which our first parents were placed was "the Paradise of God."

But Paradise was not simply a remembered name; it
was a word of promise and hope as well : for in the prophet Isaiah, it is a frequent type of the future blessedness
and glory of the people of God. "The Lord shall comfort Zion: He will comfort all her waste places: and He
will make her wilderness like Eden and her desert like
the garden of the Lord."[5] *Paradise* was the word adopted

---

[1] Smith's Dict. of Bible. [2] Eccles. ii. 5. [3] Num. xxiv. 6. [4] Neh. ii. 8. [5] li. 3.

by the Septuagint to describe this scene of beauty—"joy and gladness shall be found therein, thanksgiving and the voice of melody."

Such being the idea of Paradise in that version of the Scriptures then widely used among the Jews, and which Christ Himself probably read from in the synagogues, what promise did He intend to convey to the thief at his side when He said, "To-day Thou shalt be with Me in Paradise?" He did not explain the term; He would not tantalize His fellow-sufferer with an unintelligible reply; it must have had a satisfying meaning to the mind of a common Jew.

We have seen that the Jewish Rabbis had gone beyond the Biblical idea of the term, and had pictured Paradise as either a place of sensuous delights in the Messiah's kingdom upon earth, or an intermediate place of blessedness after death; and some of the more intellectual among them, such as Philo, had made Paradise a mere symbol of the happiness to be derived from wisdom. But shall we therefore attach to the word Paradise as used by Christ the popular notion of "a fair land cooled by ocean breezes and watered by limpid streams, where the souls of the righteous would tarry awhile on their way to heaven; or a region in the upper part of Sheol, somehow divided from the place of the wicked, but not the final resting-place of the good?" Surely Christ's method of teaching forbids us to assume that, by using a term of common speech, He would countenance the erroneous notions which the popular imagination had attached to that word. The Jewish popular belief was full of errors concerning the Messiah, and the kingdom of heaven; but Jesus neither refrained from using these terms, nor by using them did He sanction the erroneous notions which attached to them in the popular mind. Rather, He sought to reclaim such words to their proper significance. Hence inasmuch as the term

Paradise was essentially a Bible-word through its frequen
use in a translation as widely read as the Hebrew Scriptures—we must look for the meaning of Paradise, not to
the popular belief nor the fancies of the Rabbis, not to the
speculative Philo nor the credulous Josephus, but to
the fundamental idea of the first Paradise in the Old Testament, as this was illustrated by the spiritual teaching of
our Lord. It were easy to poetize or philosophize here;
but the question is one of interpretation.

The primitive Paradise—the first abode of man—embraced these elements; a state of purity or innocence; a
place of beauty, abundance and delight, or a condition of
peaceful, and entire satisfaction; the nearness of God as
the loving Father: and an implied pledge of immortality.
The true life in Paradise was without sin—for when man
sinned he was cast out from the garden; life in Paradise
was free from want and care—for toil and pain came as the
curse of sin: life in Paradise was one of plenty and delight—for the garden was planted with " every tree that
was pleasant to the sight and good for food;" [1] life in
Paradise was favored with frequent manifestations of the
presence of God—for the Lord God walked in the garden,
He talked with Adam, instructed and blessed him, making
every provision for his happiness as an expression of his
Maker's love. And this life carried with it the presumption of its immortality—for the symbolic tree of life stood
in the midst of the garden, like a covenant in perpetuity,
and death was threatened as a consequence of sin. Such a
Life, pure, peaceful, satisfying, blessed with the presence
of God and the promise of immortality, was the *Eden* of the
Hebrew Scriptures, which in popular language long befor.
the time of Christ, had come to be familiarly known as
Paradise. And the restoration of this Paradise was looked

[1] Gen. ii. 9.

for under the reign of the Messiah, whose coming would make the desert like the Paradise of God.

In the popular belief this would be a state of felicity such as poets have pictured in the golden age; but it would supercede the present condition of things, this disordered world of sin, pain, and sorrow, and would over-lap into the future state; and so the word Paradise came to signify some serene and blissful state of being, this side of heaven in the order of time and space, but conducting to heaven as a sort of middle-way.

Jesus took this word, *Paradise*, as the equivalent of Eden, and announced the realization of that state of primitive blessedness in the spirit-world which He would open to all believers. It is quite evident that Christ used the word to denote a condition *after* death. Both He and the sufferer at His side were presently to have done with this world; and Jesus intended to give to the penitent thief a promise of hope and encouragement concerning that which should survive the cross. There was for him somewhere a better world to which Christ would conduct him after death; for wherever Jesus Himself would be after the dissolution of the body, there should this believing penitent also be. Surely the promise contemplated a state of consciousness, and a desirable state; since going into some gloomy house of detention or limbo,—there to be kept in uncertainty till the end of the world—could have offered small encouragement as the boon of the Saviour to one who offered such a prayer with such a faith. The prayer was remarkable as acknowledging the supremacy of Christ, and the spirituality of His kingdom; "Lord, remember me when thou comest into Thy kingdom." Here was a soul touched with the sense of its own guilt, discerning the real majesty of Jesus through the sufferings of the cross, and anticipating for this despised King of the Jews, a kingdom of power and glory in that

invisible state to which they both were now departing.
The petition referred to a future and spiritual kingdom—
a sphere of glory awaiting the Redeemer after death; and
the answer of Christ to *such* a petition must be interpreted
in the same spirit.

The parallel expression in the Apocalypse furnishes a
key in part to this answer of our Lord. As there quoted
by John, in promising rewards to those who shall continue
faithful in His service, Christ said, "To him that over-
cometh will I give to eat of the tree of life, which is in the
midst of the *Paradise* of God."[1] To eat of the tree of Life
is to partake of immortal bliss; the Paradise of God is the
Paradise that God delights in and blesses with His presence;—the promise means that all of communion with
God, all of spiritual delight, and all of immortal hope,
life, and bliss that were lost by the fall, shall be realized
in the spirit-world where Christ now lives and reigns.

If we inquire more particularly after the location of
Paradise and the phases of existence and enjoyment there,
we find little to enlighten us in the New Testament Scriptures. Paul, in describing a frame of supernatural illumination by the Spirit of God, says that he was "caught up
into Paradise, and heard unspeakable words which it is
not possible for a man to utter;"[2] and this Paradise he
speaks of again as "the third heaven"—a phrase denoting
"an exalted region of light and blessedness, or the immediate presence of God." But where and what this was is
precisely what the Apostle has omitted to inform us; and
no speculation on our part can supply these omissions of
the Revelation.

This much then—neither more nor less—do we learn
from the word Paradise itself as interpreted by Biblical
usage:—a state of peace, security, holiness, satisfaction, blessedness, where the presence of God is more immediately

---

[1] Rev. ii. 7.   [2] 2 Cor. xii. 4.

manifested. But there are other facts or hints in the words of Christ touching the condition of departed saints immediately after death, which may here be grouped together for their combined light upon the question.

First, Christ clearly taught that the *personality* of the soul remains in conscious exercise. The parable of Lazarus and Dives shows this; so does the appearing of Moses and Elias on the Mount: so do the words of our Lord concerning the patriarchs: "He is not a God of the dead, but of the living: for all live unto Him." [1]

Again, the language of Christ to His disciples, in view of His own departure, implies that directly after death believers enter into a closer union with their Lord. We may fairly assume that the felicity promised to the dying malefactor was not exceptional; that such a one as he had been was not singled out for a favor that would not be accorded to disciples who had given proof of their devotion in their lives. This presumption becomes certainty in view of the assurance of Jesus to His disciples: "I go to prepare a place for you. And if I go and prepare a place for you, I will come again and receive you unto Myself; that where I am, there ye may be also." [2] This promise did not relate to that final Advent when Christ will gather around His person the collective host of His Redeemed; it was spoken to the eleven disciples as individuals, for whom severally a place should be prepared in the "many mansions" of His "Father's house." The consciousness of the presence of Christ, and a participation in His glory, would be the experience of these disciples when they should follow their Lord to the unseen world. [3]

From these sayings, brief and fragmentary as they are, we may gather that they who die in the Lord become immediately conscious of a nearer union with Christ than they had ever attained to in the most devout and extatic com-

<hr />

[1] Luke xx. 38.   [2] John xiv. 2, 3.   [3] John xvii. 24.

munings of this life; that after they are delivered from the burden of the flesh they do live unto God and are in joy and felicity; that dying is only the birth of the soul into a higher existence for which its qualities and powers of intelligent moral *personality* are at once an adaptation and a prophecy; and for which also, it is prepared in *character* by the grace of God,—so that to be "absent from the body" is to be "present with the Lord," consciously in the satisfying presence of Christ.

According to the psychology of the Bible, after the death of the animal part of man, there survive both the spiritual essence, which is the proper personality, and the principle of vitality, and this last enters into union with some *form* adapted to this higher state of being, some kind of vesture— though it may have no more material substance than the invisible ether. The Bible holds fast by Personality; the human spirit is not absorbed into the divine; neither does it float vaguely into space; it has positiveness, definiteness, is somehow circumscribed; or in common speech, it must have a body; not flesh and blood, for this is forever put away; not yet the spiritual body—for that comes after the resurrection; but a vesture fitted to a spiritual existence; so that "being clothed we shall not be found naked."[1] After the dissolution of our earthly house, which is only a tabernacle—a temporary abode—and which is a burden, both through its infirmities and by its inability to carry out all the aspirations of the spirit—we shall be "clothed upon with our house which is from heaven"—a form adapted to the region of spiritual life.[2] Death will only strip us of our mortality; it is not *we* that die, but our mortality; and then the soul, freed from the body of death, will be "clothed upon," clad in its proper vesture as a spiritual creature—no longer of the earth earthy—all trace of mor-

---

[1] 2 Cor. v. 1-5.

[2] For views of *Delitzsch* and others on this intermediate body, see Appendix.

tality swallowed up of life—the very soil and smell of earth gone from the shimmering gossamer, in which it floats or flies through the boundless scope of heaven. [1]

The Egyptians symbolized the departure of the soul by a bird quitting the breast of the mummy to fly away toward the Sun. When purified it returns to its mummy with the kiss of peace. In the great picture of the Communion of St. Jerome, while the expiring Saint is making his last Confession of Christ, one sees above him a bevy of cherubs fairly capering with joy as they drop their golden canopy of cloud to embrace the soul at the moment of its exit—that mortality might be swallowed up of life.

But while each departing saint, his personality unchanged, his spiritual vitality untouched by death, enters with an exalted consciousness of life and of spiritual powers, into a blissful fellowship with Christ in Paradise—there will remain for him some more glorious consummation at the resurrection of the dead. The Paradise to which he goes may be as the park that surrounds the palace of the king; he may have the freest range of the park and the gardens, and may look through the paling upon the golden House of Beauty, and behold at times the face of the King, and

[1] Dante has beautifully pictured this ethereal body as investing the soul when, at death,

> It separates from the flesh, and virtually
> Bears with itself the human and divine;
> The other faculties are voiceless all;
> The memory, the intelligence, and the will
> In action far more vigorous than before.
> And even as the air, when full of rain,
> By alien rays that are therein reflected,
> With divers colors shows itself adorned,
> So there the neighboring air doth shape itself
> Into that form which doth impress upon it
> Virtually the Soul that has stood still.
> And then in manner of the little flame,
> Which followeth the fire where'er it shifts,
> After the Spirit followeth its new Form.
> *Purgatorio.* xxv. 80–100. Longfellow's Translation.

hear the praises of the cherubim—but he must wait for
the gathering of the whole company from earth, and the
endowment of the spiritual body before the gates that
divide the palace from the park shall be thrown open that
he may enter in. His blessedness from the first will be
full even to the measure of his capacity, but the resurrection
and his transformation into the likeness of Christ's glorious
body will augment both his capacity and his means of
blessedness.

The distinction is well taken here by Nitzsch, between
the believer's entering into bliss and his consummation in
and with the whole body of the Redeemed. "The mere
duration and immortality of the soul, or the bare deliverance from its earthly habitation, does not complete Christian hope; for the consummation of the individual is by no
means perfect, so long as the entire creation and church
are not consummated with him and he with them."[1] Many
Scriptures point to the general resurrection as the enfranchisement of the creation itself—which now waits and
groans for that manifestation of the sons of God which
shall come through the redemption of the body. The
completeness of man in Christ will not be accomplished
till, by the resurrection, death shall be vanquished in our
bodies as it was in His. That event is set before us as the
consummation of the whole work of Redemption; and the
period between our departure and that Day will be for us
an intermediate state—but a Paradise of intense delights
and of conscious nearness and fellowship with Christ.
But the crowning bliss shall not be till the resurrection:
"Then cometh the end; when the Son shall deliver up
the kingdom to God, even the Father, and God shall be
all in all."[2]

In that august day "the Lord Himself shall descend
from heaven with a shout, with the voice of the archangel

and the trump of God; and the dead in Christ shall rise
first, then believers yet living on the earth shall be caught
up together with them in the clouds;"[1] then shall go up
the grand procession to the gates of the New Jerusalem
swung open in mid-air—the trumpets sounding, the vast
ether palpitating with harmonic symphonies; the sons of
God shouting for joy, the very stars, ringing out silvery
chimes for the marriage of the Lamb—the final consummation of all things terrestrial and celestial in the union
of Christ and His church in everlasting joy.[2]

This view of the state of departed saints may well
encourage cheerfulness and thanksgiving on behalf of
those whom Christ has taken to Himself. No need
have we to pray for them, seeing they are already with
Christ: no cause have we to mourn for them, seeing that
directly they are absent from the body they are present
with the Lord;—"Now that he is dead, wherefore should
I fast? I shall go to him, but he shall not return to
me."[3]

To the primitive Christians all this was reality. They
have left their faith and hope recorded upon the tombs
which they constructed in their hiding-places in the sub-
terranean excavations or quarries of the city of Rome.
In those long galleries of catacombs, where the bodies of
martyrs and persecuted saints were laid to rest, there is not
one trace of despondency or gloom. It is written over one

---

[1] 1 Thess. iv. 16, 17.

[2] Although the details of this description are borrowed from the Apostolic
writings, the germs of the whole conception are found in the teachings of
Christ; and the words of Paul are not here cited as authoritative—for we are
concerned solely with Christ's own words as the source of authoritative belief
—but as illustrating the meaning of Christ from the point of a scholar and
disciple who was versed both in the Jewish and the Pagan notions of Hades,
and who has embodied in one proportionate form the fragmentary hints of his
Lord touching the future state.

[3] 2 Samuel xii. 23.

and another "She sleeps;" "In peace;" "With Christ." The anchor, the cross, the crown, the symbols of the resurrection and immortality make those dark galleries bright with the presence of the Eternal Life.

This doctrine should inspire the Christian disciple with the glad consciousness of the nearness of his Lord at death. The effort to find for heaven a locality commonly results in placing it at an immense remove in space and time; the attempt to define its features and occupations results in vague imaginings; meantime Paradise comes floating down to us, and Jesus steps to the bedside of one whom we think *dying*, and says "I come to *receive* thee to Myself; To-day shalt thou be with Me in Paradise;" and could our vision be purged, like that of the prophet, we might see the mountains full of chariots of fire. Heaven is around us; if we are Christ's, one step and we are there! Then why let earth trouble, delude, engross, or detain us? And why should death intimidate us?

Christ's doctrine of the future opens before us the grandeur of the moral universe and of the work of Redemption. The science of astronomy has revealed to us somewhat of the stupendous scale of the physical creation; worlds circling about worlds, systems circling about systems, through millions of leagues of space; light traversing immensity with its ever-repeating waves; the laws of attraction and gravitation ruling the hosts of heaven without voice or speech; and all this ordered beauty and grandeur obedient to one Infinite and Invisible Power. But this material creation is only the theater of the moral universe; these innumerable worlds are but the many mansions in the vast house of our Father, for the home of His children; this illimitable space is but the field of their activities and joys! The physical may change and pass away; the heavens depart as a scroll; but the moral universe shall then "grow resplendent more and more;"—as we

"behold the hours
Of Christ's triumphal march, and all the fruit
Harvested by the rolling of these spheres."[1]

Then to every one who is found faithful to Christ, will it be given to "eat of the tree of life, which is in the midst of the Paradise of God."

[1] Dante, *Paradiso*.

CHAPTER XIV.

THE RESURRECTION OF THE DEAD.

CHRISTIANITY concerns itself for the restoration of the Body as well as for the redemption of the Soul. To redeem and sanctify the Soul is its first office and endeavor; but it also cherishes and honors the body as the workmanship of God and as the habitation of the soul, and the medium through which it acts upon the outer world, and receives from that impressions the most quickening, suggestive and controlling.

The natural science of the Bible finds no link of development from the monkey to the man, but the first man was formed by the direct act of God, who "breathed into his nostrils the breath of life."[1] The philosophy of the Bible is not that of the Stoics, who regarded the body as the antagonist of the soul, and its suppression or destruction as necessary to the soul's perfection—for the divine Word was made flesh and exhibited the true harmony of the body with the soul; nor is it the philosophy of the Epicureans, that made pleasure consist in gratifying and pampering the flesh—for it teaches that "the body is for the Lord," even "the temple of the Holy Ghost."[2] And this Religion which so honors the body in its origin and seeks to ennoble it with all care and culture for the present life, does not cease to regard the Body when death and the grave have claimed it. The consolation it offers as supreme is not that the soul is freed from its burden and clog, that the lower nature is dropped for the freer development of the higher;

[1] Gen. ii. 7.   [2] 1 Cor. vi. 13, 19.

but Christianity promises to cherish the buried dust as God's seed-corn, and to give this back again in the beauty and vigor of an incorruptible life. Over against the grave it writes the Resurrection; over against Death the Life Everlasting; and Jesus surrenders His own sinless body to the demand of our common mortality; yields up the ghost, is dead and buried; then comes forth in the victorious assertion of that undying Personality which unbars for us the gates of death and the grave: "I am the Resurrection and the Life." [1]

And herein Christianity shows itself in wondrous sympathy with the human heart: for much as we are taught that the true life and beauty and love are belongings of the soul, how do we cherish the body from first to last. How dear to the mother is the babe that gives as yet no sign of thought or speech; how every tiny member of that tiny form is written in her heart; what beauty she discovers in just the ordinary beginnings of a human life; and even if her child lacks physical perfection, how does the very infirmity cause it to be cherished the more tenderly! In riper years, though what we prize as our possession in a friend is the soul—the mind and heart in sympathy with our own—yet we are forever longing for the *presence*, the word, the look that continually reassure us that we do possess the soul. When sickness comes, how fondly do we cling to the wasting form: and when death has snatched it, though faith assures us that the soul has gone to live above, and reason teaches that the body without the soul is nothing, yet do we count each hour precious that we may keep that body near us, and the last tie is not severed till it is taken away; then comes the "sorrowing most of all, that we shall see the face no more;" [2] and then too come the full sympathy and power of the Gospel in the assurance of the divine Redeemer, the risen Lord, who stands weeping

1 John xi. 25. 2 Acts xx. 38.

at our side, and speaks the undying consolation " *Thy Brother shall Rise again.*" [1]

The beauty, the force, the value of this assurance are utterly broken 'by two modes of interpretation that are sometimes applied to the subject; the one makes the declaration " The Son quickeneth whom He will," [2] a figure of speech to describe the quickening of the soul into spiritual life; the other makes the promise " He that believeth in Me, though he were dead, yet shall he live," [3] refer only to the continued life of the soul after death has terminated the life of the body; making the resurrection coincident with death,—the rising of the spirit into a higher sphere of existence, where death can never come. They who hold such views, like Swedenborg for instance, believe neither in a general resurrection of the dead appointed for some remote period, nor in any resurrection or re-habilitation of the present body; but give to all the language of the New Testament concerning the rising of the dead, a symbolic meaning, applying it either to a moral renovation in this life, or to the spiritual emancipation and development of the righteous at death.

We must, therefore, settle distinctly the meaning of words—if we would understand the doctrine of Jesus touching the resurrection. The word He used, ἀνάστασις, was applied to the act of raising up or restoring that which had fallen or lay prostrate. Thus the rebuilding of the walls of a city thrown down by war was an *anastasis* or resurrection. The wall stood in the same place, and was built in whole or in part of the same materials; so that it was the same wall restored; and this word *anastasis* is used by Homer and others for the act of rising from bed, especially after sickness. It is applied also to the lifting up of suppliants who were lying prostrate before a temple. Nor are there wanting instances in classic writers where *anastasis*, or a form of the same word, is directly applied to a rising from the dead. In the Iliad of Homer, Achilles driving the Trojans before him into the river Xanthus, sees coming up the bank, as if out of the stream itself, a son of Priam whom once before he had taken prisoner, had carried away in his own ship and sold into distant slavery. Startled by this apparition, as if a dead man had come to life, Achilles exclaims :—

> " O strange! my eyes behold a miracle.
> Sure the brave sons of Troy whom I have slain
> Will rise up from the nether darkness yet." [1]

This would be a literal *anastasis* of the dead. Again in that touching scene where the aged Priam, having heard that his only surviving son Hector had been wounded, ventures alone to the camp of Achilles to beg for the release of his boy; (alas, he is already dead!) and the stern warrior replies :—[2]

> " Sorrow for thy son
> Will profit nought; it cannot bring the dead
> To life again."

Here the *anastasis* would be literally restoring the dead body to life, which Achilles declares to be impossible. A like example occurs in a tragedy of Æschylus, where, in describing a murder, he says,[3] " When the dust has drunk up the blood of a man once dead, there is no raising it up " —no *anastasis*.

This word then had no doubtful meaning; it was properly applied to the lifting up, the restoring, the setting back in its place of a person or thing that had fallen or disappeared. As applied to the dead it would naturally denote a visible restoring of the body—such a raising up that it would be felt to be the same.

---

[1] xxi. 56, Mr. Bryant's version.   [2] xxiv. 557, Mr. Bryant's version.
[3] *Furies*, 664.

A belief in such a resurrection, pronounced by these Greek poets a thing impossible, had found a lodgment in some religions of antiquity. The ancient Egyptians bestowed far more care upon their tombs than upon their houses; they called the abodes of the living *inns*, because these were occupied only for a limited period; but the sepulchres of the dead they called eternal habitations. Great pains were taken to preserve the body from corruption in order that it might again become the habitation of the soul. This is the most satisfactory explanation of the custom of embalming and the care taken to deposit the mummy in a secret and durable sepulchre. Upon some of the mummy-cases the soul is painted as a bird revisiting its former home; and the Book of the Dead,[1] a kind of sacred hymn which was deposited with the mummy, represents the body as at last awaking to the light of the sun, and exclaiming, " Hail, O my Father; I have come; I prepare this my body; I am not corrupted nor wasted away; I am not suffocated; I live, I grow, I wake in peace."

The doctrine of the resurrection of the body is found also among the Persians, as far back as the third or fourth century B. C. in a sect of Magians " who taught that man would revive and become immortal with a fine ethereal body, and would lead a life of bliss upon an earth forever freed from the corrupting influence of evil." In their sacred books a great prophet is predicted to arise toward the expiration of this world's course; who will appear as "The conqueror of death and the judge of the world." In the might of *Ormuzd* the chief divinity of the Parsee religion, this prophet will awaken the dead. An objector is represented as asking, " Since wind and water carry off the remains of the body, how shall it be restored again?"

---

[1] See an analysis of the Egyptian doctrine of the Future State, by the author in the Bibliotheca Sacra, 1868, p. 69.

But in reply, Ormuzd, the divinity, points to his almighty powers of creation; and as he is the creator of the grain of corn, which after corruption springs up afresh, so by his power also shall the resurrection take place, and but once in truth, and not a second time."[1] It would be a curious inquiry whether this clear and striking statement of the resurrection crept into the religion of the Magians from the same source as the doctrine of Daniel, who lived in the land of the Chaldees when he wrote: "Many of them that sleep in the dust of the earth shall awake; some to everlasting life, and some to shame and everlasting contempt."[2]

The belief in the immortality of the soul had slowly unfolded itself among the Hebrews from a very early period. Job and David had also foreshadowed a resurrection of the body;[3] but Daniel was the first to give this doctrine such a positive form, and after his time it was the commonly received belief of the Jews.

The *Apocrypha*, though not entitled to the place of Biblical authority, is nevertheless valuable as a testimony to events and opinions among the Jews of its time. We read in the books of Maccabees[4] of one who when put to death exclaimed to his executioner, " Thou like a fury takest us out of this present life, but the King of the world shall *raise us up*, who have died for His laws, unto everlasting life." Again it is recorded, that after a great victory, Judas Maccabeus offered prayers and sacrifices for the dead; upon which the historian comments, "doing well therein, in that he was mindful of the resurrection; for if he had not hoped that they that were slain should have *risen again*, it had been superfluous and vain to pray for the dead."[5] This testimony is complete upon the

---

[1] Döllinger, *Judenthum und Heidenthum*, i. 411.   [2] Daniel xii. 2.
[3] Ps. xvi. 9; Job xix. 26. (?)   [4] Mac. ii. 7, 14.
[5] Mac. xii. 45.

point that the doctrine of the resurrection of the body was commonly held among the Jews before the time of Christ; it appears distinctly in their literature of the second century B. C., and in the Greek version of the Apocrypha the literal resurrection of the body is described by the term *anastasis*.

The Pharisees, who were accounted the Orthodox of the nation, and who represented the popular belief, held to the doctrine of the resurrection of the dead: while the Sadducees, a much smaller sect, regarded as heretical, denied it. Martha's confidence that her brother would rise again at the last day, shows how common was this belief among the Jews.

This history of the word *anastasis* and of the popular belief in the Resurrection, has an important bearing upon the case in hand. That Jesus taught *a* doctrine of the Resurrection all agree; but some say that He spoke figuratively, of a spiritual renovation, or of the rising of the soul from the body into a higher region of life.

But in order to know the true doctrine of Jesus we must ascertain the meaning of His words in the circumstances in which He used them. We have taken the word He used,— or, if He spoke in Aramaic, we have its Greek equivalent —*anastasis*, and have shown that the great masters of the Greek tongue before His time used this term for the raising up or restoring a person or thing that had fallen or was prostrate or helpless—the object raised up being the same that had fallen: we have seen that Greek writers used this very word to describe the *revivifying a corpse*, the *anastasis* of a dead body; we have seen moreover that a belief in such a resurrection was extant in the world; that the Egyptians had it dimly, the Persians of a later period perhaps more clearly; that it was foreshadowed by Job and David, and distinctly announced by Daniel; that it became an article of popular belief among the Jews, and that the

Greek-Jews in their version expressed it by the word *anastasis*. Thus the natural obvious meaning of this word as applied to a dead person is established by usage and history.

The circumstances in which our Lord proclaimed Himself the Resurrection and the Life leave no doubt that He had this same meaning. Lazarus was dead: that was a fact; he had been sick for a good while; so sick that his sisters had sent a messenger to Jesus—then some days' journey distant—but Jesus did not come. Lazarus died; all the village knew that: he was buried, and all the neighbors were at the funeral: he was bound hand and foot with grave clothes and laid in a cave, and a stone covered the mouth of it. When Jesus arrived Lazarus had been already dead four days, and for some time buried.[1] Jesus said to Martha, "Thy brother shall rise again." Martha said unto Him, " I know that he shall rise again in the resurrection at the last day." She here expressed what was the common belief of the Jews—that at the end of the world the dead would be raised from their graves. Martha did not intend simply to assert her belief that the soul of her brother still lived, nor that he would rise spiritually to a higher state of existence ;—all this she believed; but it was the bodily presence of Lazarus she so missed and longed for, and her faith taught her that the self-same brother who lay dead in the sepulchre would come to life again— but not till that far-distant day of the general rising of the dead. In answer to that faith, and to confirm it, Jesus said unto her, " *I* am the resurrection and the Life ;" the Resurrection is made certain in and through Me : as I am the Life, having in Myself the gift of life, there is vested in Me power to raise the dead. Therefore He would have her not only believe in the possibility of the Resurrection, and look forward to receiving back her brother in the last

---

[1] It was the Jewish custom to bury very soon after death.

day, but believe in Himself as having power over death
and the grave, and able to give back her brother by His
word. The principle of *Anastasis* was in His life. After
this Jesus went to the grave, and " cried with a loud voice
Lazarus, come forth; and he that was *dead* came forth."
There was the *anastasis*—the raising up of a dead body,
by giving it life again. The Resurrection that Martha
believed in, that she hoped for in the far-off future, was
made present and palpable to her senses. The event interprets the meaning of Christ. The thing done shows
what He intended when He said "I am the Resurrection:"
I the source and giver of life will raise the dead.

Some will say, however, This was a miracle, like His
own resurrection, for a particular purpose—to show forth
His divine power and glory,—and not to be taken as
proof of a future resurrection. But the very end for which
the miracle was wrought was to confirm Martha's belief in
the resurrection at the last day, by showing that Jesus had
power to raise the dead, and would accomplish it.

His other statements upon this doctrine confirm this
view; as a running commentary upon them will show.
First we have the argument recorded by Matthew, Mark,
and Luke, in reply to the Sadducees. This sect denied
the common Jewish doctrine of the resurrection, and they
thought to confound Jesus, or at least to embarrass Him
by their famous case of the seven brothers who had mar-
ried in turn the same wife. They put the doctrine of the
resurrection in this bald literal form, and asked Jesus to
dispose of their objection. It would have met their difficulty to have replied that the Resurrection must not be
taken literally but figuratively and spiritually, as meaning
the translation of the soul to a higher sphere,—for spirits
could not be supposed to enter into a literal marriage.
But Jesus did not take that ground : He held fast by the
common Jewish belief of a resurrection, and declared that

" in the Resurrection they neither marry nor are given in marriage, but are as the angels of God in heaven ;" [1] that is He affirmed the resurrection of the body, but with such a transformation in respect of physical conditions, as will adapt it to the state in which angels live, a condition of existence in which the formal relations of this life, while remembered with joy, shall be no more necessary and no more desired. Then He went on to assert the Resurrection as set forth by Moses in the fact that Abraham, Isaac, and Jacob would ever have a recognized identity in the kingdom of God. Thus did Jesus maintain against gainsayers the doctrine of a proper *anastasis* of the dead.

In a discourse recorded by John [2] He makes this doctrine of a bodily resurrection, if possible, even more distinct and emphatic by contrasting it with a spiritual awakening from sin and its condemnation. " He that heareth My word, and believeth on Him that sent Me, hath everlasting life, and shall not come into condemnation : but is passed from death unto life :" *i. e.* "by means of faith he receives a principle of life which cannot be impaired by death." This obviously is said of the spiritual life, the renovation of the soul : for it is a process now going forward, and its effect is seen in those who believe : " Verily, verily I say unto you, the hour is coming and *now is* when the dead shall hear the voice of the Son of God ;" this awakening of men dead in trespasses and sins is now taking place : "and they that hear shall live ;" all who obey the gospel shall come to a new life in Christ.

He then goes on to speak of His quickening power upon the literally dead; and this with reference to the final judgment. "Marvel not at this; for the hour is coming"—He does not here say and *now* is—He is looking forward to the last day ; " in the which *all* "—not as before " they that hear "—but " all that are *in their graves*," and hence

[1] Matt. xxii. 30. [1] John v. 25, seq.

literally dead, "shall hear His voice, and shall come forth, they that have done good, unto the resurrection of life, and they that have done evil, unto the resurrection of damnation."[1] *Now*, whoso *will* hear has life spiritual; then, all *shall* hear. Jesus is expounding His life-power as the Son of Man. He who now *gives* life to the *soul* by faith, will hereafter *restore* life to the *body* by His power. This covers the whole ground. Jesus Himself distinguishes between the spiritual and the bodily Resurrection and teaches both; one now is, the other is coming.

Again Jesus specifies particularly the spiritual life and the resurrection as gifts to believers. " This is the will of Him that sent Me; that every one which seeth the Son and believeth on Him may have everlasting life; and I will raise him up *at the last day*."[2]

Christ's doctrine of the Resurrection was illustrated and verified by His own resurrection. For the vague conjectures of the ancients touching the possibility of such an event, He substituted the certainty of the fact; and while philosophy was, and ever will be, at fault concerning the mode of a resurrection, Jesus furnished the key to the fact in His proper personality. This is the feature that characterizes His doctrine, and removes it from the category of speculative beliefs to that of tangible facts.

Had Jesus merely given certainty to the belief in the resurrection as already held by the devout among the Jews, this had been a contribution to faith worthy of such a Teacher. Had He added to this assurance of the fact some explanation of the manner in which so great a marvel will be effected, He would have brought philosophy as well as faith under the highest obligations. Had He only repeated the declaration made in His discourse of the true

---

[1] Here is named a *set* time for the resurrection as an event distinct from all moral and spiritual changes.

[2] John vi. 40.

bread: "No man can come to Me, except the Father which hath sent Me draw him; and I will raise him up at the last day;"[1] this pledge to use His personal power in restoring the dead to life, would have been a satisfying assurance to believers, of their victory over death. But He went far beyond this, and centering in HIMSELF the fact, the doctrine, and the assurance of this stupendous miracle, He said, "I AM the Resurrection and the Life," both are linked together, both emanate from Me, both center in Me; the Resurrection is Life in victory over death; and the Resurrection that rescues from death unto life again shall issue in the Life Everlasting.

What a wealth of meaning is hidden in those words! Jesus had said to Martha, "Thy brother shall rise again." By this assurance He sought to test her faith in the resurrection as held by the Jews, without, as yet, announcing His intention to restore Lazarus to life. For this she must be prepared through the development of her faith in the possibility of a resurrection; and this belief Jesus made definite and positive, by making it individual, and meeting that question of personal identity which the heart yearns over by every open grave. "Thy brother shall rise again;" rise as thy brother to be known and loved. "I know," said the half-believing, half-wondering woman, "that he shall rise again in the resurrection at the last day:" but that is a long, long way off, and by his grave it seems so distant, so strange, so misty, that faith almost loses its hold upon it; and in wondering how it can be, I hardly keep the confidence that it shall be,—the resurrection—what? how is it?—at the last day—when shall that be? Then said Jesus, "I am the resurrection and the life; he that believeth in Me, though he were dead, yet shall he live." The creative power that gave life at the first proceeded from Me; the power of resurrection that shall bring back life from the grave centers in Me; and it needs only that you believe in ME, and distance and impossibility vanish in presence of the Life.

"I am the Resurrection." This announcement makes real and positive that which had before been a matter of speculative faith. What life is we know no better than before; but we do know whence life comes, and who imparts it. How life can be renewed in dead, buried and perished clay we do not know, any more than we know how life is given to the new-born babe or to the seed long buried under ground; but we do know *who* can give life to the dead and make that life indissoluble and perpetual. Instead of speculating how this thing can be, or searching after a principle, law, or process through which it can be accomplished, we look upon a person who can cause it to be, and who centers it in Himself as a reality. The Resurrection is not merely an event, it is a power; it is life reviving and asserting itself again where death had for a time suspended its manifestations; and this Life is not simply a fact, a phenomenon, it inheres in a Person and proceeds from a Person, so that He not only gives life, but is the life that He gives—He imparts somewhat of that which characterizes and constitutes Himself; He not only causes the resurrection to come to pass in another, He *is* the Resurrection, and as He raised himself by His own energy, so He enters by His own life-energy into the sleeping dust and raises that. The resurrection is but the application of life to that which had been dead, and He *is* the life. "As the Father hath life in Himself, so hath He given to the Son to have life in Himself;"[1]—a life that sustains itself, and can impart life to others; and so "The Son quickeneth whom He will."[2] The life is the quickening power; the raising up is but one mode of exercising that power upon a passive subject. And when

---

[1] John v. 26.   [2] John v. 21.

we have formed the idea of one who has life in Himself the resurrection ceases to be so great a marvel; it is no greater marvel than the first creation, or the original giving of life to any creature; the *Life* is the real wonder.

The declaration of Christ that He is the Resurrection was borne out by two marvellous acts of life-power—first the raising of Lazarus, and second the raising up of His own body. Twice before He had raised the dead:—the daughter of Jairus from the bed on which she died, the son of the widow from the bier on which he was being carried out of the gates of Nain. The knowledge of these and of other miracles of Christ upon infirmities and diseases of the body, had led Martha to feel and say, "Lord, if thou hadst been here, my brother had not died," and had encouraged her half-formed hope; " I ...v that even now whatsoever Thou wilt ask of God, God will give it Thee." How feeble, unformed, unreal that hope was appeared in her remonstrating at the grave against removing the stone, because Lazarus had been dead four days and must have fallen into corruption—so does intensity of grief vibrate between hope and despair. Jesus had sought to educate her to the point of implicit faith in Himself; and the circumstantiality of these details prepared the way for this crowning lesson. Let us recapitulate the incidents.

We know that Lazarus was dead; that he was buried; that his friends were mourning him; that he had been dead four days; that the sister who so yearned after him that she almost hoped for his recall, was yet unwilling that his grave should be disturbed; and when under these conditions of seeming impossibility, Jesus standing by the grave cried, "Lazarus come forth," and "He that was dead came forth bound hand and foot with grave clothes, and the napkin yet tied about his face,"—as if startled from a sleep—we feel that He who spake was the Resurrection and the life. Lazarus was raised, but Jesus was the *Resurrection;* the wonder of the Power is greater far than the wonder that it wrought. The people who heard of the miracle made this distinction. Multitudes resorted to Bethany from curiosity, that they might see Lazarus; but their wonder and faith were turned from the man who had been raised from the dead to the Man who had raised him ; and so many became His disciples that the chief priests " consulted that they might put Lazarus also to death ; because that by reason of him many of the Jews went away and believed on Jesus :"—so much greater was the author of the resurrection than the event itself.

But above all, Jesus showed that He was *the* Resurrection by raising Himself from the dead. As, to the common people, the bringing up of Lazarus from the grave where he had lain four days seemed a greater marvel than raising the young man from his bier at Nain, so the raising Himself seemed a yet greater wonder than to raise another. There were two reasons for this ; First, upon the cross Jesus had succumbed to death ; and by thus yielding in His own person to the enemy from whom He had rescued Lazarus, He had seemed to vacate His power or prerogative of life. In the presence of a vast concourse of approving spectators, He had been nailed to the cross and lifted up: He had expired of exhaustion and agony : the executioners on guard had pronounced Him dead; a soldier had thrust a spear into His heart : and His death being certified, by the authority of the governor, He had been taken down from the cross by His sorrowing disciples, buried in a new tomb, and the stone sealed and a guard set over it. Thus whatever power of resisting and overcoming death Jesus had shown in healing the sick and recalling the dead, seemed to have forsaken Him in His own extremity. Therefore that He should rise again was the greater marvel.

And there was a second reason for this, in the fact that death seemed to separate from Him that mysterious power by which He had restored others from death. When Jesus brought back Lazarus to life, He invoked His Father; He put forth His own will; He used some energy or efficiency residing in Himself: *He* was the power that acted upon another. But now He was undoubtedly dead —a lifeless body laid away in the tomb—with no power of motion or of feeling, and no symptom of vitality. That spirit-power that had broken the hold of death upon Lazarus, to human view had utterly departed when on the cross He yielded up the ghost. It seemed therefore a greater miracle that He should raise Himself than that He had raised another. And when on the third day He stood in the midst of His disciples, the same Jesus with the print of the nails in His hands and His feet, and the marks of the wound in His side, this was the sublime, the invincible testimony that He, in, by, and of Himself, was the Resurrection and the Life. This it is that gives to the Christian faith in the Resurrection the freshness and life that always attach to a Person; this is not an abstract dogma, nor a theory that might tantalize and bewilder but could never satisfy;—it is confidence in a Person who has done in and for Himself that which He promises to do for every disciple.

"He that believeth in Me, though he were dead, yet shall he live."[1] This saying applied to Lazarus in the first instance, as a *type* of true believers who had died before the redeeming work of Christ was wrought out to its visible completion. Although Christ had not been revealed to such as the giver of life from the dead, nevertheless they having had that spiritual faith which is the key to all restoration, shall partake of this benefit of Christ's coming: such an one, though like Lazarus he have died without the

[1] John xi. 25.

demonstration of the resurrection that I will give in My person, yet shall he live—come to life again through Me: and this promise, as affecting believers who had already died, was at once confirmed by bringing up Lazarus from the dead.

But there followed a far-reaching, all-embracing promise for believers from among all coming generations of men; "Whosoever liveth, and believeth in Me, shall never die."[1] This declaration has so staggered some in its literalness that they have construed it of spiritual living and dying —the life of the soul, in its felicity being secured by faith in Christ as its Redeemer. But there is nothing in the construction to indicate a change from a literal resurrection in the first clause of the sentence, to a spiritual life in the second; and if we take this last saying as meaning a spiritual life, must we not follow Swedenborg in spiritualizing the resurrection also? But our Lord applied and confirmed His declaration by raising Lazarus from the grave, thus showing that He was speaking throughout of a physical, literal resurrection, a coming back to life with personal identity.

Others have understood Him to refer to believers who shall be living on the earth at the time of His coming,— concerning whom it was a current belief that they shall be glorified or transfigured, without the process of dying. But it seems a straining of the sense to carry it forward to that distant future, when there is nothing in the context that refers to the end of the world.

Christ made a promise of universal application to those that should believe in Him. He had just spoken of true believers who were already dead; these He would redeem from the possession of death, and they as to their persons shall live again. He then spoke of all living disciples; all that then were, and all who should afterwards become

[1] John xi. 26.

disciples: "Whosoever liveth;" every believer who is yet living shall be exempt from death through faith in Me. The interpretation lies in the meaning and effect of death as changed by Christ's coming and by faith in Him. "He that *believeth* shall never *die;*" for

(*a*). To the believer in Christ death has no power of evil either through fear or through suffering. All mental disquietude is removed, and death as a process of nature taking effect in the body, is a falling asleep, a rest.

(*b*). The process of dying liberates the spirit from its mortal appendages, that it may enter upon felicity unqualified and unending. The physiological process of dying is the enfranchisement of the spirit, a triumph of the life-principle over that which is mortal. Life in this stage of existence is a perpetual struggle with opposing forces; the elements that compose our bodies tend continually to dissolution and decay. Even when no disease invades, and no accident threatens, there is a constant waste of tissue that calls for incessant repairs; and in the healthiest condition, how is the hidden vitality that we feel throbbing and yearning within us, hampered by physical conditions or fatigue. But Christ has taught that death is the liberation and expansion of the life. It is the *mortal* that dies; the spirit lives; and, moreover, shall never die—death has no more dominion. The believer will be restored from the possession of death as to the body, raised up and glorified, so that death in the sense of destruction shall never be accomplished upon anything that pertained to him. Here the question of time is nothing upon the scale of the infinite future.

How grand the scope given to Christ's work of redemption by His doctrine of the Resurrection! For that work the Son of God came into the world where sin had reigned through all the generations of men; entered into that humanity which sin had made its own; redeemed and sanctified this; went into personal conflict with Satan in the

field of his most successful temptations, and openly triumphed over him; invaded the realm of darkness and cast
out devils by His word; went down into the grave to meet
death in the field of his unbroken possession, and there
trampled under foot death, the grave, and Hades, and rose
in the might of victory. Sending forth His Spirit, He has
continued the triumphs of redemption in the world of
human thought and will, and He shall come once more to
perfect His victory by redeeming the body from the grave.
All earth and time form one grand symphony of redemption.
The world is yet in the *andante* movement, but a melody
of hope runs through the solemn tones, and the time is
already quickening; the final movement shall open with
the trump that wakes the dead, and with hallelujahs that
sweep the skies.

Hence the Christian faith is a finality in religion;
in respect of the restoration of man, his development, his
blessedness, it leaves nothing to be desired, nothing to be
thought of. It redeems man from sin, and will lead him
to perfection of character; it fortifies him against trial
and makes him the conqueror of death; it recovers him
from the grave and clothes him with a spiritual and glorious body like unto Christ's; it introduces him to fellowship with God and the society of all the holy and blessed. Thus linking man to the spiritual and eternal life,
the Christian faith gives dignity to his present and glory to
his future. The necessities of man's present condition bind
him much to the material things around him, while it is
the tendency of his appetites and passions to seek their grat-
ification in the earthly and sensual. Yet he is conscious of
intellectual wants, of spiritual yearnings and aptitudes that
show his affinity for a higher life. These the Christian
faith meets with its twin doctrines of redemption and resurrection. Redemption delivers the spirit while yet in the
body, from the dominion of the flesh, so that believers are

no longer "of the world."[1]   Resurrection asserts the final dominion of the spirit in the body itself; He that believeth, by that act of faith is born again, and by virtue of this life he shall never die.

[1] John xv. 19; xvii. 14.

CHAPTER XV.

To the power of Resurrection Jesus linked the prerogative of Judgment. The same Son whose spirit now quickeneth the soul to a new and everlasting life, and whose
voice shall hereafter quicken all the dead, will come to
judge the world; for the Father "hath given Him authority to execute judgment also, because He is the Son of
Man."[1]

In His life-time Jesus declined to act as judge in cases
brought to Him,[2] and He disavowed any judicial purpose
in His mission; "For God sent not His Son into the
world to condemn the world, but that the world through
Him might be saved."[3] The ruling purpose in the mission
of Christ was to deliver man from condemnation—for " He
that believeth on Him is not condemned,"—no longer
lies under judicial condemnation as a sinner, and shall not
hereafter fall under penalty:—" Verily, verily I say unto
you, he that heareth my word and believeth on Him that
sent Me hath everlasting life; and shall *not come* into
condemnation; but is passed from death unto life."[4]
Even to those who openly rejected Him, Jesus said, "If
any man hear my words and believe not, I judge him not;
for I came not to judge the world, but to save the world."[5]

The purpose of Christ's mission was salvation, and the
whole tone of His life was as far as possible removed from
the spirit of judgment. But although Jesus so emphatically disavowed both the act and the spirit of judgment in

---

[1] John v. 27.   [2] Luke xii. 14.   [3] John iii. 17.
[4] John v. 24.   [5] John xii. 47.

His personal life upon earth, He as distinctly proclaimed Himself the judge of mankind, and His purpose of coming again in that character, at the end of the world. "When the Son of man shall come in His glory and all the holy angels with Him, then shall He sit upon the throne of His glory; and before Him shall be gathered all nations; and He shall separate them one from another, as a shepherd divideth his sheep from the goats; and He shall set the sheep on His right hand, but the goats on the left." [1]

This scene represents a public and general judgment, at a fixed time, presided over in person by the Son of Man, whose decisions will finally determine the condition of all mankind according to character. Other declarations set forth a special fitness in the designation of Christ to the office of judge, "*because* He is the Son of man." [2] These several points cover the teaching of Jesus upon the momentous doctrine of the final judgment. In the scheme of Redemption proclaimed by Christ, the Judgment is kept ever in view, as a motive for accepting the Gospel, as a warning against rejecting it, as the fitting termination of the great drama of human life, and the final vindication of the righteousness and the authority of God before the universe—an event of everlasting moment to the moral history of our race and to the government of God. Hence all that can be known concerning the Judgment from the lips of the Son of Man, has a direct bearing upon every individual not only in his relations to that distant future, but in his present personal relations to Christ and the Gospel.

First. It was taught by Christ that there will be *a public and formal act of judgment concerning every individual of our race.* There have been attempts to explain away His teaching in this particular. They who deny that the Resurrection signifies the raising of the body with a substantial identity, though with refined adaptations to a

---

[1] Matt. xxv. 31.   [2] John v. 27.

spiritual life—who would make of the *Anastasis* nothing
more than a moral renovation here, and the liberation of
the soul by death into a higher spiritual life,—equally
deny a formal declarative Judgment, and would make the
judgment consist in the division of character effected by
Christ's word in this life, and in the natural progress of
the soul into a corresponding condition after death : in
other words, such interpreters hold, that the judgment
begins in this world in the separation of good and evil
which the word of God pronounces and the course of Providence effects, and then that this goes on, as a natural law
of progress, into the future world, there keeping separate
the good and the evil from the moment of death. Thus
death itself becomes, as it were, an event of a judicial and
retributive character ; and there is no need of further judgment.

Beyond a question these ideas of Judgment are not only
founded in Reason and in Nature, but are brought out in
the teachings of Christ. But in addition to these obvious
and natural processes of judgment, He taught that there
will be a positive act of Judgment proceeding from Himself in a formal and conspicuous manner. His word truly
does judge men day by day. This Jesus Himself stated to
be an inevitable consequence of His own preaching,
though He had not come into the world for the purpose
of judgment. The clear strong light of truth as He presented it, made more palpable the darkness of sin and unbelief, and the perversity and wickedness of such as would
not come to the light. This is the condemnation, the
χρίσις, the separation, the decisive event, the turning point
of character—" that light is come into the world, and men
loved darkness rather than light because their deeds were
evil." [1] Hence while he who believes on the Son of God
and comes to the light is freed from condemnation, " he

[1] John iii. 19.

that believeth not *is condemned* already, because he hath not believed in the Name of the only begotten Son of God."[1] This process of moral judgment, making plain distinctions of character by the test of truth, is going on continually and necessarily, as often as the Gospel is preached. It is a judgment that no man can escape : the Truth pronounces it by shining over against his character and life, and the man pronounces it upon himself by his own deportment toward the Truth. There comes a new *krisis* to every soul so often as it confronts the word of Christ. Every word of His Truth judges the soul and compels the soul to judge itself. When Christ says " Be ye perfect as your Father," His word judges us as sinful. When He says " Repent and believe the Gospel," His word judges our impenitence and unbelief; the light makes the shadows stand out. When He teaches us to pray, His word condemns a prayerless life. When He commands us to love God with all the heart, He judges our love of self and the world.

As with the word of Jesus, so also with His life. The manifestation that Jesus made of perfect holiness and of divine power and glory, brought into bolder relief the sinfulness of those that rejected Him, and showed that whatever their pretensions to piety they were radically defective at heart; for in refusing His teachings and rejecting the evidences of His divine purity and power, they showed that in heart they had really no love for holiness nor for God. " If I had not come and spoken unto them, they had not had sin." Their aversion to what is truly good and divine would not have stood out as it then did in their consciousness and to the view of others, and because of ignorance they would have been less culpable; " but now they have no cloak for their sin."[2] " If I had not done among them the works which none other man did, they

---

[1] John iii. 18.   [2] John xv. 22.

had not had sin;"[1] had not Christ appeared with His wonderful works of divine power and love attesting the truth, there had been some comparative excuse for men living in ignorance and unbelief: "But now have they both seen and hated both Me and my Father." The same principle of judgment was again enunciated to the Pharisees who sought to condemn Jesus for giving sight to a blind man on the Sabbath day. They professed to have the true law of religion and refused to be convinced by the miracle. Jesus said, "For judgment I am come into this world, that they which see not might see; and they which see might be made blind."[2] His coming into the world, His being in the world, by the normal effect of light and truth made a judicial discrimination among men as to the honesty of their feelings and the sincerity of their professions toward Truth and God. "If ye were blind, ye could have no sin; but now ye say We see, therefore your sin remaineth."[3] This judicial process—a judgment in fact though not in form—a moral judgment, goes forward day by day.

Men profess a regard for principle, for morality, for religion,—pride themselves upon their virtues;—yet when Christ appears before them the embodiment of every virtue, the manifestation of true goodness, the exponent of true religion, they render Him no homage, give Him no love, follow Him with no obedience, and so by His Presence their pretensions are judged. But this searching, discriminating effect of truth and holiness was *not the whole* of the judgment meant by Christ, as is plain from His own words; for He teaches that the self-same Truth which now reveals the characters of men and so far judges them, will also judge them hereafter. "He that rejecteth Me and receiveth not my words, hath One that judgeth him; the word that I have spoken, the same shall judge him *in the last day.*"[4]

1 John xv. 24.   2 John ix. 39.   3 John ix. 41.   4 John xii. 48.

The notion of a judgment immediately after death, a judgment which consists simply in allotting the spirit, as by a law of its own being, to a condition corresponding to its moral state, finds some warrant in our Lord's parable of Dives and Lazarus. There Lazarus is pictured in a state of felicity after death, reposing "in Abraham's bosom," and Dives in a place of torment, whose pains he endures while his five brethren are yet alive in this world. This parable clearly teaches these two things—that immediately after death the soul is found existing in a state of consciousness; and that in the state next following upon death, there is a wide distinction in the conditions of the departed which answers to the differences in their characters in this world. This is virtually a judgment; whether we regard it as the formal act of God, or the working out in their natural effects upon the frames and feelings of the soul of the dispositions formed and the habits indulged in the present life. To the extent of separating the good and the bad into distinct abodes of happiness and misery, the effect of death is judicial and retributive. What the very laws of nature in respect of all tendencies and developments, and the laws of the human mind in respect of memory, association, and conscience so obviously teach, is herein the law of God, and the rewards and punishments which take effect directly after death are of the nature of a judgment upon each soul in particular.

But in addition to this our Lord has set before us the picture of a public and formal judgment at which He will preside, and pronounce judgment in person. " The Son of Man shall come in His glory, and all the holy angels with Him; and He shall sit upon the throne of His glory." Now it is true that great providential judgments in the course of human history were sometimes prefigured by Christ as the coming of the Son of Man. Such was the destruction of Jerusalem, and the final subversion of the

Jewish polity and faith, concerning which Jesus said: " Then shall appear the sign of the Son of Man in heaven; and then shall all the tribes of the earth mourn, and they shall see the Son of Man coming in the clouds of heaven with power and great glory." [1] There were no supernatural portents of that event; its immediate effects were limited to a small territory, and after Titus had wiped out the capital of a rebellious province, the affairs of the world went on as before; yet in its moral bearings upon the kingdom of God, this was one of the great way-marks of human history. And this pictorial " coming " of the Son of Man is used only of certain signal and majestic events in history which the minds of men instinctively recognize as the judgments of God. The grandeur of the event in its moral relations justifies the boldness of the figure.

Again, the event of death is sometimes spoken of under the figure of a master coming to reckon with his servants; [2] for to each individual the time of death is the winding up of his earthly affairs, and a summons from his Lord to render up his account. But to represent the common event of mortality that occurs at every moment of every day as the coming of Christ with great power and glory, with His holy angels, the sounding of a trumpet and the setting up a throne, would be a rhetorical extravagance that no Biblical writer ever dreamed of. And however each individual may be practically judged at death, such a description as our Lord has given of His own coming in the character of Judge can mean nothing less than a public and formal act of judgment.

In the same language He teaches that this judgment will be *universal in respect of the human race.* " Before Him shall be gathered all nations " [3]—all the families of men in all their generations. This positive, formal and universal

<hr>

[1] Matt. xxiv. 30.   [2] Matt. xxv. 19.   [3] Matt. xxv. 32.

judgment is most clearly set forth in the following words: "The Father hath given Him authority to execute judgment, because He is the Son of Man.[1] Marvel not at this," said Jesus, and entering somewhat into detail, He proceeded to describe what manner of judgment this shall be;— not a judgment in this life, separating His friends from His enemies: not a judging of souls one by one, by assigning them their portion at death; but a simultaneous judging of all mankind, to follow upon the Resurrection— "The hour is coming in the which all that are in the graves shall hear His voice:"[2] that voice is elsewhere likened to the sounding of a trumpet, the signal for decampment, which wakes the sleepers for a battle or a march—"the intimation of some grand catastrophe" at hand; "ALL that are in the graves shall hear His voice, and shall come forth: they that have done good, unto the resurrection of life, and they that have done evil, unto the resurrection of damnation."[3] Thus mankind will be judged as in the body for the deeds done in the body. God's dealings with men in this world will then be unveiled in a convincing revelation of His righteousness. The interlaced influences of society will then be untwined, and each character be brought out according to its deserts. "For there is nothing covered that shall not be revealed: neither hid that shall not be known. Therefore, whatsoever ye have spoken in darkness, shall be heard in the light; and that which ye have spoken in the ear in closets, shall be proclaimed upon the house-tops."[4] How much greater moment will the public exposition of character, followed by appropriate awards, impart to the judicial verdict of the divine government, than would the silent dropping of each individual at death into his appointed place!

Christ taught further that there will be *a set time for*

---

[1] John v. 27.   [2] John v. 28.   [3] John v. 28, 29.   [4] Luke xii. 3.

this general judgment. This belongs to the very idea of it as public and universal.

In the order of events Christ placed the Judgment after the Resurrection. He spoke of it as THAT DAY,—an expression which in New Testament usage denotes the closing up of this dispensation and the ushering in of a new order of things. There is something that awakens awe in this emphatic designation of "that Day:"—"Of *that* Day and hour knoweth no man, no, not the angels of heaven;"[1] "It shall be more tolerable in *that* Day for Sodom than for Chorazin;"[2] "Take heed to yourselves lest *that* Day come upon you unawares;"[3]—a Day selected, marked, appointed, a Day which like the first day of creation, the day of the crucifixion, the day of the Lord's resurrection, shall be remembered when all other days of human history are forgotten. For this shall mark indelibly the calendar of our race, as it passes over from the doings of time into the issues of eternity—a Day so grand, so bright, so glorious, so terrible, that in all the ages after it shall be remembered as That Day!

Christ announced the judgment to follow the end of the world. "In the end of the world, the Son of Man shall send forth His angels, and they shall gather out of His kingdom all things that offend, and them which do iniquity, and shall cast them into a furnace of fire;"[4] and again He said, "At the end of the world the angels shall come forth, and sever the wicked from among the just."[5]

To sum up the doctrine of Jesus concerning the Judgment; at a fixed period in the future, marking so high and solemn an occasion as "that Day," at the close of the present order of things, the end of the world, and after the resurrection, there will be a public and general judgment of mankind which shall finally divide them into two great

¹ Mat. xxiv. 36.　　² Luke x. 12.　　³ Luke xxi. 34.
⁴ Mat. xiii. 41, 42.　　⁵ xiii. 49.

classes, and shall apportion these according to their character, to a state of happiness or a state of misery. It will be a crowning characteristic of the Judgment that the Lord Jesus in person, as the Son of Man, will preside at that august solemnity, and will utter the decisions that shall fix forever the destiny of each and all of mankind. The *Son of Man* shall come in His glory, and shall sit upon the throne of His glory: all nations shall be gathered before Him for their final award: He shall separate them one from another; He shall set the sheep on His right hand, but the goats on the left.[1] The judging shall be His; the decision shall be His; the welcome to the righteous, the sentence upon the wicked shall proceed from His lips:— "The Father judgeth no man, but hath committed all judgment unto the Son."[2]

The Humanity of Christ is made prominent in this reference to the judgment, as His Divinity was made prominent in reference to the resurrection. The dead shall hear the voice of " the Son of God "—the divine power and majesty will be most strikingly expressed through the voice that shall raise the dead; but "the Son of Man," our representative and glorified humanity in Christ, shall come into view in the solemnities of the judgment. It is easy to imagine the moral significance of this exaltation of the Christ as the Judge. His personal connection with humanity, His experience of its trials and temptations, His sympathy with its sufferings and sorrows, will throw an air of benignity and tenderness over a scene that must of itself possess so much of majesty and awe. As one has said, "Man shall be judged by his fellow, by the most gracious and the meekest man, by man who hath borne the sins of mankind, and can have compassion upon his brethren—so that it is Mercy itself that judgeth."—One may well conceive that the same sympathetic experience with our human-

---

[1] Mat. xxv. 33.   [2] John v. 22.

ity that qualified Jesus to be "a merciful and faithful High Priest," would have some corresponding relation to His office as Judge, bringing Him near to the arraigned in a compassionate consideration of ignorance and infirmities.

Moreover, as the truth of Jesus was the closest test of character, the life of Jesus the perfect model of humanity, the death of Jesus the highest expression of love, it is fitting that they who have had knowledge of Him should be brought to trial at the last before Him, and be judged by their feelings and actions toward Himself. Surely every complaint or even suspicion of severity must be silenced, when He who showed His anxiety to save men by dying for them, and who promised forgiveness to them that hated Him, shall remand unto condemnation for their sins those who would not come unto Him that they might have life.[1] Their sinful unbelief will itself be their condemnation, in the light of the character and mission of Christ, and especially in the light of the mercy that has saved others and would equally have saved them.[2] There will be a fitness also in the judgment being rendered by Him who as the Messiah appeared on earth to manifest and perfect the kingdom of God in opposition to the kingdom of darkness and evil. The judicial function of Christ will set forth His divine royalty.[3]

Back of all these considerations, as exalting and enforcing them, is the fact that God was revealed to men in His paternal love and grace through the *Incarnation* of Christ. It was through our human nature as the medium, that Jehovah manifested Himself to men as the Father ; and so wondrously was the love of God in giving His Son to save the world identified with the grace of Christ in being "lifted up" for that end, so entirely were the thoughts and

---

[1] John viii. 21, 24.　　[2] Matt. xi. 20-25.　　[3] Matt. xxv. 31.

purposes of the Father reflected in the Son, that Jesus could say "He that hath seen Me hath seen the Father." [1]

The being and attributes of God had been matter of devout contemplation in the creation; had been to philosophic minds a subject of speculative thought; had been impressed upon the Jewish people by occasional appearances of celestial glory, and special acts of divine power; but when Christ came, men saw this power over nature, over diseases, over the dead, over the world of spirits, proceeding from a personal will, and so felt the presence of God as a living, acting personality; they saw this power put forth for most beneficent ends; and so, that goodness which they had inferred from creation and providence, they saw to be the living activity of the love of God : the truth which they had spelled out upon the pages of nature and of the human mind, or heard from the lips of prophets, they now heard in the clearness, the fulness, the majesty of the voice of God.   That holiness which Reason and Revelation had alike proclaimed as the sum of the divine character, and conscience and the word of God had required as the condition of divine favor, they saw before them, a living example, in Him who was without sin, and full of every grace :—but most of all, that mercy, which nature but obscurely hinted, and reason hardly dared to guess, and the law had only shadowed through its sacrifices, was here manifested in words of tenderness and compassion, in the offer of salvation, and in the forgiveness of sins: it was in view of this intelligible and completed exhibition of the character of God, that Jesus said, " He that hath seen Me, hath *seen the Father*."

The Incarnation was the most stupendous moral phenomenon in the history of this world, and so far as we can imagine, in the history of the universe.   The physical fact

<hr />

[1] John xiv. 9.

14

of the Incarnation was the least part of the miracle: for, that the Creator of all substances and forms could adapt Himself to any, were no marvel. But the purpose of the Incarnation is the moral wonder of earth and heaven,— that God entered into humanity to redeem, ennoble, enthrone it: and this sublime wonder of the Incarnation will stand out in Jesus the appointed Judge, *because He is the Son of Man.* In that Day when all nations shall be gathered before Him, the surpassing wonder shall be the unveiling of that awful mystery, the Incarnate God, the Redeeming Man; all angels His servants; principalities, powers, and dominions gathered beneath His throne!

CHAPTER XVI.

In the dramatic representation of the Judgment recorded by Matthew, the scene opens with words of congratulation from the enthroned Son of Man to His loyal and faithful disciples: "Then shall the King say unto them on His right hand, Come, ye blessed of my Father, inherit the kingdom prepared for you from the foundation of the world."[1] A state of eternal felicity awaits the close of the believer's life as its appropriate consummation. "He that believeth on Me hath everlasting life,"[2]—the life of faith sustained upon earth by the "bread of God," at death will emerge from all the limitations of the flesh into the life of perfect satisfaction in heaven;—a continuous Life—here an immanent principle, there an immanent Power "equal unto the angels;"[3] "He that eateth of this bread shall live forever."[4] This promise of a perfected and glorified life with Himself our Lord associated with the commemorative supper, embodying it with the most expressive symbol of His love, that as often as we remember Him in His death, we may revive the assurance that we shall be with Him in His glory. The sacrament which He instituted at the first as a memorial, He declared also to be a prophecy; it was designed to link together in the thought of His disciples His departure and His coming; to connect His dying upon the cross with their living forever in the kingdom of His Father. In the anguish of parting He said to His disciples "Believe in Me; I go to prepare a place for you; and if I go and prepare a place for you, I

---

[1] Matt. xxv. 34.　　[2] John vi. 47.　　[3] Luke xx. 36.　　[4] John vi. 58.

will come again, and receive you unto Myself, that where
I am, there ye may be also." ¹ And the going and the
coming He linked together in this prophetical memorial—
the *memorial* "This do in remembrance of Me," ² the *pro-*
phecy, " I will not drink henceforth of this fruit of the vine
until that day when I drink it new with you in My
Father's kingdom." ³

To drink together of the wine-cup at the Table signifies
social communion—participation in a common festival of
love: the promise of Jesus that He will hereafter drink ·
of the same cup with His disciples, is an assurance that
they shall then be admitted to a visible fellowship and enjoyment with their Lord—that He who is now felt to be
present at this sacrament, through the spiritual perception of
faith, will then be seen in the midst of His Redeemed,
welcoming them as His brethren, and diffusing over them
the glory of His presence and the joy of His own blessedness.

The sphere of this joyous communion will be the perfected state of the Redeemed in heaven. " In my Father's
kingdom," was the time and place indicated by our Lord
for the fulfilling of this promise. The "kingdom of heaven,"
the " kingdom of God," as we have seen,⁴ began to be manifested upon earth when souls, brought into a personal
allegiance to Truth and Holiness, were united in a fellowship of spiritual love and obedience to their common Lord.
Wherever such souls are found there is the kingdom of
heaven already within them : and wherever such souls are
joined together in some visible bond of recognition and
fellowship, there is the kingdom of heaven made manifest.
As yet, however, the kingdom of heaven is but imperfectly
established in respect of its authority in the hearts of those
who have received it, and imperfectly manifested through
any communion of Christians by which it is represented to

¹ John xiv. 1–4.　　² Luke xxii. 19.　　³ Matt. xxvi. 29.
⁴ Chap. iii.

the world. The kingdom in its highest sense—as denoting the perfect rule of the divine will in a perfect community—will not appear until the final coming of the Son of Man.

It is of a time after the end of the world, after death, and the resurrection and the judgment—the time when " the Son of man shall send forth his angels to gather out of His kingdom all things that offend "[1]—that Jesus has declared, "Then shall the righteous shine forth as the sun in the kingdom of their Father."[2] The Master of the house shall "thrust out all workers of iniquity," separating the false from the true, and then shall Abraham, and Isaac, and Jacob, and all the prophets abide in the kingdom of God[3]—in a state of purity and felicity that no sin nor trouble shall ever invade: the kingdom of God purified of all the accidents of evil that have attached themselves to its external development in this world, shall then stand forth in its essential beauty and glory. That state of perfected character and beatified existence which the Scriptures describe as Heaven, our Lord here styles His Father's kingdom. It will be the crowning honor and felicity of the saints in heaven, that the Lord Jesus will then make Himself known as their friend and companion, receiving them into a personal fellowship, and sharing with them as at a high festival, His peculiar glory as the Son of Man. In that richness of immediate personal intercourse, in that fulness of love made visible by the sharing of all its gifts, will Jesus fulfill His parting word to His disciples, "I will drink new wine *with you* in my Father's kingdom."

The cup of communion at that feast will have a new flavor, and will sparkle with fresh delights—a flavor that will not as now reach the soul through the senses, but shall convey direct from soul to soul the very essence of

[1] Matt. xiii. 41 . [2] Matt. xiii. 43. [3] Luke xiii. 25, 30.

love and bliss ;—the wine of life pressed from immortal fruits, and imparting the purity, tone, and freshness of celestial joy. It will be a "new" and more exalted mode of spiritual intercourse;—where now this cup, as a symbol, addresses the imagination and helps us to conceive of Jesus as spiritually communing with us, there Jesus will give us in His own person the tokens of fellowship that shall cause us to realize that we are with Him and possess Him forever.

It will be new, also, as the cup of greeting differs from the cup of parting. In the cup of parting we give all good wishes, all kindly feelings, and pledge ourselves to mutual remembrance, and to sympathetic, spiritual communing; yet with all this there is blended a feeling of sadness at the separation. But in the cup of greeting, we cannot stay to speak of good wishes and good feelings, and promises of fidelity, for the joy we have in coming together face to face. The new wine will beam with the reflection of that joy.

And this parting promise seems to foreshadow a peculiar joy of Christ in the fellowship of His redeemed held in reserve, as it were, until that day of reunion. This cup of blessing He does not share with the angels. There are sympathies and communings, tender and inexpressible blendings of soul between Jesus and His disciples, which only the Humanity that He redeemed can know. Hence the significance of the negative as well as the positive terms of the promise; "I will *not* drink henceforth of this fruit of the vine, until that Day when I drink it *new* with *you* in My Father's kingdom."

And there is another deep spiritual meaning here: namely that the saints in heaven shall forever refer their felicity to the Redemption wrought for them by Jesus through His death upon the cross. Upon the eve of offering Himself up for their redemption, Christ gave to all who should

believe on His name, this cup as the symbol and memorial
of His blood " shed for the remission of sins." With the
parting injunction " This do in remembrance of Me," He
coupled the promise of meeting them again in the higher
fellowship of heaven. But there too, the joy of meeting
their Lord, the bliss of being saved, would be presented
under the symbol of a cup; and though the wine would be
new—the first interview there in wonderful contrast with
the parting here—yet would the wine, the cup, link all
the blessedness of that reunion in heaven, to the tender
memories of the sacrifice on earth—link the salvation
yonder to the Redemption here; and so, in the long interval Jesus Himself will not partake of the cup, until the
memorial of suffering shall be transformed into the greeting of reunion, with all " the travail of His soul " [1] gathered about Him in His Father's kingdom.

Under this exquisite figure of a festival of love begun
on earth to be renewed and perfected in heaven, did the
Lord Jesus set forth the fruits of His redemption to all
believers. His doctrine of the Final State of the Righteous is that, after the Resurrection and the Judgment, they
shall dwell in perfect bliss and glory, amid the constant
tokens of His presence and love. However high their
joys in the intervening Paradise, there must come to them
some wondrous augmentation when the Son of Man sitting on the Throne of His glory, with all nations gathered before Him,—shall say unto them upon His right
hand, " Come ye blessed of My Father, inherit the kingdom prepared for you from the foundation of the world;" [2]
—blessed with the Saviour's welcome, blessed with His
immediate presence, blessed of His Father, possessors of
that " kingdom " for which they were created at the first
in the divine image, and were renewed as the spiritual
sons of God.

---

[1] Isaiah liii. 11.   [2] Matt. xxv. 34.

A collocation of the words of Christ touching the final state of all believers teaches as the sum of His doctrine: (a). That one element in that state of blessedness which is promised them hereafter will be *the near Presence of the Lord of their life and love.* " I go," said He, " to prepare a place for you, and I will come again and receive you unto Myself, that where I am, there ye may be also." [1] In His last prayer for His disciples Jesus anticipated their coming to be with Himself, and His desire for this breathed to the Father was also the determination of that will which was always the will of God. He was about to return to that visible glory and blessedness in the heavenly mansions, which He had with the Father before the world was; but that glory would henceforth be brightened by His work of Redemption, and by the participation of His followers in the triumphs of His Resurrection: " Father, I will that they whom Thou hast given Me be with Me where I am ; that they may behold My glory which Thou hast given Me." [2]

The victorious leader of the American army, the second saviour of his country, with an honest pride summoned his son from West Point to witness his inauguration as President, that he might behold and enjoy his father's honor; yet the son of the President could share the glory of his father only through its reflection upon him morally; nothing of the military renown, nor of the political distinction was his; and when the father's term of office shall expire, the son will be of no more consequence in Washington than any other man. But the beholding of Christ's glory promised to His disciples is a sharing as well as a seeing; for Jesus has so identified Himself with His Church that His glory will pervade His people as being identified with Himself. " I am glorified in them;" [3] " I in them and Thou in Me." [4]

---

[1] John xiv. 3.   [2] John xvii. 24.
[3] John xvii. 10.   [4] John xvii. 23.

(*b*). A second element in this coming blessedness will be *the exaltation of believers in honor, through their union with Christ.* They shall "inherit a kingdom;" not only shall they find themselves amid the visible splendors of the kingdom of God, bathing in the light and glory of His presence; but they shall know that all this is theirs for an eternal possession. All that God can communicate to them of honor and blessing, filling their nature to repletion, shall be theirs. He made man at the beginning to have dominion over other works of His hands: He crowned him with glory and honor and put all things under his feet.[1] But man uncrowned himself by sin—subjecting his soul with its divine instincts of knowledge and spiritual power, to the dictation of the body and its appetites, he cast away his lordship over nature, and became its servant. By redeeming man from sin, Christ has restored him to that spiritual power and dominion which from the foundation of the world were designed to be his; and into the fulness of that kingdom the Redeemed shall enter in the heavenly state; dominion over the powers of nature, so that nothing shall harm them; dominion over evil spirits so that these shall no more tempt them; dominion over time and space through the powers of an unwearying and unending life.

"Kingdom" is not mere position and sphere of action, but the consciousness of power, of capacity and exaltation; "The kingdom of God is within you." Could we for instance, transport ourselves, without external helps, at our own will, from star to star, we should have the kingdom over space; the spirit-power would control distance, gravitation, all that pertains to motion and place. Some such joyous freedom of conscious power in respect of nature and her laws, may be a portion of the kingdom of the saints.

(*c*). Another element of the final state of the righteous as promised by Christ is, that *they shall have the approving*

[1] Ps. viii. 6.

benediction of His Father, and so shall dwell in conscious fellowship with God. "Come, ye blessed of my Father."[1] "Then shall the righteous shine forth as the sun in the kingdom of their Father."[2] To be acknowledged as children of God denotes the completeness of the restoration which Christ has accomplished in believers. Sin severed the spiritual union of the soul with God and effaced His spiritual likeness; sin made man no longer a child of God save in origin and name; and so completely does a moral resemblance set aside all resemblance by mere derivation or title, that to the Jews who, while calling themselves the children of God, denied the truth and the Son of God, Jesus said "Ye are of your Father, the *devil*."[3] But to them that believed on His name, Jesus imparted the glory of a sonship in privilege and promise analogous to His own: "The glory which Thou gavest Me I have given them; that they may be one, even as we are one."[4] This filial relationship will be acknowledged and crowned with open benediction in that heavenly home. Then shall be fulfilled in its highest meaning that declaration of Christ, "He that loveth Me shall be loved of My Father."[5] "For the Father Himself loveth you, because ye have loved Me, and believed that I came out from God."[6] As one has said, "God neither hopes nor believes, but knows and loves;" therefore love is greater than faith or hope, because it does not, like these, only relate to God as an object, but belongs to God as a nature, so that in loving Him we share Him also. That beatific union Christ will proclaim at "that Day;" saying, "Come, *blessed* of My Father."

And His Father is their Father also. While they were yet in this world, if we may so speak, He had appropriated them as children; they had come to Him because the Father drew them; receiving the Spirit of Christ they had

---

[1] Matt. xxv. 34.   [2] Matt. xiii. 43.
[3] John viii. 44.   [4] John xvii. 22.
[6] John xiv. 21.   [6] John xvi. 27.

become "the children of the Highest,"[1] and now the unspeakable blessedness of heaven, in the reciprocative love of God, shall be theirs by the gift of the Father.

Other elements of heavenly felicity are set forth in the writings of the apostles, especially by Paul and John; but the plan of this treatise restricts us to the personal teachings of our Lord, and therefore we enumerate only those features of heaven which Jesus Himself has delineated. For the same reason we refrain from all speculation upon the nature of existence in the heavenly state and its modes of occupation and enjoyment. We would not introduce one breath of mere conjecture to mar the serene beauty and dignity of the declarations of Christ. Yet few and brief as those declarations are, what higher heaven can we conceive than Jesus has promised, in a perpetual feast of love and joy, under new conditions of existence, not subject to partings and sorrows; in His own near and abiding Presence; in the sharing of His glory; in the honor of a kingdom; in the blessing of His Father, and a welcome to all the good His love can provide and all the joy that it can bring.

This blessedness is traced directly to His Redemption. This cup—the New Testament in His blood shed for the remission of sins—will be brought into remembrance at the threshold of that heavenly festival, because only by that blood could we have remission, and only through remission of sins can we have life and heaven. "As Moses lifted up the serpent in the wilderness even so must the Son of Man be lifted up that whosoever believeth in Him should not perish, but have eternal life."[2]

But though Christ Himself is the only door into heaven, and no man cometh to the Father but by Him,[3] yet there are conditions of mind and of action to be fulfilled on our part, in order that we may be numbered with the saved. Two such conditions Christ Himself laid down with empha-

[1] Luke vi. 35.   [2] John iii. 14, 15.   [3] John xiv. 6.

sis in His solemn description of the last Judgment and the
awards that shall follow it; these are, confessing the name
of Christ, and acting from the love of Christ. " Whosoever shall confess Me before men, him will I confess also
before My Father which is in heaven. But whosoever
shall deny Me before men, him will I also deny before My
Father which is in heaven."[1] This confessing may take
many different forms, and it is not the form of it that is essential as a condition, but the thing itself as truly and heartily
done—not making a confession, but confessing Christ.
To confess Christ is first of all to acknowledge Him in the
soul as Redeemer and Lord; to confess one's need of Him
to take away sin; to confess one's dependence upon Him
for salvation; to confess one's admiration of Him and
homage toward Him; to confess Him with the full sur-
render of heart and life to His service. And one must
likewise confess Him before men; by a Christian tone and
spirit in the family and in society; by Christian principles
in business and a Christian deportment in the common
life. And in addition to these modes of confessing Christ,
one should honor Him by some sort of public acknowledgment and testimony. The obvious way of making such
confession is to join His Church; and if one's reason for
not doing this is an unwillingness to confess Christ, how
can such an one hope that Christ will confess him?

The other condition of admission to the heavenly blessedness is a life of active benevolence prompted by love to
Christ. In the commendation bestowed upon the righteous in the day of judgment, their welcome to the kingdom
seems to proceed upon the ground of the good works they
had done.[2] Did our Lord then teach or imply a doctrine
of salvation by works, or of merit? The very statement
contradicts that supposition; for they who do such works
have no thought of merit in them; they are astonished and

---

[1] Mat. x. 32, 33.   [2] Matt. xxv. 34-37.

overwhelmed at the enumeration; "Lord, *when* saw we
Thee an hungered and fed Thee? or thirsty, and gave
Thee drink." [1] What they did was not in the endeavor to
merit heaven, or to work out or work *up* a salvation, but
was the acting out of a true love to Christ in dependence
upon Him. These good works were not meritorious but
evidential : "The works of love performed by the righteous
are the proofs by which they evince their calling to the
kingdom of God. As works of true love these presuppose
living faith : faith and love are as inseparable as fire and
warmth : the one cannot exist in its real nature without the
other. External actions of charity may be dead works ;
but our Lord speaks of the affluence of the inward tide of
love in acts of holy charity." "Ye have done it unto
Me :"—without thought of personal reward, without a calculation of merit, under the promptings of the Saviour's
love, they had carried out His spirit in ministering to
others. To act in all things from love to Christ denotes
that vital union with Christ which qualifies the participant
for the felicity of heaven. And since heaven consists more
in spirit than in place, more in character than in condition, this doing the will of Christ in the daily life is not
so much a formal preparation for the life to come, as it is
the present experience of that principle of holy living
which shall find its proper consummation in the Life Everlasting.

[1] Matt. xxv. 37.

CHAPTER XVII.

WE have traced the doctrine of Christ step by step from His first preaching of the necessity of repentance and the new birth, and His promise of eternal life to all who should believe upon the Son of Man as lifted up upon the cross, to the announcement of the day in which He will come again to judge the quick and the dead ; and pausing as it were at the threshold of the eternal state, we have heard the words of final greeting, " Come, ye blessed of My Father, enter into the kingdom prepared for you from the foundation of the world."[1] Would that we might close our contemplation of that scene with these thrilling words of invitation!—that there were no alternative to be looked upon, no contrast to the picture that Christ has given of Himself embosomed in the midst of His glorified disciples at the festival of the new wine, the feast of immortal life and love in His Father's kingdom. But since He has stated the alternative and drawn the contrast, we must follow His teachings in all fidelity to the end. Already at the beginning of His ministry, in the first proclamation of the Gospel, the alternative was presented, the contrast was foreshadowed. He came that " whosoever believeth in Him should not perish, but have eternal life ; " and this clearly implies that they who would not believe must perish ; which, indeed, was expressly declared in that " he that believeth on Him is not condemned; but he that believeth not is condemned already."[2] And the contrast

---

[1] Matt. xxv. 34.   [2] John iii. 18.

which was thus pointedly stated at the beginning of the Gospel, runs through our Lord's discourses and parables to the close; and is there drawn out in the form of results that are positive, visible, and unchangeable.

The issue of life or death, salvation or condemnation, was always present to the mind of Jesus in preaching the Gospel. A future state of rewards and punishments formed a back-ground of·motive and warning in every discourse, and in some discourses was brought most impressively into the foreground. Self-denial, the renouncing of besetting sin was urged for the reason that "It is better to enter into life halt or maimed, than that the whole body should be cast into hell."[1] Courage in acknowledging Christ was urged by this plea: "Fear not them which kill the body, but are not able to kill the soul; but rather fear Him who is able to destroy both soul and body in hell."[2] His hearers were exhorted to "enter in at the strait gate, for wide is the gate, and broad is the way, that leadeth to destruction, and many there be which go in thereat."[3] They were exhorted to "make the tree good," the heart right, because "every tree that bringeth not forth good fruit is hewn down and cast into the fire."[4] They were warned that mere professions could not save them, for even "children of the kingdom," born of the seed of Abraham—for not receiving Christ, shall be "cast out into outer darkness, where shall be weeping and gnashing of teeth;"[5] for while in this world much that is evil is gathered into the visible church, "at the end of the world the angels shall come forth and sever the wicked from among the just, and shall cast them into the furnace of fire."[6] The Pharisees and all hypocrites were warned of "the damnation of hell."[7] Dives having lived a sensual, worldly life, on dying went to a place of misery, and "was in torments;"[8]

[1] Matt. xviii. 8. [2] Matt. x. 28. [3] Matt. vii. 13. [4] Matt. vii. 19. [5] Matt. viii. 12
[6] Matt. xiii. 42.   [7] Matt. xxiii. 33.   [8] Luke xvi. 23.

" What then is a man profited, if he shall gain the whole world, and lose his own soul?"[1] The foolish virgins, having no oil of grace in their lamps, shall knock and cry in vain at the door of heaven, forever shut against them.[2] "Many will say to Me in that day, Lord, Lord, have we not prophesied in Thy name? and in Thy name have cast out devils? and in Thy name done many wonderful works? And then will I profess unto them I never knew you; depart from Me, ye that work iniquity."[3] "All that are in the graves shall hear the voice of the Son of Man, and shall come forth;—they that have done good, unto the resurrection of life, and they that have done evil, unto the resurrection of damnation."[4] "These shall go away into everlasting punishment, but the righteous into life eternal."[5] "For the Son of Man shall come in the glory of His Father, with His angels; and then He shall reward every man according to his works."[6]

All these are the very words of Christ. The doctrine of a coming judgment, at which a direct recompense from God shall be rendered to men individually according to character, is not an invention of a malignant theology. It was the constant teaching of Jesus Christ, and distinguishes Christianity as a moral system, with positive awards, from systems that refer all evils to purely natural causes.

That penal consequences follow upon the transgression of physical laws, and that these are intended to have a moral effect in restraining transgression, is written in the whole constitution of Nature and of Man. Some maintain, however, that the penalties of transgression are limited to the operation of natural laws; that these may be retrieved at any time in the future by a change of conduct on the part of the sufferer; or will work themselves out at

---

[1] Matt. xvi. 26.   [2] Matt. xxv. 1 seq.   [3] Matt. vii. 22.
[4] John v. 23.   [5] Matt. xxv. 46.   [6] Matt. xvi. 27.

last in his atonement and purification. In other words, by the doctrine of natural consequences, sin and its effects are simply a question between man and the general system of laws within which he exists. Certain actions are followed by certain effects. Whoever therefore, transgresses the laws of his being or the laws of the universe must expect to take the consequences. This doctrine of natural consequences is true so far as it goes; and this alone should suffice to deter men from transgressing the laws of their being. But Christ taught that the punishment of sin will embody the additional element of a positive retribution from His hand as the righteous Judge of the world ;—that He Himself will reward every man according to His works; and that these awards will be final and everlasting.

Exception is taken to this doctrine of a direct and positive retribution as inconsistent with the wisdom and goodness of God, and with the plan of salvation ; it is styled a dogma of a hard and arbitrary theology. But since this feature is made so prominent in the Gospel, since it is a doctrine most emphatically pronounced by Jesus Christ Himself, it cannot be set aside except by setting aside the whole of Christianity ; it is linked with the doctrine of Jesus from first to last ; and it must be in harmony with the divine justice and love that beam from every page of His Gospel.

Our Lord's doctrine of retribution differs from the doctrine of natural sequences in two material points. First, in place of a natural law of cause and effect, it sets before us a personal judge whose word declares the penalty ; and secondly it makes that penalty a positive infliction upon moral grounds, because of character and not the mere issue of a natural law. We have already in part discussed this distinction, [1] but it is so striking and momentous that it

---

[1] See Chap. xv.

deserves a further consideration. It marks the difference between a machine-world in which things move on by mere natural routine, and a moral government in which the Creator and Head of the universe maintains His authority over intelligent creatures by moral laws with their proper sanctions.

Recalling for a moment the scene of the final judgment, as portrayed by Christ, we there behold Himself sitting upon the throne of His glory, and all nations gathered before Him; He separates mankind into two classes by the test of character, and He Himself pronounces the final award; He addresses the one class as " Blessed of His Father," and welcomes them to " the kingdom " reserved for them; this He does as King and Judge, with an authority whose effect is immediate and final; then this same judicial authoritative voice says to those upon the left hand, " Depart from me, ye cursed, into everlasting fire." And the result of this solemn proceeding is summed up in the words—" These shall go away into everlasting punishment, but the righteous into life eternal."[1] Now it may be said this scene is pictorial, and that much of the language is the drapery of a poetic description. Grant this, but of *what* is it a picture? and what instruction is it designed to convey? Does it picture the mere working of natural laws, by which at death men one by one drop into their respective places in a future state of existence? Can this vivid and impressive picture be reduced to a mere parable of natural distinctions and natural sequences? How then shall we dispose of the central figure—the living personal Christ? How dwindle down the collective multitudes, divided by character, into a mere succession of individuals passing off the stage each in his own time and way? This is a picture indeed, but a picture whose corresponding reality is a formal, definitive judgment, which the Saviour in person will pro-

nounce upon men according to their deeds.[1]—This certainly
is the doctrine of Christ concerning the future retribution;
and if we compare this in detail with the doctrine that all
punishment is the result of natural causes, we shall find it
more than that in accordance with the reason of things.

(a). Both views agree as to the fact of penalty. Strictly
speaking there is no sect in religion nor school of philosophy
that absolutely denies that sin incurs penalty. Those who
hold that there is no retribution after death—if there are
any such—argue that sin receives its whole punishment
through the evils of the present life, or that Christ has
cancelled these indiscriminately for all; and those who hold
to the final restoration of the wicked to holiness and heaven,
admit that there will be a future retribution, but argue
that this will at length satisfy itself, or will work the reformation of the offender. In either case then it is admitted
that law has a penalty for transgression; and the difference
between all these schemes of natural sequence and Christ's
doctrine of retribution lies in the form of the penalty and
the manner of inflicting it.

The fact that penalty is affixed to the laws of nature is
too obvious to require proof. He who violates the laws of
health, in respect of air, of food, of sleep, of exposure, of
labor, must take the consequences in suffering, in debility,
in premature death. He who disregards the known properties and effects of the substances and elements of nature,
who puts his hand into melted lead or takes strychnine
into his stomach, must suffer in consequence. Every child
knows that a world of laws must be also a world of penalties. In the fact of penalty, therefore, all theories agree.

(b). It is agreed also, upon both theories—the natural
and the Christian—that penalty for the violation of law is
just;—that is just in the principle of it, for we are not here
speaking of manner or degree. Those who accept Christ's

---

[1] See Chap. xv.

teaching of course believe this, for they believe in the righteousness of God. And those who regard all suffering as simply the consequence of violating natural law, do not accuse nature of injustice or cruelty because of the suffering that follows disobedience. Now the benevolence of God might just as well be impeached because of these penalties of natural law, as for a positive retribution. But how absurd we should think it, if a man who had burnt his hand by his own carelessness, should go up and down in a raging passion against the cruelty of nature in making fire burn. We use all the great agents of nature, fire, steam, chemical forces, subject to the risk and the penalty of violating or abusing them; and the penalty of disobedience or disregard which all men see to be a *fact*, men also admit to be just. "You should have known better," "You should have taken care,"—these and like phrases impute the evil not to the law but to the transgressor. The pain which is incidental to the violation of the law renders even physical law a means of moral discipline.

(c). Both theories—the natural and the Christian—agree that natural evil may be fitly made a penalty for moral disobedience. When the mother warns her child not to go near the fire, and lays her strict commands upon him, if he goes and burns himself, she teaches him that his suffering comes not only from disregarding the properties of fire, but from disobeying her command. A drunkard violates not only the laws of his physical constitution, but the laws of reason and of conscience, the laws of good society, the moral law of God; and though the penalty comes chiefly in the form of physical suffering and degradation, we yet attach this to moral as well as to physical law.

Human laws annex physical penalties to moral offences. Theft, though committed upon inanimate things is a breach of morality; murder, though committed upon the physical body, is a crime of deepest moral die. The law punishes these crimes with physical pains and privations that have no connection with the physical objects violated. Hence it is absurd to say that all penalty comes merely in the way of natural sequence from natural laws; it attaches itself also to the great principles of moral law.

Thus far, then, the theory that penalty comes in due course of nature, and the doctrine of Christ that it is inflicted by God as a righteous governor for the infraction of His laws agree in these successive steps :—(d). that there is penalty, as a matter of fact, in the system under which we live, whether we call this nature or providence; (e). that as a principle, the infliction of penalty for transgression is wise and just; (f). and that penalty, though coming in the form of natural evil, often stands visibly connected with the infraction of moral law. But from this point the doctrine of Christ goes farther, and teaches that penalty shall be pronounced directly from Himself as Judge, aside from or in addition to the natural course of things, and as the fit and just conclusion of this very dispensation of grace. The rule or principle here laid down for the infliction of penalty is the rule of absolute justice. Each man shall be judged according to what he has or has not done; and "that servant which knew his Lord's will, and prepared not himself, neither did according to His will, shall be beaten with many stripes." [1]

Man's relations to the moral law, and to all law in his character as a moral being are far superior to his relations to physical law. The soul no less than the body has its own laws. In his own free actions, his moral conduct, man is bound to do right by an obligation as strong surely as that which binds him to observe the laws of nature in the care of his body; and as a moral being he must be amenable to moral law. This law has certain penalties that

[1] Luke xii. 47.

come as matter of course, as certainly as the sequences of
physical laws—such as remorse of conscience; the loss of
self-respect; a sense of unhappiness; the apprehension of
evil. The principle of penalty for disobedience here distinctly applies.

In threatening to inflict a direct positive penalty for
sin, in distinction from its natural sequences, Christ announced beforehand a rule of perfect justice. It is that He
will try men solely by their own actions, and will recompense them according to the tenor of their spirit and conduct. This is a rule of perfect equity. If any have
obeyed the law, they could desire no more favorable rule
than to be rewarded according to their deeds. And for
such as have broken the law there could be no rule more
just and equal than that they shall be dealt with exactly
according to their conduct; that they should receive simply that which is their due. The Judge of infinite righteousness, of perfect knowledge, goodness, and truth, will
do *right* in dealing with men according to their deeds.
And if, moreover, they have had opportunity given them
to escape penalty by repentance, and have refused this, it
will be perfect justice to deal with them upon their own
ground.

Hence the rule of *personal* reckoning here laid down is
proper and equitable. Men are not to be judged collectively or in classes, by some general sweeping act, but
each and every man according to that which he hath done.
The formative influences of society upon personal character, the circumstances in which a life was molded, the
relative degrees of darkness and light in each individual
case, the temptations to sin, the allurements to virtue, all
that affected the man in the course of his earthly conduct,
will enter into the judgment upon that conduct; and in
the light of all these conditions and circumstances, each individual case will be made up for its own issue. This is

the fairest rule of judgment that can be imagined. What could any man ask for himself, or what could he conceive of as a principle of judgment, more scrupulously just than this—that each and every man be judged according to his personal conduct?

We now come to the gist of Christ's doctrine of punishment. The fact of penalty and its justice being recognized, it being also established that natural evil may properly be used as a penalty for moral transgression; and the rule of judgment by personal conduct being absolutely just, it remains only to consider the reasons for a positive judgment and retribution in distinction from the natural consequences of violated law. Such a judgment is due to the transcendent worth and dignity of moral interests in the universe, and to the claims of public justice and right in a moral government. Man's highest dignity and worth is in the sphere of morality. Here it is, as a being capable of moral choice, of knowing truth and obeying virtue, capable of principles of action as lofty as the mind of God and enduring as His throne, in a word capable of holiness and its immeasurable blessedness, it is in this that man is allied to angels and to God. Build one broad and stable pyramid of physical laws; if it were possible heap into one stupendous mass all the matter now shaped and distributed into ten thousand worlds; above this place again the noblest powers and attainments of intellectual life—indeed, if this were possible, the accumulated powers and products of mind in its highest spheres; still above these must we place in sublime pre-eminence a pure and perfect moral character, as the crown of all excellence, the height of all dignity, the seat of all true power and grandeur, the nearest approach to the divine. "Man partakes of all that is below him, and becomes man by the addition of something higher: this is, the rational and moral life by which man is made in the image of God. For in man, as thus con-

stituted, we first find a being who is capable of choosing
his own end; or rather, of choosing or rejecting the end
indicated by his whole nature. Up to man every thing is
driven to its end by a force working from without, or from
behind; but for him the pillar of cloud and of fire puts
itself in front, and he follows it or not, as he chooses." [1]

And now for a being with these majestic endowments,
with these sublime possibilities, has the Creator no recognition, no rule, no administration higher than the laws of
the physical creation? Has this rational image of God,
laws of digestion, and laws of locomotion, but no laws of
moral action? Shall a stone give him pain if he strike
his foot against it, shall his body suffer for any infraction
of mere physical law, and shall there be for his soul, with
its voluntary powers, no moral government of the Creator
having sanctions commensurate with the interests of a
moral universe? Is this soul, by which alone man is
man, governed down at the low level of the animal nature
with which it is associated—subject to law and amenable
to penalty only so far as it comes into contact with the
physical creation? Has the wise and good God committed
such a solecism in government, that He has made everything subject to law except that which alone is great
enough to comprehend law and intelligently obey it?—that
the lowest animal, the meanest plant, the very stones
beneath our feet have laws corresponding with their
nature, but the soul of man has no government appropriate
to itself? Is it credible that there is no moral government
over the universe of intelligent beings? Nothing but a
machinery of physical law? Is it credible that God has
not made known to man the law that should govern his
higher nature, or that He will not show His regard for
that law by sanctions conformed to its worth and proceeding from Himself? Surely as God is great, as the soul is

[1] Rev. Mark Hopkins, D. D.

great in His image, as a universe of moral beings is great above all the greatness of God's other works, there is a government based upon the grandeur of virtue, there is a law embodying holiness as the rule of man, and there are penalties answering to the greatness of these parties and the grandeur of these interests.

Moreover, the claims of public justice and security in a moral government demand that there be a positive retribution upon sin from the Ruler Himself. Society recognizes this principle in all criminal law. Doubtless the criminal suffers certain natural consequences of his crime, in remorse of conscience, in terrors of imagination, in the consciousness of social ignominy. But he stands not alone ; he is related to society as a whole ; and justice is the strength of the social organism. The criminal owes therefore a debt to public justice as well as to natural law. If a man poisons his wife that he may be free to live a life of shame, is that a private affair of his own household? Society takes notice of it as a crime against itself, and law has a penalty. We measure the moral tone of society by the sure and impartial justice it metes out to such a crime. If to evade legal penalty the criminal poisons himself, should this be accepted as making the account square with justice ? Is the moral law satisfied by another crime? Would the social law of the universe be satisfied by the transportation of the criminal to heaven ? When we read that " the Son of Man shall send forth His angels, and they shall gather out of His kingdom all things that offend, and them which do iniquity," [1] we feel that the mercy that offers salvation to all who in faith and holy love will seek the kingdom of God is enhanced by that righteousness which shall hereafter separate the evil from the good.

But it is objected that the doctrine of eternal punishment cannot be reconciled with the goodness of God. We, however, are not here in a position to judge of the relation

[1] Matt. xiii. 41.

of sin to the whole moral universe, nor of what the equilibrium of mercy and justice—which is essential to the restoration of a moral system once disordered by sin—may require alike of the wisdom, the goodness, and the righteousness of God. And the only question now before us is, what did Christ teach? If He distinctly taught the eternal punishment of the wicked, then if upon speculative grounds we reject that doctrine, we cannot with propriety claim to be His disciples.

Much that Christ said concerning future punishment was in the form either of metaphor or of parable; and it has been aptly said, "If we are to turn rhetoric into logic, and build a dogma on every metaphor, our belief will be of a vague and contradictory character." But the metaphors and parables of Christ were intended to convey some substantial truth—the metaphor represented a corresponding reality, the figure had a basis of fact. Taken literally, His metaphors would neutralize one another;—"the outer *darkness*," and "the everlasting *fire;*" "the fire that never shall be quenched," would seem to mark the utter destruction of sentient being; while the "torments" of Dives, and the "worm that dieth not," suggest the consciousness of suffering. But shall we, therefore, infer that "hell" is altogether a figure of speech, and that these vivid pictures have no corresponding reality? The laws of language require us to understand from these very metaphors, that the future state of the ungodly will be one of conscious and irremediable misery—the "darkness" of banishment from God, the "unquenchable fires" of memory, the "undying worm" of remorse—a state of mental anguish pre-figured by physical emblems, which neither the imagination of Dante nor of Milton could fully interpret, neither the pencil of Tintoretto, of Michael Angelo, nor of Doré could worthily represent. The emblems of future punishment used by Christ were not like the material images that painters and poets have addressed to the eye and the imagination, but were designed to suggest realities in spiritual experience too awful for fancy to dwell upon. These address themselves to the soberest judgment, and with a higher solemnity as proceeding from the lips of the compassionate Son of God.

Moreover, Christ did not always speak of future punishment in words of metaphor. He used no figure of speech, no terms of rhetoric, when in closing His description of the last judgment, He said with the simple directness of a judicial sentence—"These shall go away into everlasting punishment; but the righteous into life eternal:"[1]—$Εἰς$ $κόλασιν$ $αἰώνιον$ on the one hand, $εἰς$ $ζωήν$ $αἰώνιον$ on the other. The term $κόλασις$ means strictly not destruction, annihilation, but chastisement or punishment; thus the Sanhedrim threatened Peter and John, and let them go, "finding nothing how they might *punish* them,"[2] $κολάσωνται$: it sometimes denotes the apprehension of pain and suffering;—thus "fear hath *torment*,"[3] $κόλασιν$. The Septuagint uses this word to describe a variety of punishments inflicted upon the wicked, both individually, and as communities or nations. Thus, to the house of Israel it was said "Repent; so iniquity shall not be your ruin"— $κόλασιν$:[4] and again, to be "tormented by beasts" was a $κόλασις$.[5] Plato in his Gorgias uses the word in its primitive sense of *pruning* or *restraining;* thus—"Is not to restrain one from what he desires to *punish* him?" $κολάζειν$, and "to *punish* the soul ($κολάζεσθαι$) is therefore better than unrestrained indulgence."[6] Again, he says, "no one *punishes* ($κολάζω$) the unjust because he has been unjust, but for the sake of the future, that he may not again do unjustly."[7] It is plain from both Biblical and Classical usage that $κόλασις$ has no affinity with annihila-

---

[1] Matt. xxv. 46.   [2] Acts iv. 21.   [3] 1 John iv. 18.   [4] Ezek. xviii. 30.
[5] Wisdom xvi. 2.   [6] Gorgias 505 B., and C.   [7] Protagoras, 324, B.

tion, but denotes a punishment the subject of which continues conscious under its infliction.

Will then the punishment inflicted upon the ungodly at the last judgment be of a disciplinary nature, having in view their reformation and their final restoration to the estate of the good? This view is precluded by the term αἰώνιον—the punishment will be "eternal." This word, indeed, is sometimes used vaguely for "duration," whether indefinite or limited; an Æon however protracted may still have a definite end. But the Greek language has no other word that so fully and properly expresses that which is unlimited as to duration; it is used by Plato for the ceaseless course of things as contrasted with the limitations of time; and in the New Testament αἰώνιος is the word that expresses the eternity of God's being and the everlasting felicity of the righteous. And in the words now under consideration, the two states of "life" and "punishment" are made to run parallel in an endless duration; "these shall go away into punishment αἰώνιον, but the righteous into life αἰώνιον. It is impossible here to limit in the one case that which is unlimited in the other. If we believe that the life promised by Christ to the righteous shall last forever, then are we shut up to the literal meaning of His alternative words; and when we consider what it must be to go away from Christ, to go away from His love, His glory, His blessed presence; to go away under His condemnation; all His dread imagery of wo—the "fire," the "darkness," the "tormenting flame," the "undying worm" —is justified by this final sentence, "These shall go away into everlasting punishment." [1]

---

[1] See the Author's *Love and Penalty ;* also Appendix iii.

CHAPTER XVIII.

MANY a reader of the last chapter may be ready to say " this is an hard saying, who can hear it." But Jesus uttered many sayings that seemed hard to minds but little exercised in spiritual things; and of just such hard unbearable words He said, " They are spirit and they are life." [1]

All the teachings of Christ were spiritual in their intent, and as such were a life-power to the soul. Never touching upon philosophy, physics, or political economy, He addressed Himself throughout to the spiritual nature of man, with a view to reviving, ennobling, sanctifying this, and hence His words were not merely instruction, counsel, knowledge, doctrine, but Life. Christ was the most spiritual of teachers, and His doctrine both has vitality in itself and gives life to them that receive it.

The same is true of the Sacrament that He instituted to perpetuate Himself in the memory of His disciples ; this is the embodiment of a Truth that is Life in proportion as it is spiritually received—" The words that I speak unto you are spirit and are life." This was said of the words He had just spoken concerning eating His flesh and drinking His blood, as the means of dwelling in Him, and of obtaining spiritual and eternal life. He had described Himself as the " bread of God," [2] the " bread of life," [3] the " true bread from heaven," [4] " the living bread which came down from heaven ;" [5] and had said, " If any man eat of

[1] John vi. 63. [2] John vi. 33. [3] v. 35. [4] v. 32. [5] v. 51.

237

this bread, he shall live forever." [1]   The bread He then defined more literally as His *flesh*, which He would give for the life of the world.

These sayings caused much perplexity to the Jews, who at length broke out into a strife about His doctrine as unnatural and absurd, saying " How can this man give us His flesh to eat?" [2]   But instead of toning down or explaining away His words, Jesus made them even more literally sensuous than before: saying " Except ye *eat* the flesh of the Son of man, and *drink* His blood, ye have no life in you; whoso eateth My flesh, and drinketh My blood, hath eternal life; and I will raise him up at the last day. For My flesh is meat indeed, and My blood is drink indeed. He that eateth My flesh and drinketh My blood, dwelleth in Me and I in him :" [3] and then as if to challenge their captious criticism to the utmost, He put the doctrine in this bald statement, " He that *eateth* ME, even He shall live by Me." [4]

Even His disciples were troubled by such words; and " many said, this is a hard saying, Who can hear it?" [5] Jesus perceiving their murmurings, said, " Doth this offend you? What and if ye shall see the Son of Man ascend up where He was before?" [6] The resurrection and ascension of Christ would confirm His statement that He came down from heaven, and would show also that He had within Himself the power of life; the witnesses of those events would understand the spiritual meaning of His words and the spiritual value of his death. And hence there was a life-power in the words He had just spoken, when they were spiritually apprehended.

It will be easier to understand His use of this bald, almost sensuous literalism about eating His flesh and drinking His blood, if we bear in mind how extensively the language of spiritual ideas is based upon sensible objects, and how

[1] John vi. 51.   [2] vi. 52.   [3] vi. 53, 57.   [4] vi. 57.   [5] vi. 60.   [6] vi. 62.

naturally the mind when seeking a strong expression for a spiritual truth, in order to present it more vividly and effectively, seizes upon something in nature as its symbol, and teaches the inward by the outward. " Words are signs of natural facts. The outer creation gives us language for the beings and changes of the inward creation. Every word which is used to express a moral or intellectual fact, if traced to its root, is found to be borrowed from some material appearance. *Right* means *straight; wrong* means *twisted.* We say the *heart* to express emotion, the *head* to denote thought. An enraged man is a lion, a cunning man is a fox, a firm man is a rock, a learned man is a torch. A lamb is innocence: a snake is subtile spite. Light and darkness are our familiar expression for knowledge and ignorance, and heart for love. Thus words are fastened to visible things ; and the moment our discourse rises above the ground line of familiar facts, and is inflamed with passion or exalted by thought, it clothes itself in images taken from nature." [1]

In this view our Lord's saying, so far from being hard and mysterious was as natural as it was forcible. He was dealing with men who were carnal in their feelings and desires; who followed Him for the excitement of seeing His miracles and for the present benefit they hoped to receive from these. " Ye seek Me, because ye did eat of the loaves and were filled." It was in vain to talk to such men about the superiority of spiritual ideas and aims to carnal desires, or of the spiritual design of His mission, the thing must be put before them baldly at their own level ; and the spiritual conveyed to them in the form of bodily figures. And so Jesus said to them, You must eat the true bread ; it is not enough that you see what I do and hear what I say ; you are to be saved by receiving Me ; you must take Me as I am, you must eat Me.

[1] R. W. Emerson, *Essay on Language.*

Neander has given an interpretation of these words, which accords equally well with the uses of metaphor by Christ, and with the spiritual philosophy that pervaded His teaching. "Jesus tells the Jews that He would give them *a* bread which was to impart life to the world; hence that the bread which He *was about* to *give* was, in a certain sense, different from the bread which He *was;* different, that is, from His whole self-communication. *And the bread which I will give is my flesh.* This bread was to be the self-sacrifice of His bodily life for the salvation of mankind. The life-giving power, *as such*, was His Divine-human existence; the life-giving power, *in its special act*, was His self-sacrifice. The two are inseparable; the latter being the essential *means* of realizing the former; only by His self-sacrifice could His Divine-human life become the bread of life for men.

"The Jews wilfully perverted these words of Christ into a carnal meaning; and therefore He repeated and *strengthened* them : *Except ye eat the flesh of the Son of Man :—* 'except ye receive My Divine-human life within you, make it as your own flesh and blood, and become thoroughly penetrated by the Divine principle of life, which Christ has imparted to human nature and Himself *realized* in it, ye cannot partake of eternal life.'

"When He had left the synagogue, and was standing among persons who, up to that time, had been His constant attendants, He said, 'I have spoken to you of eating My flesh; *doth this offend you?* What then will you say when the Son of Man will ascend into heaven? You will then see Me no more with your bodily eyes; but *yet* it will be necessary for you to eat my flesh and drink my blood, which then, in a carnal sense, will be plainly impossible.' It is obvious, therefore, that Christ meant no material participation in His flesh and blood, but one which would have its fullest import and extent at the time specified.

" He then naturally passes on to explain the spiritual import of His life-streaming words. It is the spirit that giveth life ; the flesh is nothing ; hence I could not have meant a sensible eating of My flesh and blood, but the appropriation of My spirit, as the life-giving principle, as this communicates itself through My manifestation in flesh and blood. As My words are only the medium through which the Spirit of life that gushes forth from Me is imparted, they can be rightly understood only so far as the Spirit is perceived in them." [1] Such is the true significance of eating the flesh of Christ, and drinking His blood.

These words do not countenance that literal sensuous view of the Sacrament which is given in the notion of the real presence or transubstantiation taught by the Roman Catholic Church. That doctrine is that " our Lord Jesus Christ, true God and man, is truly, really, and substantially contained in the sacrament of the holy eucharist after the consecration of the bread and wine, and under the form of these sensible objects." By the priestly act of consecration, or by some miraculous influence which attends that act, it is claimed that " the whole substance of the bread is converted into the substance of the body of Christ our Lord, and the whole substance of the wine into the substance of His blood." [2]

[1] *Life of Jesus Christ,* by Augustus Neander, Am. Ed. pp. 267–269.

[2] The Council of Trent, in the Decree of Session xiii. *De sanctissimo Euchar-istiæ Sacramento,* has declared it to be the binding faith of the Church, "that immediately after the consecration, the true body of our Lord, and His true blood, together with His soul and divinity, do exist under the species of bread and wine; His body under the species of bread, and His blood under the species of wine, by virtue of the words of consecration; His body also under the species of wine, and His blood under the species of bread, and His soul under each species, (through that natural connection and concomitance by which all the parts of Christ our Lord, who has risen from the dead, no

16

This notion is based upon a literal interpretation of such sayings as these: "This is My body, which is broken for you;" "This cup is the New Testament in My blood;" and again, "My flesh is meat indeed, and My blood is drink indeed." But such an interpretation supposes physical impossibilities and absurdities which would make nonsense of the words of Christ; such as that, He while sitting before them a living man in His proper flesh and blood, was at the same instant present as to His body in the bread, and as to His blood in the wine; or that He who is now absent as to His body in heaven is yet present in body in the sacrament, so that His body yet remaining in heaven is at the same moment created anew in ten thousand places upon earth, or wherever the sacrament is observed. It is idle to class this pretense among miracles, for no miracle of our Lord ever involved a contradiction in the nature of things. His language does not call for any such interpretation. He said, "I am the *door*." "I am the *light* of the world." "I am the true *vine*;" and pre-Raphaelites have attempted to depict Him under these various symbols; yet no one dreams of taking such expres-

more to die, are closely joined together);—and even His divinity is there also, through the wonderful and hypostatical union thereof with His body and soul." *Cap.* iii.

By this it is taught that the *substance* of the bread and the wine completely disappear—only the *species* or appearance of either remaining—and that under this is the real substance of the Lord Jesus Christ, body and blood, soul and divinity. Whoever shall deny this, or shall affirm that Christ is present, "only in a sign and figure, or by His power" is declared accursed.

Dr. Moehler, one of the most able and judicious expounders of the Roman Catholic faith, says, "Catholics firmly hold that Almighty God who was pleased at Cana, in Galilee, to convert water into wine, changes the inward substance of the consecrated bread and wine into the body and blood of Christ. This belief in the real presence of Christ in the Eucharist, forms the basis of our whole conception of the mass. Without that presence, the solemnity of the Lord's Supper is a mere reminiscence of the sacrifice of Christ, exactly in the same way as the celebration by any society, of the anniversary of some esteemed individual, whose image it exhibits to view, or some other symbol, recalls to mind his beneficent actions." *Symbolism,* § xxxiv.

sions literally. The Church is His body; do we, then, eat the Church in the sacrament?

The Jews rebelled against Christ's doctrine of His flesh and blood, because they insisted on taking it literally and making it absurd. But Jesus said of these very words, They are spirit and life; you must look beneath the form for the meaning.

But they should not be pressed so far in the opposite direction as to take away from the sacrament its real basis and force as a symbol. A highly respectable body of Christians—the Society of Friends—reject altogether the outward sacraments of baptism and the Lord's Supper, and regard the baptism of the Spirit, and a spiritual communing with Christ by meditation, as all that Jesus intended to be preserved among His disciples. But how shall we then account for the solemnity with which, at the last Passover, He took the bread and the cup, and with prayer and thanksgiving set these forth as symbols and memorials of His body and blood, and said to His disciples, " *This* do in remembrance of me." [1] This surely meant that they should go on to do as He then did; that is, should set apart bread and wine as a memorial.

The disciples acted upon this from the day of the Lord's death; and the Apostle Paul, while correcting some abuses that had crept into the observance of the Supper, recognizes the sacrament itself as appointed by Christ to be perpetual in the outward form of it, and not simply a spiritual communion. He recalls the formula by which our Lord instituted the Supper, and repeats with emphasis His injunction, "This do in remembrance of Me." [2] Clearly then what Jesus said concerning the spiritual meaning of His words was not meant to supersede a service which He established with so much solemnity in the form of it. That were to spiritualize into nonentity. There are other

[1] Luke xxii. 19.   [2] 1 Cor. xi. 24.

bodies of Christians, who while they keep up the observance of the Lord's Supper, make this simply a memorial
of the fact of His dying, and attach no sacrificial meaning
to the death.   These understand His reply to the Jews as
refining the whole transaction of the cross into an heroic
martyrdom for the truth, which was destined to exert a
spiritual influence upon mankind, but had nothing of the
sacramental or redemptive quality which belonged to the
sacrifice under the Old Testament.   This view takes the
extreme point of opposition to the Roman Catholic doctrine of sacrifice, as the view of the Friends is at the
extreme of opposition to form.

These three views have points of analogy as well as of
contrast.   That of the Roman Catholic Church makes
much of the form, because the purport of the sacrament
is to transform the bread and wine into the body and
blood of Christ.   Opposed to this is the view which—to
get rid of so gross a superstition—does away with the form
altogether, and would trust the remembrance of Christ
entirely to the heart without external signs, and would
seek communion with Christ solely in and through the spirit.

Again, the Roman Catholic view makes the sacrament a
literal repetition of the sacrifice of Jesus upon the cross,
and therefore holds up the consecrated wafer for adoration.
Protesting against this idolatry, the third view mentioned
goes to the extent of denying any sacrificial meaning to
the sacrament, and keeps it up in form only as a memorial,
just as one observes a birth-day festival, or any other form
of commemoration.   It is a memorial but not a *symbol.*

Now each of these views results from pressing to an extreme particular words or phrases uttered by Christ, without regard to other expressions which have equal authority
and significance, and which must be considered in making
up a complete view of His doctrine of the sacrament.   He
did say, " Except ye eat of the flesh of the Son of Man

and drink His blood, ye have no life in you, for My flesh is meat indeed, and My blood is drink indeed;" and directly after, He said, "It is the Spirit that quickeneth; the flesh profiteth nothing; the words that I speak unto you, they are spirit, and they are life." These two sayings qualify and interpret each other. The second does not annul the first by depriving it of all meaning; Jesus did not intend by this, You must take my words entirely in a spiritual sense, and thus attach no significance to the terms flesh and blood. Why did He repeat these words so often, and with such solemnity of impression, if they were to be set aside as absolutely of no account? What He said was, "There is a spiritual life *in* these words that I have spoken;" and therefore we should neither take them grossly as a literal eating of flesh and blood, nor set them aside for some refined spiritual conception which has no relation to such eating and drinking; but we must get out of these very words the spiritual life that is in them; these very words that speak of eating His flesh, and drinking His blood, *are* "spirit and life," when one takes them rightly. They teach that the Lord Jesus gave His flesh, His life for the life of the world; His death was a sacrifice as the means of life and salvation.[1] But this sacrifice does not take effect for any individual from the mere fact of its having been offered; it does not stand simply as an event of history, to exert a moral influence upon mankind: but it gives life to him who eats and drinks it;—that is, to him who appropriates it to his own case *as the provision upon which the life of his soul depends*—just as the life of the body depends upon food and drink. He who so receives the death of Christ—makes this application of that death as the necessary means of his soul's life—will find that Christ becomes to him as his very flesh and blood.

The death of Christ was a literal, physical event: there

[1] See Chap. V.

is no doubting that fact, and the glorious truth of the resurrection depends upon it.   But this death did not come
in the course of nature, nor merely as a consequence of natural laws; neither was it simply an effect of human violence: for Jesus laid down his life: [1] suffered Himself to
be put to death; and in the discourse under review He
said, "The bread that I will give is My flesh, which I will
give for the life of the world."   This made His death a
sacrifice.   He gave His life, and by that giving brought
life to the world.   But the practical benefit of the sacrifice
can be had only by accepting it as a sacrifice in our stead;
by appropriating it with a full heart as the means of life;
and this it is to *eat* Christ, so that His life becomes ours.
Hence the stress laid upon receiving the *life* of His sacrifice.   "The flesh profiteth nothing."   It is of no avail to
belong to the body of Christ—the church—unless the
soul is a partaker of His life.   There are benefits from
church membership to one who is truly a disciple; but
membership in the church gives no warrant of salvation,
and will rather be a hindrance if made, in any wise, a substitute for Christ.   "He that eateth Me shall live by Me."
Hence the virtue of the sacrament is found only in feeding
upon Christ.   It is not "he that eateth this material
bread," but "he that eateth Me;" not eateth Me in the bread
but who in the act of eating the bread brings *Me* home to his
soul as his food, his life, his portion, his salvation.   Hence
the very essence of the sacrament consists in the doctrine
of Christ that it embodies, and which through an expressive sign-language, it brings to the soul as its spiritual life.
The Doctrine is the true Sacrament.

If in coming to this sacrament we realize through it the
nearness and the fulness of Christ, if we thereby receive
afresh into our hearts His living truth and grace, then do
we feed upon Him.   As we speak of devouring a book

[1] John x. 15, 17, 18.

whose thoughts please us, devouring the letter of a friend, devouring that friend himself in an extasy of love, so we take Christ into our hearts and feed upon Him and thereby receive new strength of spiritual life.

Food and drink fill and satisfy. They make blood and tissue ; they sustain life, and fill our corporeal nature with the sense of satisfaction. So the doctrine of redemption embodied in the sacrament fills our souls with life from Christ. He is the life; He gave Himself to be our life ; and so completely does His life enter into us by faith, that it becomes to us the eternal life, swallowing up death itself in the fulness of His resurrection. He who has ascended up where He was before—the living, reigning Son of Man— will lift us up to the same life and glory, if we will truly keep His sacraments. The words that He speaks unto us are Spirit and are Life.

CHAPTER XIX.

" I HAVE given unto them the words which Thou gavest Me; and they have received them, and have known surely that I came out from Thee, and they have believed that Thou didst send Me." [1] Such was the testimony of Christ to the source of His doctrine and to the quality of discipleship. " The Words which *Thou* gavest Me." So Jesus constantly affirmed that His teaching was an express communication from God, to be therefore received as having divine authority. He did not evolve from His own brain a system of doctrine, and after thirty years of reflection in His quiet village home—in communion neither with books nor men, but with His own soul, with nature, and with God—announce this as a new theology for the world : but from the beginning of His teaching He said, " My doctrine is not Mine, but *His* that sent Me." " If any man will do His will, he shall know of the doctrine, whether it be of God, or whether I speak of Myself." [2] While He spake only that which He Himself knew to be the truth, this knowledge was not the mere conviction of logic, nor simply the intuition of His human consciousness, but " as My Father hath taught Me," He said, " I speak these things." [3] " I have not spoken of Myself, but the Father which sent Me, He gave Me a commandment, what I should say and what I should speak: and I know that His commandment is life everlasting:

[1] John xvii. 8.   [2] John vii. 17.   [3] John viii. 28.

whatsoever I speak therefore, even as the Father said unto Me, so I speak." [1] In thus claiming to speak the mind of God, Jesus asserted much more than the general accordance of His teaching with divine truth—such an accordance as might be shown by comparison and inference —He meant that He spake directly as the mouth of God; not commissioned, merely, to deliver a message, nor inspired to perceive and utter certain truths, but having such a union with God and such a knowledge of God, that the mind of God found expression through His words, the voice of God uttered itself through His lips. "The words that I speak unto you, I speak not of Myself; but the Father that dwelleth in Me, He doeth the works. The word which ye hear is not Mine, but the Father's which sent Me." [2] "The peculiar import of His doctrine," says Neander, "consists in its relations to Himself as a part of His self-revelation, an image of His unoriginated and inherent life. His power lay in the impression which His manifestation and life as the incarnate God produced; and *this* could never have been derived from without."

What Jesus constantly declared to men concerning the source of His teachings, He reaffirmed when summing up His life in the solemn act of prayer to the. Father. "I have manifested Thy Name unto the men whom Thou gavest Me out of the world: Thine they were, and Thou gavest them Me; and they have kept Thy word. Now they have known that all things whatsoever Thou hast given Me are of Thee. For I have given unto them *the words* which Thou gavest Me;" [3] and again, "I have given them *Thy word*." [4] What Jesus taught was the absolute, the infallible, the authoritative truth of God —this, and nothing short of this; this, and nothing else than this.

But the question here arises, How fully did Christ present

[1] John xii. 49. [2] John xiv. 10, 24. [3] John xvii. 6, 7. [4] John xvii. 14.

the truth of God? To what extent did He convey to men the truth that God would have them to know, for the right improvement of the present life, and for salvation in the life to come? That He omitted to speak of many subjects concerning which we are curious and anxious to be informed, the heart knows too well which has gone to His word with troubled questionings about its future, only to meet there a new demand upon its faith. But was this omission of accident or of design? Was it owing to some limitation upon His knowledge, or to the brevity of His life, or the lack of opportunity? or was it a purposed withholding according to the will of God? Had Jesus lived say ten or twenty years longer, may we infer that He would have thought out some subjects more fully and have expanded these in His discourses? or that occasion would have arisen for discoursing upon topics now left untouched? or that in any way He would have added to the sum and substance of the truth that He actually declared? In other words, did He die before He had communicated *everything* to mankind that the Father intended to reveal by Him when He brought His first-begotten into the world? Would the prolongation of the life and ministry of Christ have afforded any solution of problems and mysteries now left unsolved?

Take for instance three questions,—which perhaps more than any others have occupied the speculative theology of the Church, and tasked the faith of individual believers.

(*a.*) What is the nature of God and how stand the Father and the Son related to this nature in common? Jesus coming from the bosom of the Father declared Him, "manifested" Him, and taught the oneness of the Father and the Son:—but the metaphysical conception of the divine essence and unity He never touched upon, nor would He have enlightened us in that direction had He continued to preach for thirty years. "All things," said

He, "are delivered unto Me of My Father; and no man knoweth the Son, but the Father, neither knoweth any man the Father, save the Son, and He to whomsoever the Son will reveal Him."[1] But while Jesus did reveal the Father morally and spiritually, He gave no answer to the questions which metaphysical theology is evermore raising concerning the essence of God and the consubstantiality of the Son with the Father : and this because such questions did not lie within the purport of the mission for which God sent Him into the world.

(b.) Take next the question of Christ's second coming—the time of it and the manner of His kingdom—questions which in every succeeding age have agitated the Church, and divided its faith. Such questions our Lord expressly declined to answer ; saying to His over-curious disciples, " It is not for you to know the times or the seasons which the Father hath put in His own power."[2]

(c) And once more, how reticent He was upon the whole class of questions that come thronging into the mind, in view of death and the hereafter—those exciting, perplexing, agonizing questions: Where *is* the spirit? Does it yet know me? Shall we meet, and know, and love again? How naturally could all such questions have been answered by our Lord as He conversed of the death of Lazarus, and when He stood by his grave ; but concerning the physical or metaphysical conditions of existence after death both His lips and the lips of Lazarus were sealed, while yet He proclaimed to the whole dying race of man, " I am the resurrection and the life—he that believeth in me, though he were dead, yet shall he live."[3]

The revelation of Christ then was not abbreviated by His opportunities, by His death, nor by any known limitation whatsoever. The Scriptural view of His mission gives no reason to suspect that He failed to communicate any part of

[1] Matt. xi. 27.   [2] Acts i. 7.   [3] John xi. 25.

that truth of God which it had seemed good in the sight of the Father should be revealed ; but on the contrary we are told that the Lord Jesus did make known all that the Father would communicate to mankind with respect to their salvation from ruin unto life eternal. The revelation was perfected and completed in Him, and He could say, " *all* things that I have heard of my Father, I have made known unto you ;" and in His last prayer, Jesus, addressing His Father said, " I have finished the work which Thou gavest me to do." [1]

Prominent among the elements of His work was, proclaiming the truth of God, and bringing men into the kingdom of God through allegiance to that Truth. This is the undertone of that wonderful prayer [2] in which our Lord uttered His own conception of His mission, and—in what He had accomplished for His disciples, and what He supplicated on their behalf—declared He had finished the work that His Father had given Him to do. He had come into the world that He might recover men to God ;— the work of reconciliation, as to the form of it, would be consummated by His death :—this He had foreshadowed in His discourse to His disciples, and this finishing stroke was about to be given to the life and doctrine of the Son of God. But while His death is present in His own thought as the finishing act by which the Son of man shall be glorified, and God shall be glorified in Him, that which Jesus makes prominent in His prayer is the *doctrine* of divine love and restoration, by whose renovating and sanctifying power He had gathered and yet would gather His Church into a blissful oneness of life, in Himself and the Father.

He had glorified the Father by bringing men out of the power of the world, sin and death, into that true spiritual life which shall be eternal ; but this He now defines to be—

[1] John xvii. 4.   [2] John xvii.

knowing the only true God and Jesus Christ—knowing
with that knowledge which makes its object real, and receives it into the life as a possession and a power. This
knowledge Jesus had imparted by manifesting the Father
to His disciples; giving unto them the words that the
Father had given Him; and the proof of the divine life in
them was, that they had received this word of God and
kept it. He prayed that they might be sanctified and perfected through this same word of truth; and closed His
petition with the words, "O righteous Father the world
hath not known Thee; but I have known Thee, and these
have known that Thou hast sent me: and I have declared
unto them Thy name, and will declare it: that the love
wherewith Thou hast loved me may be in them, and I in
them."

This declaring the truth from God in such wise as to
bring men into a true life in the knowledge and the love
of God, was so integral and vital in the work of Christ
that He gave it to Pilate in evidence of His royal commission : "Art thou a *King?*"—"To this end was I born,
and for this cause came I into the world, that I should
bear witness unto the truth;"[1] and having set up the
kingdom of truth in believing souls, to be perpetuated
through their testimony, and by the power of the Holy
Ghost, Jesus could say to His Father, "I have glorified
Thee on the earth, I have finished the work which Thou
gavest Me to do."

The comprehensive completeness of the doctrine of
Christ in all that concerns the restoration of man to God,
his spiritual well-being and his eternal life, assures us
that as the Son of God sent to give light to the world, He
finished His work in His personal ministry upon earth.
All that the apostles did afterwards, under the guidance
of the Holy Spirit, all that the Church has since accom-

[1] John xviii. 37.

plished through her teaching ministry and her schools of theology, has been simply in the way of interpreting, unfolding, and applying that which Jesus Christ Himself gave in its substance, and with a germinating power capable of such expansion to the thought, and such application to the life of all after ages. "The teaching of Christ presented seeds and stimulants of thought. It must, therefore, by no means surprise us to find that the full import of most of His words was not comprehended by His contemporaries; such a result, indeed, was just what we might expect. He would not have been Son of God and Son of man, had not His words, like His works, with all their adaptation to the circumstances of the times, contained some things that were inexplicable; had they not borne concealed within them the germ of an infinite development, reserved for future ages to unfold. It is *this* feature which distinguishes Christ from all other teachers of men. Advance as they may, they can never reach Him; their only task need be, by taking Him more and more into their life and thought, to learn better how to bring forth the treasures that lie concealed in Him."[1] The study we have devoted to the doctrines of Christ, one by one, has prepared us to appreciate this, by now grouping these doctrines in various lights for a general survey of their range and bearing, their significance and moment, their thoroughness and depth, their practical scope and influence.

How comprehensive was the doctrine of Christ in the range of topics which it embraced, and in the bearing of these upon the supreme end of His mission—the recovery of man to holiness. All intelligent beings of whose existence we have any knowledge, or whose existence had been shadowed in the creations of poetry and philosophy—wherever found in the peopled realms of space—were brought within the range of His doctrine, in their rela-

[1] Neander: *Life of Jesus Christ,* ？ 65.

tion to man's spiritual condition, whether of sin and its
conflicts, or of salvation and its hopes. Man himself in
his personal character, his condition, his wants, his desires,
his aims, his temptations, his perils, his possibilities; man
in his relations to his fellows, to the community, to the
race; the angels as messengers of love, rejoicing over the
returning prodigal, witnessing the confession of the penitent, representing little children before the face of God in
heaven, bearing the child of God from want and wretched-
ness here to Abraham's bosom, attending upon the solemnities of the last judgment and welcoming the redeemed to
the glory of the Father; the devil and his angels cast out
from heaven, infesting the earth to possess the bodies and
the souls of men, and awaiting their malignant triumph in
the condemned of the last day;—God in His supremacy
as Creator, Lord and Judge of all; in the infinitude of
His presence and the plenitude of His power; in His spiritual nature as the object of worship; in His holiness to
be revered, in His paternal bounty to be praised and loved;
in His gracious nearness as the hearer of prayer: in the
habitation of His glory, prepared for the home of His
children;—God in the mysterious unfolding of Himself
through the only begotten Son, and the Holy Comforter,
while yet He retains the ineffable oneness of His being—
this immense scale of existence from lowest to highest, and
from worst to best, was all covered by the doctrine of
Christ, bringing the whole moral universe into relations of
good or evil with mankind. And as all beings, so too
all worlds were brought within the compass of His doctrine;—this world with all its creatures, as under God's
providential care; the world of spirits, subject to His control; the world of the dead, obedient to His voice; and
that yet more intangible, impenetrable sphere, where spiritual influences act upon the thoughts and the hearts of
men, to enlighten and sanctify, or to delude and destroy.

And as with all beings and all worlds, so with all periods of duration—these were brought into the doctrine of Christ so far as related to the main question of human redemption. The history of this world as a preparation for Him of whom Moses and the prophets did testify; the unwritten history of that kingdom prepared before the foundation of the world, known to Him whose consciousness went back to the glory of the Father before the world was; the coming ages to be illumined by His gospel, the nations to be made His disciples, the end of the world, the raising of the dead, the judgment, and the eternal state and destinies beyond, these all were brought in line within the doctrine of Christ. What other teacher—even though enlightened by His guidance—has taken such a grasp upon all being, all time, all worlds, and gathering within His thought all things visible and invisible—heaven, earth, hades, hell, the eternity before the world was, the ages gone, the ages to come, and the eternity beyond—has converged and concentrated all upon the focus of man's restoration to his true position in this vast circle of beings, powers, ages, worlds?

The completeness of the Revelation in Christ appears also in the significance and moment of His doctrines. All truth is important to be known; all knowledge has some value and use for its possessor; and he who makes any discovery, settles any fact, establishes any principle, not only enriches himself, but is in some particular a benefactor of mankind; and the reward of discovering truth, the advantage of acquiring knowledge, is a stimulus to that application of the mental powers which is itself a benefit of no mean value. But were the question one of sending a messenger from heaven clothed with divine wisdom and authority, to communicate to men a knowledge of truth as known absolutely to God, there would be a choice among truths, in respect both of subjects and the manner of imparting knowledge. Were one invited to an evening with a distinguished scholar, poet, artist, he would not care to hear him talk of the weather, of the Pacific Rail-road, the Cabinet, or the financial policy of the country, but would crave to hear from him something upon that which he knew so much better than any one else. One would not wish Plato to talk about the climate, nor Shakspeare about the crops, nor Raphael about the currency, nor would it be worth while an angel's coming to converse for an hour upon any problem of physical or mental science—the squaring of the circle or the law of the association of ideas. There are things of so much higher moment upon which he might enlighten us from a knowledge unattainable by man, that to occupy his discourse with our human science and affairs were below the dignity of his mission. The value of truth is relative in respect to the subjects, the occasion, the opportunity; and that which for the moment seems of absorbing interest, may dwindle to nothingness in presence of some illustrious person about to speak upon the highest themes.

Suppose now the Son of God, having in full, clear vision, all truth, all knowledge, all wisdom, to have come into the world for the purpose of giving light to men:—of what should He speak? What themes, what doctrines and lessons, would be worthy of so stupendous a miracle, so ineffable a mystery as this divine incarnation? Should He speak of the destruction of that Roman Empire that then ruled the world? of the rising in after times of another empire whose victorious Cæsar should sweep the fields of conquest from the Tagus to the Tiber, from the Rhine to the Moskwa? Should He announce the discovery of America, the invention of printing, the rail-way, the telegraph? Should He lay down a science of government and of political economy for the regulation of human society, or a philosophy of the mind in respect to sensation,

17

reflection, consciousness, intuition? But knowledge such
as this, so important and useful in regard to earthly interests, was sure to come, in the progress of events, under
the stimulus of necessity or the opportunity of research,
bringing with it a healthful development of the race by
the very act of investigation and discovery.

There were questions deeper, broader, higher, for the solution of which the wisdom of ages was unequal, but which
the Son of God could illumine with a word. With what
feeling does God look upon man a sinner? How can the
just and holy God, offended in His justice and holiness by
the impiety of men, be approached with hope of favor?
How can a man be just with God? How rise to intercourse
with the Father of his spirit? How escape the condemnation that he knows is over him, that he feels within
him? How find entrance to the paradise of purity, peace,
and love which is still the dream and hope of a fallen
world? How meet death and that which is after death?

Questions such as these, of the restoring and perfecting
of the soul that shall outlast all empires and all ages, were
the questions to be answered when the Son of God stood
face to face with a sinful dying world, to speak the words
that had been given Him of the Father. And questions
of such infinite moment filled the thought of Christ and
imparted to His discourses a fulness of significance and
value that can pertain to no wisdom of man. In the
supreme matter of man's recovery to God, to holiness and
heaven, no point is left untouched, no question unsolved.

The completeness of Christ's teaching appears further,
in the thoroughness and depth of His doctrines. He laid
the axe at the root of the tree: He drove the plowshare
down under the soil. He did not talk of the overturning
of the Roman empire; He overturned it by the principles
which He set in motion against its oppressions, its vices,
its crimes. He did not furnish a philosophy of social

order; He reconstructed society by a few simple truths concerning the individual, the family, the neighbor, the state, the Church. He did not deliver a treatise on trade or political economy, but He gave rules that rendered injustice, fraud, dishonesty impossible within His kingdom and disgraceful outside of it. What He taught took hold upon the innermost thoughts, feelings, passions, motives, imaginations of the human heart, to work there a revolution deep and radical. And His doctrines still confront the soul as a finality in respect to its character, its needs, its duties and its hopes. These words of Christ strike the soul with awe, for by them it shall be judged. Not all the volumes of moral science written since His days, not all the legislation of united Christendom, could weigh upon us with so much of authority as we feel in the few little sentences of the Sermon on the Mount.

From the survey we have now taken, how comprehensive is the doctrine of Christ. The word of Christ is that God is a Spirit—to be worshipped therefore in spirit and in truth; that He is holy—and therefore to be glorified by the fruits of holiness in the lives of men; that He is a Father, and therefore to be approached with filial faith in prayer, to be acknowledged with filial gratitude in all the blessings of life, and to be trusted, with a filial confidence, under all trials and cares.

The word of Christ is that the heart of man is sinful; that out of it as from a fountain flow all corrupt and bitter streams; that from it as a root proceed all evil and bitter fruits: and, therefore, that man must be born again, and made pure from within or he cannot see God.

The word of Christ is that He was with the Father in His glory before the world was; that He and the Father are one; that by virtue of His original divine nature, He has all power in heaven and in earth, the power of life and of death, power to forgive sins. The word of Christ is that this eternal Son of God, came into the world to seek and to save that which was lost;—came, sent by the Father's love; came, not to condemn the world but that the world through Him might be saved. The word of Christ is that He draws men to Himself by being lifted up upon the cross; that He gave His flesh, that is His life, for the life of the world; that, like the corn of wheat, He must die in order that the fruit of His coming might appear.

The word of Christ is that He is the resurrection and the life; and that whoso believeth on Him shall not perish but have everlasting life, and shall be raised up at the last day. The word of Christ is that He, the Son of Man, shall come again in the glory of the Father, to judge the world; that He will raise the dead; that He will separate the sheep from the goats; that they who by faith have lived righteously, shall be blessed of His Father and welcomed to His kingdom; but they who have been unbelieving and unrighteous shall go away into everlasting punishment. All this body of truth is the word of Christ.

If we formulate Christ's teachings as *doctrines;* we find here the doctrine of God's spiritual essence, of His absolute perfection, of His infinite love; the doctrine of the divine personality of Christ Himself; the doctrine of man's sinful and lost condition: the doctrine of the redemptive sacrifice of Jesus for the sin of the world; the doctrine of the new birth or regeneration by the Holy Spirit, as indispensable to our admission into the kingdom of heaven; the doctrine of the resurrection of the dead, of the general judgment and of the awards of life and of death, alike final and eternal. All the great doctrines known in theology as the doctrines of grace,—doctrines that revolve around the central truth of man's deliverance from sin and death and hell through the sacrifice of the Son of God—the doctrines of sin and reconciliation, of re-

pentance and faith, of pardon and salvation through the
cross of Jesus, of regeneration and sanctification through
the Spirit, of the resurrection of the dead and eternal judgment—these doctrines, stripped of technical phraseology
and of human philosophy, are the word of Christ.

The word of Christ is preceptive as well as doctrinal;
it is His word that we be humble and meek, merciful and
pure, peaceable and holy, prayerful and charitable; it is
the word of Christ that we seek righteousness and the
kingdom of God; it is the word of Christ that we love
one another, and do good unto all men; it is the word of
Christ that we glorify our Father in heaven through the
abounding fruits of righteousness.

The word of Christ is a word of promise also. It is
the word of Christ that He will send the Comforter to
teach, enlighten, console, and sanctify us: it is the word
of Christ that He and the Father will abide in the believing, gentle, loving soul; it is the word of Christ that in
the work of saving men through His gospel, He will be
with us alway even to the end of the world; it is the
word of Christ that whatsoever we ask the Father in His
name He will give it us: it is the word of Christ that
His peace shall be ours, and His joy shall be fulfilled in
us; it is the word of Christ that He will prepare a place
for us in His Father's house, and will come again and receive us to Himself.

All that the Gospel contains for our instruction in righteousness; for our elevation in character; for our consolation under trial; for our hope in the future; for our joy
and peace on earth, and our final felicity in heaven, is the
word of *Christ.*

The completeness of the revelation by Christ appears in
the practical scope and influence of His doctrines. In the
vast range covered by His teachings, while these touch at
intervals upon themes of thought the most abstruse and

matters most remote from human experience, there is yet nothing mystical, nothing speculative, nothing for mere abstract contemplation; but every doctrine, whether concerning man, angels, God, this world or that to come, takes right hold upon human life and character, upon duty here and destiny hereafter. Beginning with the heart, the personal soul, the individual life, the truth as Christ gave it works out into all the lines of human action, into all phases and conditions of society, into all business, all pleasure, all intercourse, all official place, all relationships, all plans and all obligations—past, present and to come. One can be nothing, do nothing, speak nothing, think nothing, to which this truth does not apply, with a commanding, a controlling power.

It is this comprehensive completeness of Christ's teaching in the essential point of character, that makes Him indeed the WAY, the TRUTH and the LIFE. As He came from God to lead us to God, and has pointed the way fully and clearly, nothing outside of Him can be the way. As He brought to us the words of the Father to light us up to God, there can be no truth proper or needful or useful for salvation, that is not embraced in His teachings. And as His light was the life of men, there can be no life apart from Him. To receive Christ as teacher is to receive Him in His fulness as the law of life, the way of salvation.

"This is the work of God, that ye believe on Him whom He hath sent;"[1]—this is the sum of faith and of duty. "I know not," says Schleiermacher, "where we can find any passage, even in the writings of the Apostles, which says so clearly and significantly, that all eternal life in men proceeds from nothing else than faith in Christ."

There can be no improvement upon Christianity as this was presented at the first by Christ. To say that *theology*, in the meaning of a human science of interpretation, and of

[1] John vi. 29.

logical definition and construction applied to the doctrines of Christianity, can be improved, is only to say that human imperfection, which mars whatever it touches, attaches to any system that man can frame, even though the materials furnished him be perfect and divine. But when men speak of outgrowing Christianity, of finding a truth more perfect, a way more simple, a salvation more complete, they might as well talk of dispensing with sunlight by some new patent of science for consuming the oils, gases or metals of the earth. The very truths purporting to be in-tuitions of consciousness, that are brought forth to supplant Christianity, are either unconsciously derived from Chris-tianity, or find in it full recognition and confirmation. As the strokes of the hammer that bound to its bed the last link of the Pacific Rail-road rang clear and musical upon the telegraphic bells all over the continent, proclaim-ing the way opened from sea to sea, so the words of Jesus, proceeding from the central point of human history—where this world was linked once more to heaven—vibrate through the ages, in every clime and tongue, making mu-sical the soul that listens for their coming. The words that the beloved disciple caught and treasured for such as had not seen the Lord and yet had believed, were written for us also, that we might believe that JESUS IS THE CHRIST, THE SON OF GOD ; and that believing we might have life through His name. [1]

[1] John xxi. 31.

APPENDIX I.

I. CHARACTERISTICS OF THE FOURTH GOSPEL.

THE Theology of Christ is largely derived from the Fourth Gospel, commonly known as the Gospel of John. This Gospel has certain peculiarities that distinguish it in a marked manner from the other three, commonly called the Synoptics. In the duration it assigns to the ministry of Jesus, in the number of His recorded visits to Jerusalem, in the date of the Last Supper, and in other minor points of detail, there are differences between the fourth Gospel and the Synoptics that have tasked the ingenuity of critics in arranging a harmony of the Gospels. These points are discussed at length in recent critical commentaries on John, and in learned and able monographs upon the genuineness of the fourth Gospel, but they are only incidental to the line of inquiry pursued in this volume.[1]

A more important distinction between the Fourth Gospel and the Synoptics is found in the style and subjects of the teaching of Christ, and in the representation of His person and character. In the Synoptics Jesus appears mainly as the Son of Man, who teaches moral truths and practical virtues by parables and sententious sayings. Even the sermon on the mount, though linked together by a subtile law of association and development, is a series of apothegms rather than a consecutive unfolding of doctrine. But in the Fourth Gospel, which opens with the doctrine of the Logos, Jesus appears more commonly as the Son of God, declaring and vindicating His Messiahship and His personal relations to the Father, and in extended discourses

---

[1] See Alford, *Com. on John;* Meyer's *Kom. über das Evang. des Johannes.* De Wette's *Kom. über das Evang. des Johannes.* Weiss, *Lehrbuch der Bib. Theologie des N. Testaments.* Bleek's *Einleitung in das N. T.* This standard work is now accessible in English, through Clark's "Foreign Theological Library;" it is distinguished by candor, learning and ability. De Groot, *Basilides als erster Zeuge für alter und autorität Neutestamentlicher Schriften, insbesondere des Johannesevangeliums;* and the Essays of Prof. George P. Fisher, D. D. on *the Supernatural Origin of Christianity.*—To these Essays, as well as to Bleek's Einleitung, I have been specially indebted in preparing this Appendix.

264

and dialogues setting forth the deepest doctrines of the spiritual life. This last feature has given rise to the theory that the author of the fourth Gospel was a Hellenic Christian, of the Alexandrine school, who constructed a fictitious life of Christ under the name of John, in order to give to his theological scheme the semblance of apostolical authority. A candid survey of the whole range of evidences, both internal and external, will, we think, show the falsity of this theory, and result in the conviction that the fourth Gospel was the work of the apostle John.

II. THE VIEW OF STRAUSS.

Strauss maintains that it is impossible to deduce the faith of Jesus from the fourth Gospel :—the tone of dogmatic assertion and of self-glorification in which Jesus there speaks of Himself and His relations to the Father, is incompatible with the historical representation of His character given by the Synoptics, and must have proceeded from an enthusiastic and posthumous worshiper of Jesus, who put his own Gnostic conceptions of the " Word " into the mouth of his divinized Master. [1]

From an examination of the external evidences relating to the first three Gospels, it results that, a little after the commencement of the second century, one finds certain traces, if not of their existence under their present form, at least of the existence of a great part of the materials that entered into their composition ; and moreover, the more ancient narratives had their origin in the very country which was the theater of the events which they recount. As to the fourth Gospel the results are far less favorable. This did not begin to be known until after the middle of the second century, and everything indicates that it had its origin in a foreign country, and under the influence of a philosophy unknown in the primitive Christian society. In the first three, in view of the interval of several generations between the events that they narrate and their definitive composition, the possibility of the addition of legendary and fabulous traits must be admitted ; in the fourth the alloy of philosophical speculation and meditative fiction is more than possible—it is probable.[2]

III. VIEW OF BAUR.

The strength of the negative criticism upon the fourth Gospel is concentrated in Dr. F. C. Baur, the acknowledged leader of the Tübingen School. Baur's conception is that the fundamental idea of

[1] Strauss *Das Leben Jesu* (1864) § 33.   [2] *Leben Jesu* (1864) § 13.

this Gospel, in the mind of its author, was to portray the unbelief of
the Jews, as the principle of darkness, opposing itself to the divine
principle of light and of life, incarnate in Jesus; and that its plan is
to follow out step by step the conflict of these two principles under
the form of an historical drama. He assigns its composition to the
epoch when Gnosticism and Montanism flourished, when the Church
attempted to defend herself at once from these two extreme tendencies,
and was agitated as to dogma, by the application of the idea of the
word to the person of Christ, and as to discipline, by the question of
the celebration of the Passover. Without any positive leanings, the
Gospel concluded within itself all the contrasts of its time, in one
central and higher conception, and hence was received with universal
favor by all parties. It was written about A. D. 160–170.

The author of this Gospel, strong in his own convictions, persuaded
that he knew better than the primitive evangelists—who were still
held in the prejudices of Judaism—the true spirit of Christianity and
of Christ, with entire good faith modified the evangelistic history,
accommodated it to the spirit of the time, and placed in the mouth of
Jesus discourses that corresponded with the evolution of the Christian
ideas; and confident of having penetrated and revealed to the world
the inner glory of Christ, he felt authorized, if not to declare it in
express terms, at least to let it be understood with sufficient clearness,
that he was the beloved disciple of Jesus.[1]

To sum up briefly the view of Baur, it is that "the fourth Gospel
was not written with an historical aim, but in advocacy of certain
doctrinal ideas; and the writer made use of the Gospel tradition
already before him, especially in the first three Gospels, in a very
free and arbitrary way. The author, who was not certainly a Jew
by birth, lived in Asia Minor, or more probably in Alexandria, in
the second century, at a time when the Church was agitated and
divided by conflicting parties, by the Gnostic controversies, by that
concerning the doctrine of the Logos, by that concerning Easter, and
by those of Montanism."[2]

IV. INTERNAL EVIDENCES.

Both Strauss and Baur have admitted the clearness, consistency,
and unity of the Fourth Gospel—that it is true to its own conception

---

[1] *Krit. Untersuchungen über die kanon. Evangelien* 1847, and *Theol. Jahr-
bücher* 1844, 1847, 1851, 1854.

[2] Condensed by Bleek. Int. § 63.

of Jesus and His mission—though they deny that either its doctrines or its miracles could be imputed to the Jesus of the Synoptical Gospels. But this denial is in both instances based upon a dogmatic assumption. It is *assumed* that the "Son of Man," who appears in the Synoptics setting forth in simple parables the practical relations of the kingdom of God to this world, could not also have uttered the lofty and somewhat mystical doctrines of the Fourth Gospel concerning the Son of God. Not to dwell here upon the marked diversity of method often found in the same teacher—which will be considered under the head of "style"—this assumption is set aside by the simple fact that "declarations of Christ are recorded in the Synoptics perfectly corresponding with what we find in John concerning the divine dignity of the Son of God, and His relation to the Father." Thus Matthew and Luke declare the intimate union of the Son with the Father in language exactly parallel to the type of such declarations in John : "All things are delivered unto me of my Father; and no man knoweth the Son but the Father; neither knoweth any man the Father, save the Son, and he to whomsoever the Son will reveal Him."[1] In showing how David had called Him Lord, He declared His pre-eminence and His pre-existence.[2] In giving His last commission to His disciples, He asserted the plenitude of His power and the perpetuity of His being; and at the same time conjoined Himself with the Father, upon equal terms, in the formula of baptism.[3] Before the Sanhedrim, in answer to the demand, "Tell us whether thou be the Christ, the Son of God," He acknowledged the title, and said "Hereafter shall ye see the Son of Man sitting on the right hand of' power, and coming in the clouds of heaven."[4] For this assertion of divine attributes He was charged with blasphemy and adjudged "guilty of death." The relation of His death to the life of the world was clearly announced in that saying, recorded by Matthew and Mark, "The Son of man came not to be ministered unto, but to minister, and to give His life a ransom for many."[5] Thus the germs of the most important doctrines of Christology embodied in the Fourth Gospel are found in the Synoptics; and that John, writing his Gospel at a later date, should have given greater prominence and amplitude to this class of Christ's sayings, was in accordance with that divine wisdom that evolves life in its highest organization from the simplest germ-cell.

---

[1] Mat. xi. 27, Luke x. 22, comp. John vi. 46 and x. 15.   [2] Mat. xxii. 41. Mark xii. 35. Luke xx. 41.   [3] Mat. xxviii. 18.   [4] Mat. xxvi. 63, 64.   [5] Mat. xx. 28 ; Mark x. 45.

The objection to the genuineness of the fourth Gospel from the miracles that it records, brings into a question of pure criticism a foreign element of dogmatic speculation, and is well met by Bleek. [1] "We must be content not to determine for ourselves beforehand, or à priori, how far the influence of God's Spirit may extend, or how far not; we must admit that it may operate not only on animate and human nature, but upon inanimate nature likewise. It is only self-deception to think that we can set up a barrier or line of demarcation, determining what miracles are possible and what impossible, or that it is by no means necessary to infer this from the character of the miracles themselves, trustworthily attested and recorded. It is quite unreasonable, on the ground merely that St. John's Gospel records miracles as wrought by Jesus, which do not come within our arbitrarily pre-conceived notion of a possible miracle, to deny to it that trustworthiness and historical genuineness which it so evidently possesses in so many points. It is not unimportant to observe that the accounts given of miracles in the fourth Gospel are comparatively rare, and by no means so frequent as in the Synoptics; and this should awaken in the minds of persons who so argue a pre-judgment in favor of St. John. In those cases, moreover, wherein a comparison can be instituted, the account given by St. John is much simpler than that in the Synoptics; and bearing in mind the comparatively late composition of the Gospel, this tells all the more in favor of the opinion that the writer was himself an eye-witness and participator." [2]

Robert Browning has well hit this nice balance in John's narrative between the faith that springs from love and the faith that comes only of miracles.

> "I fed the babe whether it would or no;
> I bid the boy or feed himself or starve.
> I cried once, 'That ye may believe in Christ,
> Behold, this blind man shall receive his sight!'
> 'Repeat that miracle and take my faith?'
> I say, that miracle was duly wrought
> When, save for it, no faith was possible.
> So faith grew, making void more miracles
> Because too much: they would compel, not help.
> I say, the acknowledgment of God in Christ
> Accepted by thy reason, solves for thee

---

[1] Introd. § 79.

[2] See the account of the walking on the sea, John v. 15; Matt. xiv. 22; Mark vi. 45; and of the voice from heaven, John xii. 24.

All questions in the earth and out of it,
And has so far advanced thee to be wise. [1]

The perfect accord between the doctrines and the miracles—the word of Jesus and His works—in the fourth Gospel, and the naturalness with which they supplement each other, is an evidence of the historical character of the Gospel.

The question of style in this Gospel as compared with the Synoptics need occasion no difficulty when we reflect how the same author or teacher may vary his style for different hearers or objects. The Synoptics testify that Jesus discoursed with His disciples in a style different from that which He used before the people. [2] " It is well known," says Bleek, "how widely the representations differ that are given us of the person and teaching of Socrates in Plato and Xenophon respectively. Some, supposing these irreconcilable, have held Xenophon's account only to be historically true, and have declared the Platonic Socrates to have been the creation of Plato himself. The narrowness and erroneousness of this opinion is now acknowledged; for if Socrates were a teacher only, as Xenophon describes him, if he was not also the speculatist and philosopher that Plato describes, we could not explain how so many schools of speculative philosophy sprang from his teaching and influence. Both descriptions of Socrates are true, and are only different aspects of one and the same character. Now, if a wise man, who was merely human like Socrates, could thus present such manifoldness in unity that two of his pupils could give such contrasted yet true pictures of his teaching, surely the same is possible in the case of Christ—in the case of Him whose office and work was to be the Redeemer of men of all shades of character and life; surely in His person and life there must necessarily have been a far richer fullness." [3]

The prevailing similarity of style in the discourses of Jesus and the narrative of the evangelist, may be accounted for quite naturally by the overmastering influence of the thought of Jesus upon the mind of the susceptible and loving John. Such unconscious influence, where there is neither imitation nor invention, is by no means uncommon between master and disciple.

Indeed, the reporting of an oral discourse may depend as much upon the receptivity of the hearer as upon the phraseology of the speaker.

[1] *A Death in the Desert*—a fictitious representation of John vindicating his gospel on his death-bed.
[2] Matt. xiii. 10, 34.   Mark iv. 11, 33, 34.   Luke viii. 10.
[3] *Introd. § 76.*

Two reporters of different temperaments and different degrees of culture may present quite different phases of the same speech ; each correct as far as it goes, each incomplete as an embodiment of the thought of the speaker, yet each important for the impression it will make upon its own circle of readers, while both are necessary to a philosophical estimate of the speaker and his discourse. John appears to have fed upon certain phases of Christ's doctrine till these not only possessed his soul as a personal faith, but pervaded his thought and style.

"Let any only yield himself," says Neander, "to the impression of the Sermon on the Mount, and then ask himself whether it be probable that a mind of the loftiness, depth, and power which that discourse evinces, could have employed only *one* mode of teaching ? A mind which swayed not only simple and practical souls, but also so profoundly speculative an intellect as that of Paul, could not but have scattered the elements of such a tendency from the very first. We cannot but infer, from the irresistible power which Christianity exerted upon minds so diversely constituted and cultivated, that the sources of that power lay combined in Him whose self-revelation was the origin of Christianity itself. Moreover, the other Gospels are not wanting in apparently paradoxical expressions akin to the peculiar tone of John's Gospel, *i. e. Let the dead bury their dead.* Nor will the attentive observer find in John alone expressions of Christ intended to increase, instead of to remove, the offence which carnal minds took at His doctrine.

"Still it is true, that such passages are given by John much more abundantly than the other Evangelists. But there is nothing in his Gospel purely metaphysical or impractical; none of the spirit of the Alexandrian-Jewish theology; but everywhere a direct bearing upon the inner life, the Divine communion which Christ came to establish. Its form would have been altogether different had it been composed, as some suppose in the second century, to support the Alexandrian doctrine of the Logos, as will be plain to any one who takes the trouble to compare it with the writings of that age that have come down to us. The discourses given in the first three Gospels mostly composed of separate maxims, precepts, and parables, all in the popular forms of speech, were better fitted to be handed down by tradition than the more profound discussions which have been recorded by the beloved disciple who hung with fond affection upon the lips of Jesus, treasured His revelations in a congenial mind, and poured them forth to fill up the gaps of the popular narrative. And although it is true that the image of Christ given to us in this Gospel is the reflection of Christ's impression upon John's peculiar mind and feelings, it is to be remembered that these very peculiarities were obtained by his intercourse with, and vivid apprehension of, Christ himself. His susceptible nature appropriated Christ's life, and incorporated it with His own."[1]

As to the names *Son of Man* and *Son of God*, Neander shows that Christ employed these antithetically: "they contain correlative ideas, and cannot be thoroughly understood apart from their reciprocal relation."

The fourth Gospel exhibits throughout intrinsic evidences of being the production of an eye-witness. The minute yet unstudied description of persons, places, events, the natural and life-like manner in which the story is told, are marks not only of the historical character of the narrative, but also of the interest of the writer in all that he narrates, as a matter of personal testimony. These characteristics are very striking in the account of the closing scenes of the life of Jesus:—the manner of the disciples when Jesus announced at the Supper that one of them should betray Him: the fact that John, being "known unto the high priest" went into his palace, while Peter remained without, until John came and brought him in; the circumstantiality of the details about the weather, the fire, and what was transpiring in the judgment hall and in the outer court; these are marks of personal recollection. The same characteristic appears in the account of the visit of Peter and John to the Sepulcher.[2]

V. EXTERNAL EVIDENCES.

It is admitted by all parties, that before the close of the second century the fourth Gospel had come to be acknowledged as a canonical work, and was by many accepted as a work of the Apostle John. *Irenæus*, bishop of Lyons, *Clement* of Alexandria, *Tertullian* of proconsular Africa, and *Polycrates* of Ephesus are conclusive witnesses to this fact. Irenæus argues the necessity for four Gospels from the mystical analogy of the four divisions of the world, the four winds, the four cherubims:[3] Clement speaks of "the four Gospels which have been handed down to us;"[4] Tertullian enumerates the four;[5] Polycrates names John as "he who leaned upon the bosom of the Lord."[6] These witnesses prove that in the last third of the second century the fourth Gospel was acknowledged in all the churches as

---

[1] *Life of Jesus Christ*, Am. edition, § 71.

[2] Prof. Fisher has grouped together very effectively many passages in John's Gospel that exhibit "the air and manner of an eye-witness and participant in the scenes recorded." *The Supernatural Origin of Christianity*, pp. 84–95.

[3] *Hær.* iii. 11.   [4] *Strom.* iii. 13,   [5] *Marcion.* iv. 2.   [6] *Eusebius*, v. 24.

the work of the apostle John. Going back a step further in the
literature of the primitive Church, we find conclusive evidence of the
existence of the fourth Gospel in the first half of the second century.
According to Hippolytus, *Valentinus*, the founder of a Gnostic sect,
quoted from this Gospel as the saying of Christ, "All that came before Me are thieves and robbers;" [1] and also applied to Satan the
title "Prince of this world." *Marcion* rejected the Gospel of John,
as he also mutilated Luke's Gospel, because he thought it inconsistent
with the doctrines of Paul; [2] but his rejection of it as not favoring
his theological scheme, shows that it was already current in the
Church as the work of the apostle John.

We are indebted to Hippolytus for the resuscitation of another
witness—*Basilides*,[3] a Gnostic leader who flourished at Alexandria
in the fore part of the second century. In his discussions Basilides
says, "Thus it is said in the Gospel; This was the true light that
lighteth every man that cometh into the world:" [4] and again, "The
Saviour said, My hour is not yet come." [5] It is impossible to doubt
that Basilides had before him the Gospel of John, and regarded it as
of apostolical authority.

A yet earlier and more important witness is *Justin Martyr*, who
lived between A. D. 89 and 160. Justin speaks of the Gospels collectively as "the authoritative memoirs of the Apostles;" he declares
that Christ was "the only-begotten of the Father of all things,
being properly begotten by Him as His Word and Power"—a conception apparently founded upon John; and he uses the language of
John's Gospel, with only such slight verbal variations as would
occur in quotations from memory. In particular in his account of
baptism, Justin says, [6] "For indeed Christ also said: 'Except ye be
born again, ye shall not enter into the kingdom of heaven.' And
that it is impossible for those who are once born to enter into their
mother's womb, is plain to all." Such an approximation to the language of John can hardly be accounted for by a current tradition of
Christ's conversation with Nicodemus; and, moreover, such a tradition would go to confirm the Gospel narrative as a history, for the
Gospel reports with a matter-of-fact particularity the interview of
the Master in Israel with the Teacher come from God.

VI. CONCLUSION.

The whole argument is well summed up in the following extracts
from Bleek :

[1] Hippol. vi. 35.   [2] Tertullian, *adv. Marcion* iv. 3.   [3] Hippol. vii. 22, 27.
[4] John i. 9.   [5] John ii. 4.   [6] *Apol.* i. 61.

" We have now to consider the *design* and *occasion* of this Gospel. The former John himself seems to tell us in his closing words.[1] What he here declares to be his object in writing, viz., to further faith in Jesus as the Christ and the Son of God, and everlasting life in those who believe, may, as thus generally stated, be regarded as the highest object of the other evangelists, and indeed of all Christian teachers whether writers or speakers. But it is one thing to awaken faith, another to confirm and guard it against error on all sides. Accordingly the authors of the Gospels might have different points of view, and give to their works a correspondingly different form. Their purpose might have been either the furtherance of faith in the Son of God—and this would influence them more or less in their selection of facts, and in the characteristic execution of their task— or they might content themselves simply with the trustworthy relation of occurrences just as they happened. Among the Synoptics, the latter character seems to belong more to Luke and Mark, the former more to Matthew. But unquestionably this former character belongs in a far higher degree to John, and certainly not simply through pointed references in him to the fulfilment of Old Testament expressions and in virtue of his own remarks and observations, but also through his selection of matter for record, especially such as the discourses of the Lord, which refers far more than those in the Synoptics to the person of Jesus as the Son of God and the Messiah. More than any other of the evangelists might John have declared it to be the simple purpose of his writing, that his readers might believe Jesus to be the Christ, the Son of God. Still it would be a very great mistake to argue from this manifest intention in the Gospel against its historical reality and purpose, and to speak of it as purely dogmatic and apologetic, as has so often been done even by the latest interpreters and critics. So far is this from the truth, that if we may treat any one of our Gospels as an historical work, we may emphatically so treat the Gospel of John. In the statement of external facts, John is frequently more exact than the Synoptics. Not less is his account of events recorded by himself alone distinguished by great precision and clearness, even when he gives prominence to what has manifestly no direct dogmatic significance ; e. g. the conversation with the Samaritan woman, the healing of the man born blind at Jerusalem, the raising of Lazarus, etc. Especially is the historical character of his Gospel proved by the clearness with which it unfolds, in its gradual development, the catas-

18   [1] John xx. 31.

trophe which terminated in the death of Jesus the Redeemer.
Here pre-eminently, from the very beginning of the Lord's public
life onwards, care is taken to show how by His deeds and words the
Jewish feeling concerning Him was formed, alternating for a long
time between approval and dislike, until at last it took such a course
as to give up even eagerly to crucifixion Him on whom but a short
time before it had joyfully fixed its expectations.

"The whole Gospel shows us how the popular opinion respecting
Jesus was formed; how, for a long time, it swung between approval
and dislike; how the people, entirely filled with the Jewish notions
respecting the Messiah, sometimes thought He was the One for
whom they were waiting, and then again became determined and
bitter against Him; how the Sanhedrim resolved to make away with
Him, and how this resolution was affected by a real or pretended fear
of the Romans.   Especially is it from John that we learn how it
came to pass (a) that the people greeted Jesus on His entrance into
Jerusalem with such rejoicings, (the fact itself is recorded by the
Synoptics; but it is only in this Gospel that we learn its motive, in
the raising of Lazarus shortly before); and yet (b) that their feeling so
quickly altered respecting Him, through the discourse following the
entry, from which it could be seen how little He thought of being a
Messiah in the Jewish sense of the word.   This change of feeling is
also related by the Synoptics, but not so as to show very clearly how
it was brought about. [1]

"We need not be surprised at finding no quotations from St.
John's Gospel in the apostolic fathers; for they do not usually make
any quotations from the Gospels, though they certainly must have
known them.   There are indeed some passages which seem indirectly to refer to sayings in our Gospel, but we cannot affirm this
with certainty. . . . . .My conviction is that an unprejudiced
consideration of the external testimonies leads to the certain conclusion that our fourth Gospel was recognized as a trustworthy authority, and a genuine work, in the various churches of Christendom
before the middle of the second century.

"It must, as we have seen, have existed and been known in the
church (a) before the Easter controversies; (b) before the appearance of the Valentinian Gnosis in Egypt and elsewhere; (c) before the
rise of Montanism in Asia Minor; (d) before the time of Marcion
himself.   The position which the contending parties in all these controversies allowed to our Gospel, can be historically explained only

[1] Bleek, *Int.* § 115.

upon the supposition that it was known and recognized in the Church at large some decades of years before the middle of the second century, if not from the very beginning of it; and this fact, in turn, can only be explained upon the supposition that it is a genuine and apostolic work. Whatever may be difficult and strange in the history of this Gospel in the Church, in its contents or in its exposition, is only of such a nature as to become tenfold more difficult and more strange upon the supposition of a later and non-apostolic authorship. Our investigation has confirmed us in the steadfast conviction, which is irresistibly urged upon us ever and anon from different considerations, that this fourth Gospel is really the work of St. John, the trusted and beloved disciple of the Lord." [1]

APPENDIX II.

DR. J. J. VAN OOSTERZEE'S THEOLOGY OF THE NEW TESTAMENT.

THE most judicious and satisfactory treatise that has yet appeared in the recent science of Biblical Theology, is the *Manual of the Theology of the New Testament* by Dr. Van Oosterzee, Professor in the University of Utrecht, Holland. This was first published in Dutch in 1867, and a second edition appeared in 1869. A German translation, made under the author's sanction, was published at Barmen in 1868; [2] a full account of the work, with a translation of several sections appeared in the *American Presbyterian Review* for July, 1870; [3] and a translation of the entire work is in course of publication in the *Theological Eclectic*. [4] This translation, by Prof. George E. Day, D. D., is made directly from the Dutch, and promises to be both precise and elegant; when completed, it will be published as a distinct volume, and will form a useful text-book for Bible-classes.

For convenience of reference I have here compiled from the German edition an abstract of that portion of Van Oosterzee's work which treats specifically of the Theology of Christ.

[1] Bleek, *Intro.* § 89.

[2] *Die Theologie des Neuen Testaments.* Ein Hand-buch für academische Vorlesungen und zum Selbst-studium. Von J. J. Van Oosterzee. pp. 268.

[3] Vol. ii. New Series, pp. 434–459.   [4] Published by Judd & White, New Haven.

Section first, in the form of an introduction, defines the Biblical Theology of the New Testament as a science, carefully distinguishing it from Christian Dogmatics. The latter inquires, not only what the Christian Church in general or any one of its branches confesses as truth, but above all, what within the domain of Christian faith one really should or should not hold as truth. The former, on the contrary, asks only what is set forth as truth by the writers of the New Testament. From its point of view, it has to do, not with the correctness, but only with the import of the ideas which it finds in the teachings of Jesus and the Apostles. *Elle ne démontre pas, elle raconte.* As for the exegete, so for the Biblical theologian, the main question is, How readest thou?

§ 2, treats of the history of this science, showing that it arose at a comparatively recent period—largely under the impulse of rational-istic investigation—and is "distinctively Protestant" in its origin and methods of inquiry, making the Bible its sole text-book and authority.

§ 3, points out the method to be pursued in this study. The The-ology of the Lord Jesus Christ must be distinguished from that of the Apostolic writers, and the former discussed before the latter. Here, too, the difference between the sayings of the Lord in the Syn-optics and in the fourth Gospel comes before us. The apostolic writings should receive a like discriminating treatment—bringing out in succession the theology of Peter, of Paul, and of John. And, moreover, since the doctrine of Christ and His apostles grew like a plant out of the soil of the Old Testament, as a preparation for understand-ing that doctrine, we must acquaint ourselves with the religion out of which Christianity sprang, with the expectations which it realized, and with the condition, the ideas and the wants of the age in which Christ and His apostles lived. These points, *Mosaism, Prophetism,* and *Judaism,* as distinguished from the earlier *Hebraism,* Dr. Oosterzee groups together under the name of " Old Testament foun- · dation."

The treatise proper opens with a chapter on this " Old Testament Foundation," under which § 4 treats of Mosaism—the religious-po-litical constitution [1] for which the people of Israel were indebted to Moses; its foundation, a special revelation, its character monothe-

---

[1] " Die *religios-politische* Einrichtung ;" a constitution which did not simply combine within itself ecclesiastical and civil institutions, but in which the re-ligious idea was the key of the civil polity, and the whole political structure was based upon religious truths and erected for a religious end:—not " re-ligious and civil," but "religious-political."

istic, its form theocratic, its worship symbolico-typical, its tendency purely moral, its standpoint that of external authority—though at the same time it is thoroughly conscious that it is a preparation for a higher development. Blending the religious and the ethical, the Mosaic economy is founded not in legalism but in morality; the absolute holiness of the king is the ideal of the subject; the love of Jehovah is ever in the foreground, and religion is most intimately united with the life. Yet the law could not itself produce the holiness that it required.

Prophetism, § 5, which can as little be accounted for on the rationalistic theory as on that of magic, was both the support and the fulfillment of the earlier revelation. It built the way for the Gospel of the New Testament, exerted an important influence upon the matter and form of its preaching, and exalted its high worth above all reasonable doubt. It insisted upon the spiritual nature of the law and the necessity of spiritual consecration; it proclaimed the universality of the kingdom of God, a golden age upon earth, and the resurrection and the judgment after death. By upholding Monotheism, by quickening and sharpening the sense of sin, and thus awakening the longing for redemption, by setting over against the terrors of the law the consolation of promise and hope, it prepared the way for the Gospel.

Judaism, § 6, describes the moral and religious state of the Israelites after the Babylonian captivity—a state of degeneracy from the original Hebraism, when speculation, legalism, and formalism had supplanted the early enthusiasm for spiritual truth. Although in this period there was a general expectation of the Messiah, yet there was nothing in Judaism from which the personal character of Christ or the matter of His Gospel could have been developed.

Part Second brings us directly to the Theology of Jesus Christ:— the essence of the doctrine of God and divine things as given by Christ during His earthly life. While Jesus drew much from nature and from the Old Testament, His personality, more than anything else, was the source of His doctrine, and determined both the form and the matter of His teaching. The remainder of this chapter, from § 10 to § 17, is devoted to the conception of the Kingdom of God as found in the Synoptical Gospels. The several topics are, the kingdom itself, its founder, the King of kings, the subjects of the kingdom, salvation, the way of salvation, the consummation.

§ 10, on the Kingdom, has already been given in the note on p. 30. The founder of this kingdom Dr. van Oosterzee regards as none other than Christ Himself,[1] who even in the Synoptical Gospels, appears as the Christ, the Son of the living God, and as such is not only a true and spotless man, but is also a partaker of a super-human nature and dignity which no creature in heaven or earth can lay claim to. At the same time, § 12, He proclaims the Father as the only true, the personally living and continually acting God, who reveals Himself especially through the Son to men, and through the Holy Spirit produces in them every really good thing.

§ 13. Men only are the proper subjects of this kingdom—the holy angels being its servants, and the spirits of darkness its enemies. Christ teaches the personality of Satan, the Evil one, assumes the universality of sin in the hearts of men, and sets forth the guilt and ruin of the transgressor.

§ 14. Salvation consists in the enjoyment of temporal and spiritual blessings, which begins here, and shall be perfected in the hereafter. The earthly appearing, the active life, the redemptive death and the heavenly glory of Jesus Christ, together had this distinct purpose— to bring this salvation to all.

§ 15. Though all are invited to the salvation of the kingdom of God, yet sinners can partake of it only through repentance, faith, and a renewal of heart which manifests itself in the rectitude of the whole life. All who enter upon this way constitute together a spiritual community, which on account of its peculiar constitution, but above all on account of its character and tendency is high above every other, and shall extend and endure till the end of the world.

§ 16. Then shall come the consummation. The salvation of the subjects of the kingdom of God survives their death, but will first reach its consummation at the Advent of the Lord, at which the glory of the King shall be manifested, and those of His subjects who have been found faithful shall be rewarded with the full rewards of grace. This Advent will be ushered in by impressive signs, accompanied with stupendous changes in the cosmical and moral spheres,

---

[1] That Christ did not really *found* the kingdom of God, but revived the normal conception of that kingdom in the Old Testament, and filled out the prophetic ideal, I have already shown at p. 31. This view of the original spirituality of the Old Testament kingdom is essential to a true understanding of the preaching of Christ. The apostasy of the Jews from their primitive Theocracy, and their glorification of the forms of the law in place of the spirit of allegiance, rendered necessary the removal of their system, in order to the re-establishment and glorification of the true Theocracy. "The kingdom of God," says Neander, "could not be founded from without. It needed first a proper material; and this could not be found in human nature, estranged from God by sin."

and followed by the definitive separation of the good and the bad which shall put an irrevocable end to the present state of things.

Thus far the elements of the Theology of Christ as given in the Synoptical Gospels. His words in the fourth Gospel exhibit a character so entirely peculiar, as to require a separate treatment. It is important also to distinguish as far as possible the utterances of the Johannean Christ from those of the Christian John. Here, in the words of Christ Himself, we move in quite another sphere of thought. In the Synoptics it is the kingdom of heaven that is prominent, here the King Himself; there, the human, here the divine side of the Person of the Redeemer; there, the blessedness of redemption beyond the grave, here, upon this side of the grave. This is the theme of § 17, which opens the second part of the Theology of Christ.

§ 18, treats of the Son of God in the flesh. The self-consciousness which utters itself in the fourth Gospel is that of the only Son of God who appears as true and sinless man, to be the Messiah of Israel and the Saviour of the world, but who at the same time, during His stay on earth stands personally in a relation to heaven altogether peculiar.

§ 19. As the Son of God the Lord declared that He was from eternity, was the constant object of the love of the Father, and the sharer of His nature, majesty and power, who had in the Father the ground and the end of His life, who revealed His name in the fullest degree, and by consequence could lay claim to a homage and dignity which could not be accorded to a creature without blasphemy

§ 20. The name of the Father was revealed by the Son to a world which through sin and the powers of evil was under the dominion of darkness, but which received from God in Christ new light and life. He imparted this light and life through His coming and all His works, but especially through His sufferings and death. Yet in order personally to enjoy their benefits, a heart-faith is indispensable, and this though required upon sufficient grounds, nevertheless for moral reasons will by no means be found in all.

§ 21. They who are given to the Son by the Father, and by consequence have come to the Father through the Son, are united with the Son, and through Him with one another in a living Communion, whose peculiar character can be understood only by means of a spiritual experience, and whose benign effects are manifested in the whole course of their inner and outer life.

§ 22. That eternal life, which already here is a fruit of personal abiding fellowship with Christ, survives death and passes over into unending felicity. Also according to the Johannean Christ we must look for a resurrection of the dead, a general judgment, and an irrevocable separation at the last day. The discussion of these relations of the Son of God to the Father, to the world, to His Disciples, and to the Future, completes the second division of Van Oosterzee's treatise on the Theology of Christ.

The third part considers the apparent differences between the Synoptics and John's Gospel, in their reports of Christ's teachings, as really conducting to a higher unity. His doctrine is communicated by the four evangelists in an harmonious many-sidedness, and is on the one hand the unfolding, amplification and fulfilment of the word of God spoken by Moses and the prophets, and on the other the foundation and starting point of a series of Apostolic declarations in respect to the way of salvation, which under various modifications, in turn embody, interpret and strengthen the doctrine of Christ.

The Petrine, Pauline, and Johannean theologies are severally discussed, and the work closes with a chapter upon the agreement of the apostles with one another, the agreement of the apostles with their Lord, and the agreement of Christ and His apostles with the writings of the Old Testament.

APPENDIX III.

DR. WEISS ON FUTURE PUNISHMENT.

FOR a full discussion of the questions of the annihilation of the wicked, the final restoration of all mankind, and the adjustment of eternal punishment with the equity and the goodness of God, the reader is referred to the author's volume " *Love and Penalty.*"

The statement of Christ's doctrine of hell and eternal perdition given by Dr. Weiss in his Compendium of New Testament Theology is so clear, condensed, and in the main so exact—though I dissent from his opinion that there will be no resurrection for the wicked—that the entire section is here translated for the benefit of readers who may not have access to the original. *a.* " According to the Orthodox-Jewish view (that of the Pharisees) retributive punishment began immediately upon the death of the individual, when the soul entered into Sheol (Hades). In the oldest Gospel Hades is mentioned, Matt. xvi. 18, and its "Gates" serve for a popular symbol of that which is most firmly closed, since the kingdom of the dead lets out again no one whom it has once swallowed up: and in Matt. xi. 23, where in opposition to heaven as the highest, Hades is represented as the lowest. In the parable given in Luke xvi. 19–31, is brought out the idea of the diverse fates of souls in Sheol. The rich man and Lazarus find themselves in Hades (ver. 23) but the one in a place of torment (vers. 23, 28) where he is tortured by the greatest heat of burning thirst (ver. 24), the other, on the contrary, rests in Abraham's bosom (vers. 22, 23) and enjoys a blessedness which causes him to forget all the misery of earth (ver. 25). The places of their several abodes are divided by an insurmountable gulf (ver. 26.) The abode of the righteous in Hades is called Paradise, (Luke xxiii. 43.) That the robber shall be there with Jesus is the token of his forgiveness. There is also already in Sheol a retribution for the soul, which however, does not exclude a final decision upon its definitive fate.

b. The Messianic judgment decrees eternal punishment which forms the antithesis to eternal life. (Matt. xxv. 46). In this antithesis it is undoubtedly implied, that this punishment consists in the privation of eternal life, and this is identical with "destruction:" since the narrow way that leads to life stands in contrast to the way that leads to destruction (Matt. vii. 13 ἀπώλεια). The verb lying at the root of this word most commonly signifies a violent killing (Matt. xxi. 41, xxii. 7, also ii. 13, xxvi. 52, xxvii. 20), or perishing in a sudden and unnatural manner (Luke xiii. 3, 5. Mark iv. 38). But such an end is in itself a judgment of God (Luke xvii. 27, 29), and so the judicial punishment upon the impenitent nation could be represented as a destruction in this sense (Luke xiii. 3, 5), especially since this is commonly conceived of as destruction through the hand of an enemy (Matt. xxiv. 15–22). Likewise the judgment upon the world living in carnal security, according to the analogy of the flood, is represented as a sudden destruction, which in the end of the world bursts forth upon all who were not delivered from it. Evidently also "destruction" is frequently represented as bodily death, especially under some violent and unnatural form in which the divine judgment executes itself upon sin. But physical death only separates the soul from the body without pronouncing upon its definite fate. Since Jesus spake of the salvation of souls, there must be a destruction that falls upon disembodied spirits, and this must either be some definite destruction or destruction simply. This destruction the incorporeal demons feared (Mark i. 24) and according to Matthew x. 28, it is not the destruction of the body but that of the soul that is to be feared. (Compare Matt. x. 39 and Mark viii. 36, 37.) To this destruction were the

whole people liable on account of their sins, inasmuch as the Messiah
came to deliver them.   But only the elect should be delivered from it
(Matt. xxiv. 22, x. 22, Mark x. 26, Luke xiii. 23) while their souls,
(after the destruction of their earthly corporeity) through being re-
clothed with the body, would be conducted to the true eternal life.

  c. According to a frequent mode of representation those who are
shut out from the kingdom of God in its heavenly perfection find
themselves in Hell (Mark ix. 47 : γέεννα)—the name of a valley south
of Jerusalem, where once the idolatrous Israelites offered their
children to Moloch (Jer. vii. 31 : גֵיא בֶן־הִנֹּם 2 Kings xxiii. 10,) and
as the judgment of God would break forth upon this horror (Jer. vii.
32, 33) this was transformed into a symbol of the place where destruction would overtake those who should be condemned in the last
judgment (Mat. x. 28) : hence this judgment is called ἡ κρίσις τῆς γεέν-
νης (Mat. xxiii. 15, 33).   Yet one may not conclude from Mat. v. 29,
30, and x. 28, that the wicked shall be raised, to suffer the pains of
hell in their restored bodies.   Rather do such utterances sufficiently
explain themselves in this, that at the second coming of the Messiah
to hold the final judgment this will overtake the current generation
while yet in the flesh.   Certainly the sinners of ancient times shall
receive their definitive sentence at the Messianic judgment (Mat. xi.
22, 24. Luke x. 12, 14).   But though their souls are in Sheol, and the
question concerns the fate of their souls under this final judgment, it
by no means follows from this that there will be a resurrection of
such.   This of the kind described in Mark xii. 25, can be had in view
only for the pious.   Undoubtedly Hell is described as a place of fire
(Mat. v. 22), and its fire is explicitly called eternal (Mat. xxv. 41,
Mark ix. 43), which Mark (ix. 48 following Isaiah lxvi. 24) explains
to the effect that their worm dieth not and their fire is not quenched.
But it is by no means meant by this that sensible torments shall
afflict the bodies of the wicked raised from the dead.   Rather is the
fire a symbol of the judicial wrath of God [Mat. iii. 11] whose terrors
were thus depicted ; for the end of sinners is more dreadful than the
most dreadful death (Mat. xviii. 6. Luke xvii. 2)—it were better
for them had they never been born, (Mark xiv. 21.)   Should a real
fire be conceived of, that would call for eternal bodily torment, while
it would burn without consuming ; and this would make an obvious
contradiction, since elsewhere those who are shut out of the kingdom
of God are said to be thrust out into darkness (Mat. viii. 12).   But
this darkness again, upon the basis of Old Testament imagery, is only
a common symbol of evil and terror.   (Job xxx. 26. Is. v. 20. viii.
22. ix. 2. 1. 10).   This much therefore lies in both images—that the

condemned will suffer a fate of whose terrors they are by no means unconscious—rather will they suffer this with wailing and gnashing of teeth, (Mat. viii. 12). The subject of this experience, however, may properly be conceived of as the disembodied soul, inasmuch as the incorporeal demons feared these torments (Mat. viii. 29) and the dead in Sheol experience both pain and happiness.

(d.) These two representations of the endless fate of the condemned (see in b. and c.) accord perfectly together. The destruction of the soul, indeed, (see b.) might be conceived of in itself as a complete annihilation; but then it would not have been better for the condemned never to have been born. (Mark xiv. 21, note c.) This destruction consists rather in this—that the soul which, separated from the body, tarries in Sheol until the final Judgment, after by that judgment upon itself it is deprived of all prospect of an awakening to true life (through the Resurrection, which awaits the godly alone) remains forever in the bodiless and therefore shadowy condition in which physical death placed it. The duration of the soul as such, according to this conception is no happiness, but involves eternal punishment, inasmuch as the disembodied state of the soul, which was before dreaded as a transition state, when definitely apprehended concludes within itself the greatest unhappiness. The destruction of the soul, which in this condition is forever precluded from the true life (which cannot be conceived of apart from corporeity) may therefore be signified by the same word as the separating of the soul from the body by corporeal death (see b.), because this, when it comes upon the wicked in the day of judgment—at which the pious dead shall be separated from them by the resurrection—involves their condemnation to remain in death, that is in the bodiless condition of the soul. But this bodiless state by no means excludes the lasting consciousness of its unhappiness, since the soul as such is and remains sensitive, (see c). The fire of hell therefore cannot signify complete annihilation, for these reasons:—that the fire itself cannot be regarded as material is obvious from the representation that it is an eternal fire, (Mat. xxv. 41, Mark ix. 43, 48); that it cannot consume the subject of the punishment, since then it would cease to burn. The eternity of punishment in hell in this sense is the correlative of the statement that the decision in the Messianic judgment is definitive. It comes also undoubtedly as a logical consequence of the doctrinal teaching of Christ, for where there is one sin which can never be forgiven, (Mat. xii. 32) there must also be an eternal punishment."[1]

[1] *Lehrbuch der Biblischen Theologie des Neuen Testaments*, § 38.

APPENDIX IV.

THE INTERMEDIATE STATE.

DR. DELITZSCH, in his *System of Biblical Psychology*—a work which, in its English dress,[1] fully justifies De Quincey's complaint of "the barbarous effect produced by a German structure of sentence, and a terminology altogether new "—regards the descent of Christ into Hades as a turning-point in the condition of the righteous dead, both past and to come. "He appeared in the world of the dead as a spirit, while His incorruptible but not yet glorified and risen body was at rest in the grave; but He appeared none the less in the undissolved unity of His divine-human person as the Prince of Life breaking through the bands of Hades and the grave.

" Thus manifesting Himself to the dead in Hades, He preached to them (ἐκήρυξεν) the victory that had now come to pass.   He preached to the Old Testament dead the New Testament gospel (νεκροῖς εὐηγγε- λίσθη) of the now completed redemption (1 Pet. iii. 19, iv. 6.).   There the fallen angelic powers beheld Him as the Conqueror; the Old Testament saints, as the Redeemer; those who had died in the attitude of hardening themselves, as the Judge; and for many who, as in the judgment of the deluge, had been swallowed up by Hades in very unequal measure of sin, there were glimpses of deliverance still pos- sible.   There also the soul of the penitent thief beheld Him in the bliss of Paradise.

" Then ascending out of Hades, arising out of the grave, and rising towards heaven, the Lord led captivity captive (ᾐχμαλώτευσεν αἰχμα- λωσίαν): the gifts which the Exalted One sends down, are the fruits of His victory; and, as it were, benefactions out of the spoils of a triumphant victor (Eph. iv. 8).   For He has triumphed over the angelic powers (Col. ii. 15); and when He had subjected to Him- self the spirits that rule in the kingdom of death and of darkness, He led the men who in Hades honored Him as a redeemer with Himself toward heaven (Mat. xxvii. 51–53) and from that time forth the Paradise is above the earth (2 Cor. xii. 1–4).[2]

---

[1] Translated for Clark's *Foreign Theological Library*, 1867, by Rev. Robert E. Wallis, Ph. D.

[2] This descent into Hades is the subject of a bold and effective picture by Bronzino, in the *Uffizi* at Florence. The style is hard and mannered, but the moral impression is powerful. Christ, the central figure, is preaching deliver- ance to these imprisoned souls. The devils shrink back affrighted. Some of

" The hope that the souls of the righteous are in God's hand, and in the enjoyment of rest and peace, has now its heavenly seal: the curtain is rent, and the new and living way is opened, on which henceforth all the faithful follow their Redeemer, without being compelled to pass further through any veil, to the place where God's loving presence is revealed in glory (Heb. x. 19). Thither look the eyes of the dying: thither, when their eyes fail them, their hands still point; there they are in the presence of their risen and glorified Saviour, who guarantees to them their own resurrection and glorification, even in their disembodied state, blessed and waiting in peace the dawning which will make even their bodies alive again. They are in the enjoyment of the peace of blessed inward contemplation, and blessed exaltation. They are in the heaven of glory, but this glory is still awaiting an increase. The history upon earth must first have passed away before the completion in heaven comes on."—(Chap. VI. Sec. III).

Delitzsch holds that in this intermediate state the spirit has a certain "phenomenal corporeity and investiture." Maintaining the three-fold distinction of Biblical Psychology,—" body, soul, and spirit "—he regards the soul as the principle of bodily life derived from the spirit. This, although immaterial, probably adopts the form of the body, which the spirit through it ensouls; as it is the outside of the spirit, so it is the inside of the body, and continues in the other world in that form which, as the living principle of the body, it had assumed. Its appearance remains a corporeal one, though immaterial. In this way Delitzsch accounts for the appearance of Samuel to the witch of Endor, and of Moses and Elias upon the Mount of Transfiguration.

Dr. J. P. Lange defines the soul as "a kind of robe for the spirit." He believes that in the spirit there is a tendency towards the assumption of a body; and hence, in the intermediate state, the spirit will assimilate from the materials of its dwelling-place, what will be fitted to itself, and thus will assume an organization adapted to its sphere. [1]

Though such speculations have no basis of certainty, they find

the spirits are incredulous, others look up in grateful wonder. Eve is meekly transported, and eager to follow her Deliverer,—the long-hoped-for "seed of the woman." In one corner of the picture a beautiful boy is helping a companion out of Limbo, and many are assisting others to escape, while the door of hope is open.

[1] *Stud. und Krit.* vol. ix. pp. 693–713. Translated in *Selections from German Literature* by Professors B. B. Edwards and E. A. Park.

sufficient warrant in hints or suggestions of the Scriptures, to stimulate curiosity upon a point of the most intense personal concern. And the Bible seems to impose no limit upon such speculative inquiry, provided only that we hold fast our faith in Him who is the resurrection and the life.

INDEX OF TEXTS OF SCRIPTURE.

287

19

INDEX OF SUBJECTS.